A-Z MIDDLESBROUGH

CONTENTS

Motorway	A1(M)		
A Road			†
Proposed		**Fire Station**	■
B Road	B1365	**Hospital**	⊞
Dual Carriageway		**Information Centre**	🈺
One-way Street Traffic flow on A Roads is indicated by a heavy line on the driver's left.	→	**National Grid Reference**	⁴45
		Police Station	▲
Restricted Access		**Post Office**	★
Pedestrianized Road		**Toilet** **with facilities for the Disabled**	▽ ♿
Track & Footpath	====		
Residential Walkway	⋯⋯	**Viewpoint**	米 米
Railway	Level Crossing / Station / Tunnel	**Educational Establishment**	◰
		Hospital or Hospice	◰
Built-up Area	STONE ST.	**Industrial Building**	◰
Local Authority Boundary	— · — ·	**Leisure or Recreational Facility**	◰
National Park Boundary		**Place of Interest**	◰
Posttown Boundary		**Public Building**	◰
Postcode Boundary Within Posttowns	— —	**Shopping Centre or Market**	◰
Map Continuation	▲ 18	**Other Selected Buildings**	◰

SCALE 1:15,840

```
0          ¼              ½              ¾ Mile
0    250      500      750 Metres   1 Km
4 inches (10.16 cm) to 1 mile    6.31 cm to 1km
```

Copyright of Geographers' A-Z Map Company Limited

Fairfield Road, Borough Green, Sevenoaks, Kent TN15 8PP
Telephone 01732 781000 (Enquiries & Trade Sales)
01732 783422 (Retail Sales)
www.a-zmaps.co.uk
Copyright © Geographers' A-Z Map Co. Ltd.

Ordnance Survey®
This product includes mapping data licensed from Ordnance Survey® with the permission of the Controller of Her Majesty's Stationery Office.
© Crown Copyright 2006. All rights reserved. Licence number 100017302
Edition 6 2007

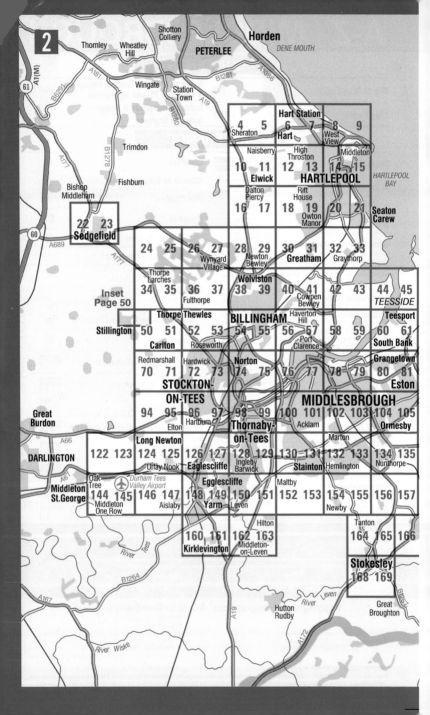

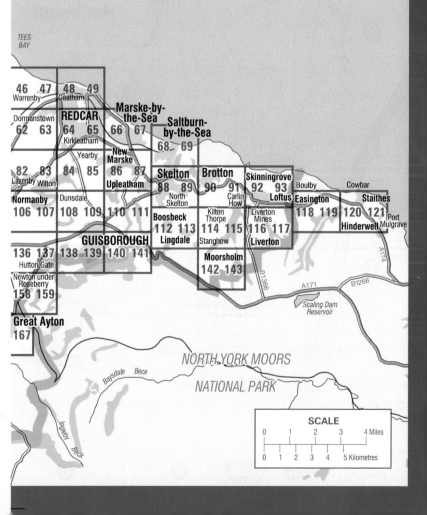

KEY TO MAP PAGES **3**

NORTH SEA

TEES BAY

46 Warrenby	**47**	**48** Coatham **49**

Marske-by-the-Sea

Saltburn-by-the-Sea

| 62 | 63 | **REDCAR** 64 Kirkleatham | 65 | 66 | 67 |

Yearby

New Marske

| 82 Lazenby | 83 Wilton | 84 | 85 | 86 Upleatham | 87 |

Skelton 88 89 North Skelton

Brotton 90 91 Carlin How

Skinningrove 92 93 Loftus

Boulby

Cowbar

| **Normanby** 106 107 | Dunsdale 108 109 | 110 111 |

Boosbeck 112 113 Lingdale

Kilton Thorpe 114 115 Stanghow

Liverton Mines 116 117 **Liverton**

Easington 118 119

Staithes 120 121 Port Mulgrave

Hinderwell

| 136 137 Hutton Gate | **GUISBOROUGH** 138 139 | 140 141 |

Moorsholm 142 143

Newton under Roseberry 158 159

A171 B1266

B1366

A174

Scaling Dam Reservoir

Great Ayton 167

NORTH YORK MOORS

NATIONAL PARK

Baysdale Beck

Ingleby Beck

SCALE				
0	1	2	3	4 Miles
0	1 2	3	4	5 Kilometres

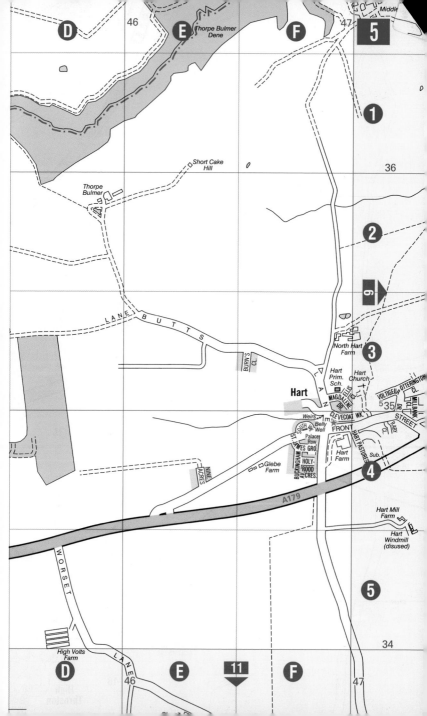

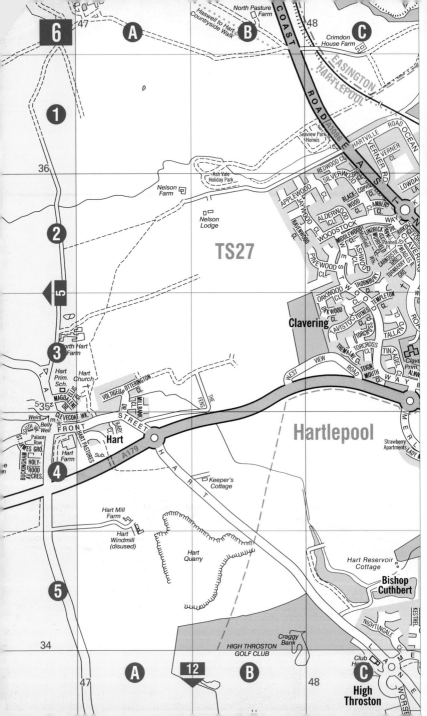

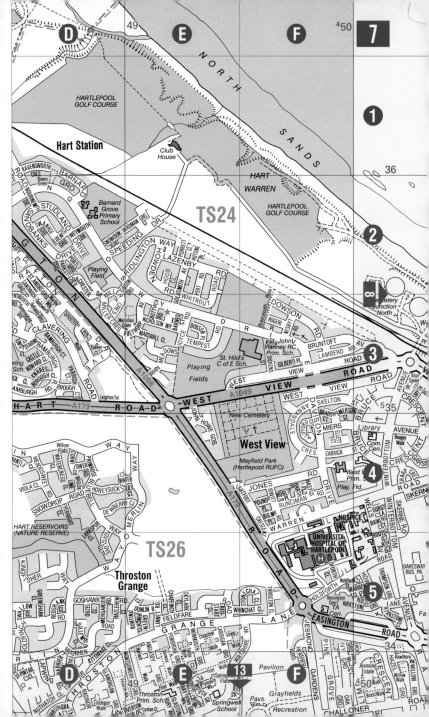

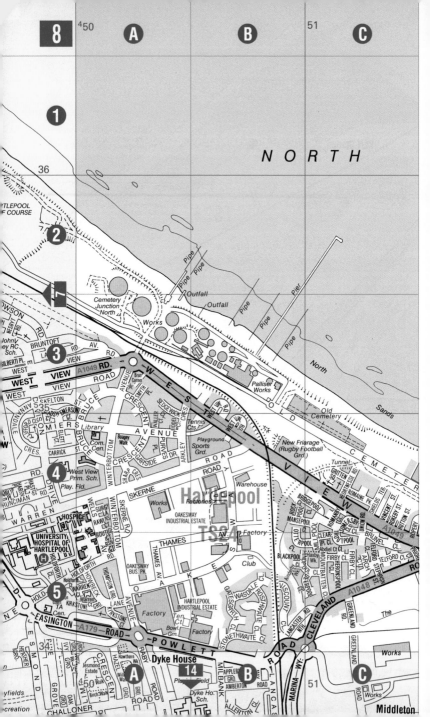

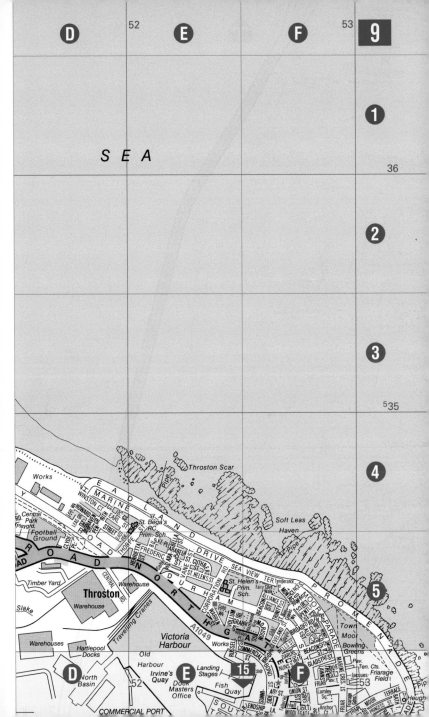

D 52 **E** **F** 53 **9**

1

36

S E A

2

3

5 35

Throston Scar

4

Works

Central Park Playgrd.

Football Ground

St. Bega's RC Prim. Sch.

Soft Leas Haven

5

MARINE DRIVE

HEADLAND

Timber Yard

St. Helen's St.

St. Cuthbert's Prim. Sch.

Fairy Cove Walk

SEA VIEW TER.

Temperance

Throston

Warehouse

Warehouse

Slake

NORTH ROAD

DURHAM

CORPORATION RD.

PROMENADE

Town Moor

Bowling Greens

Warehouses

Hartlepool Docks

Travelling Cranes

Victoria Harbour

A1049

Works

Pav.

Ten. Cts.

Friarage Field

34

D 52 North Basin

Old Harbour

Irvine's Quay

E Dock Masters Office

Landing Stages

Fish Quay

15

F 53

Lumley Sq.

Friar St.

FRIAR

MOOR TERRACE

Heugh

COMMERCIAL PORT

SOUTH

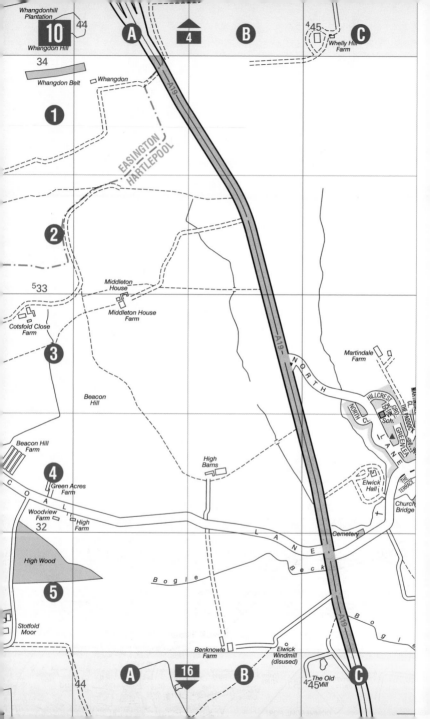

Whangdonhill
Plantation

10 44

Whangdon Hill

34

Whangdon Belt

□ Whangdon

1

EASINGTON
HARTLEPOOL

2

5 33

Middleton
House

□ Middleton House
Farm

Cotsfold Close
Farm

3

Beacon
Hill

Beacon Hill
Farm

4

Green Acres
Farm

Woodview
Farm
High
32   Farm

C
O
A
L

High Wood

5

L
A
N
E

Bogle   Beck

Stotfold
Moor

Benknowle
Farm

Elwick
Windmill
(disused)

A   **4**   **B**   4 45
Whelly Hill
Farm

C

A19

NORTH

Martindale
Farm

HILLCREST
NORTH CL.
CVM Sch.
GR.
CL.
PADDOCK
GREENER

North

ILAND

MARTINDALE

THE TERRACE

Elwick
Hall

Church
Bridge

Cemetery

A19

Bogle

A   **16**   **B**   Elwick
Windmill
(disused)   **C**
The Old
4 45 Mill

44

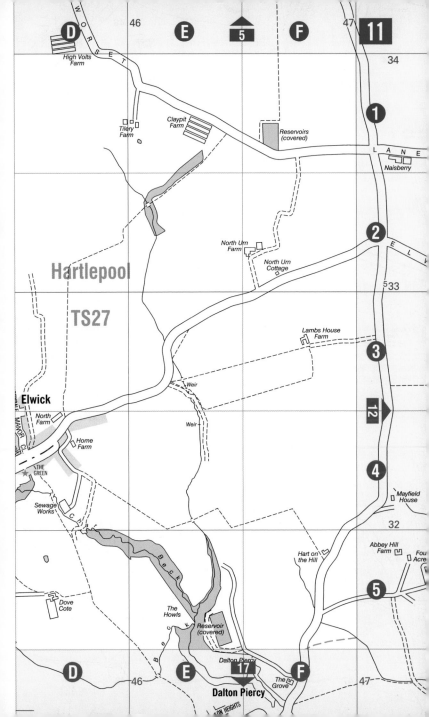

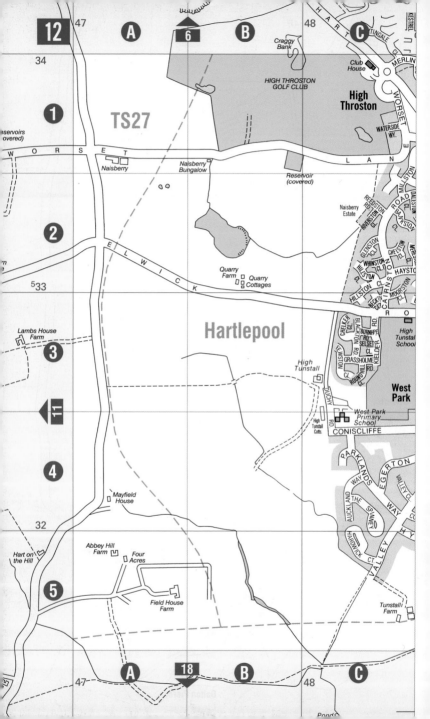

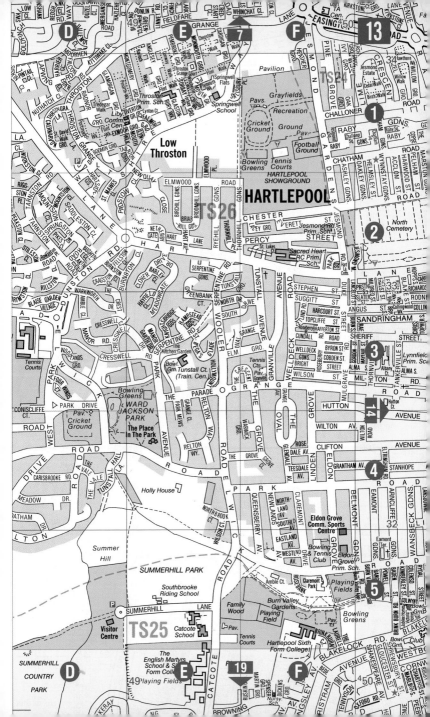

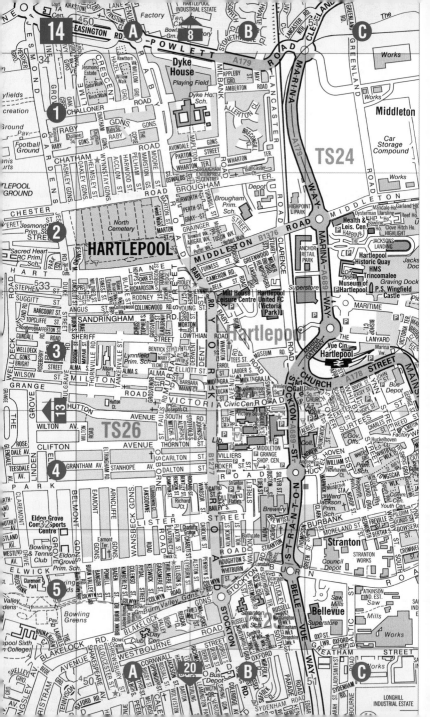

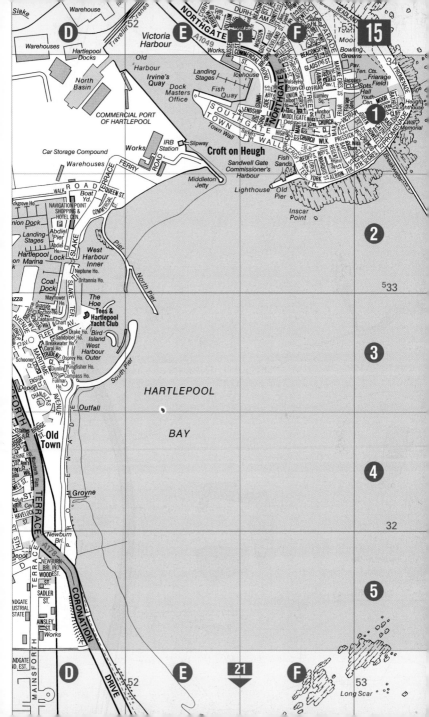

Slake
Warehouse

Travelin Cranes 52

Warehouses
Hartlepool Docks

DURH BEACON
COOP PC
GOOD
DARL BEAM
OPE
RUSSEL ST
MORISON
CLEVELAND RD
COMMERCIAL
PENTU
HEADLAND

College
PENTU
PARADE
53 T.S
MOOR
34

FRIAR
Friarage
Field

North Basin

Old Harbour
Irvine's Quay

Dock Masters Office

COMMERCIAL PORT OF HARTLEPOOL

Landing Stages
Icehouse
Fish Quay

GLADSTONE ST
BEACONSFIELD ST

MARINE CRES
Pav.
Ten. Cts.
Spts.
Cen.
Youth Cen.
Hall

Heugh Lighthouse
War Memorial

PROMENADE

Wolsey Ho
Priory Ct
SUNNI
VICTORIA
UNION
TALBOT
HALL
MIDDLEGATE

WELLS
DARIN
MARINE CRES
FRIAR
Jacques
Ct.
MKR

ABY
FRIEN
MCH
CL

ANCH
CHURCH
WLK
BAPTIST

Car Storage Compound
Warehouses

Works
IRB Station
Slipway

SOUTHGATE
TOWN WALL
Town Wall
Barkers
HIGH ST

Croft on Heugh

Sandwell Gate Commissioner's Harbour

Fish Sands

REGENT
SACRA
MARQUIS
PRISSICK
CL
STH. CRES

ST. HILDA
CCL
BREAKWATER

ROAD

FERRY
TERRACE
QUEEN ST.
COMMERCIAL ST.

Works
ROAD
Middleton Jetty

Lighthouse
Old Pier

York St
ALBION TER.
STH. CRES.
BEDFD'S
LOYD'S
BAPTIST

WALK
R O A D

Boat Yd.
NAVIGATION POINT SHOPPING & HOTEL CEN.

Inscar Point

Arkgrove Ho.
Union Dock
Landing Stages

Abdiel Pier
Abdiel
SLAKE

PIER

TERRACE
COMMERCIAL ST.

West Harbour Inner
Neptune Ho.
Britannia Ho.

North Pier

5 33

Hartlepool Marina
Lock

Coal Dock

SLAKE TER.

Mayflower Ho.
Quayside
Anchor Ho.
Captains Wlk
Chart Ho.

The Hoe
Tees & Hartlepool Yacht Club

Piazza

AVENUE
FLEET
PAVO
MARITIME

Drake Ho.
Sandpiper Ho.
Breakwater Ho.
Coral Ho.
TRIDENT
Osprey Ho.
Dunlin Kingfisher Ho.
Fulmar Ho.
Compass Ho.

Bird Island
West Harbour Outer

South Pier

Schooner
Ct.

ENSIGN
Depot
CHANDLERS

Outfall

HARTLEPOOL

SEAFORTH

Straithe
PAV
Depot

BRIDGE
ST.
KATHERINE RD
ST. Ann's
ing's Wlk
AMES ST.

Old Town

G R O Y N E

BAY

Adult
Train. Cen.
HAVELOCK ST.
STH.

TERRACE

Groyne

Newburn Bri. P.

STH.
Depot

NEWBURN BRI. IND.
WOOD ST.

A179

MAINSFORTH
TERRACE
CORONATION
DRIVE

ST.
SADLER ST.

AINSLEY ST.
Works

NDGATE INDUSTRIAL ESTATE

NDGATE IND. EST.

18 47 **A** Field House Farm **12** **B** 48 **C** Tunstall Farm

1

D a l t o n

Pond

Dalton Nook Plantation

Hartlepool

Horse Close Plantation

2 TS27

Pond

Four Ace

17 Meadow Bungalow Marite

Tees View

B R I E R T O

3 Cherry Tree Cottage

Brierton

⁵30 Brierton North Farm Brierton Farm

Brierton Farm

B e c k

Leahills View

4 Owton Grange

D A L T O N

Billingham

LINDSA
LINDSA
LANARK RD
LAMONT ERD
Lennox RD

Mine Walk
MILNE
MLN Rd
MIDLOTHIAN
ROY ROAD
RD

MACRAE
MONKTON
M O F F A T
ROD

TS22

5 B A C K

Blue House

L A N E

⁵29 Greatham

West sture

47 **A** **30** **B** 48 **C**

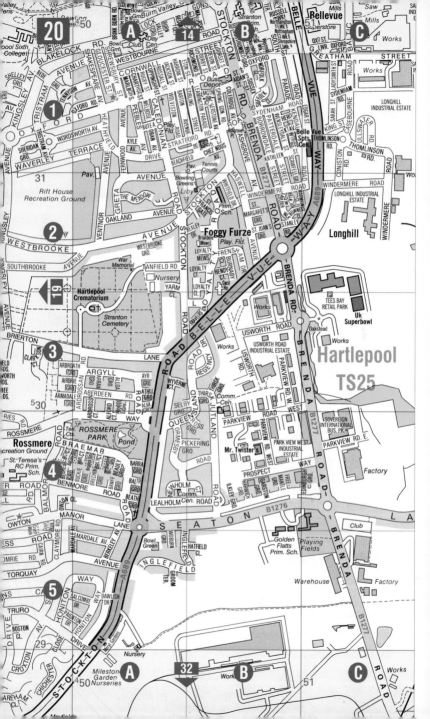

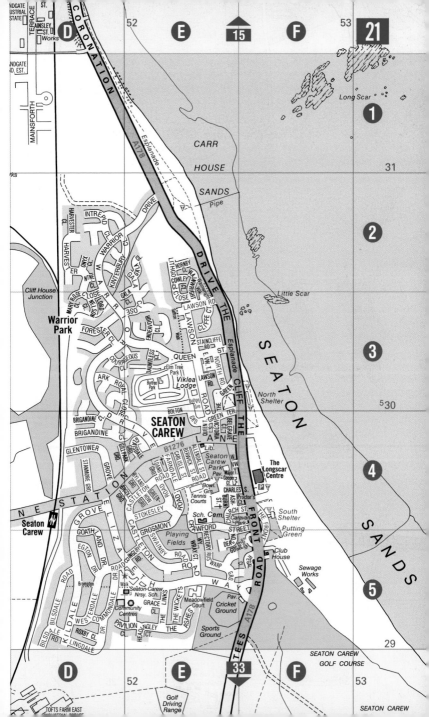

22

34 **A** Sprucely Plantation **B** **4**35 **C**

Carr Wood

1

Knotty Hill
Knottyl Hill
Club House
Golf Driving Range
Dogkennel Plantation
Knotty Hill Plantation

KNOTTY HILL GOLF CENTRE

A177 DURHAM ROAD
WELLGARTH
ST.
WEL
Turnpike WK
TURNPIKE
STALL
FARFIELD MNR
MEADOW HILL

B1278

530

Green Knowles

SEDGEFIELD HOSP.
H

Low Hardwick

2

South Durham Hunt Kennels

CHINNINGHAM CT.
NEVILLE CR.
KERR
THE GARTH
DURHAM DRIVE

Brick Kiln Plantation

3

Hardwick Hall

MILBOURNE CT.
WOLFE CT.
MITFORD CT.
WALLINGTON DR.
RELSN C.
MATEEL CT.
NORTH PARK
BOYNE
NORTH PARK ROAD
LEA
HARDWICK'S

Pheasant Plantation

HARDWICK HALL COUNTRY PARK

A177 DURHAM

SEDGEFIELD

29

Temple (Ruin)
Serpentine Lake
P
P

HARDWICK PARK
Sedgefield Showground
Lambton

PARK LANE
END
NORTH
Town Farm Ct.

4

Brakes Farm

Pav.
Cricket Ground
STATION
Claremont GR.
HASLEDON GR.
Play Field

ROAD WEST
PARK WEST
DUNELM CT.
LAMBTON CRES.
ROABY

SANDY BANK
STATION A689 **ROAD**
Sands Hall Roundabout

West Lodge East Lodge

QUEENS

DRIVE

5

Bath Plantation

Home Farm
Sands Hall

A689

SPRING

28

Sands Farm

SEDGEFIELD RACE COURSE

34 **A** **B** Grandstands **4**35 **C**

Stables

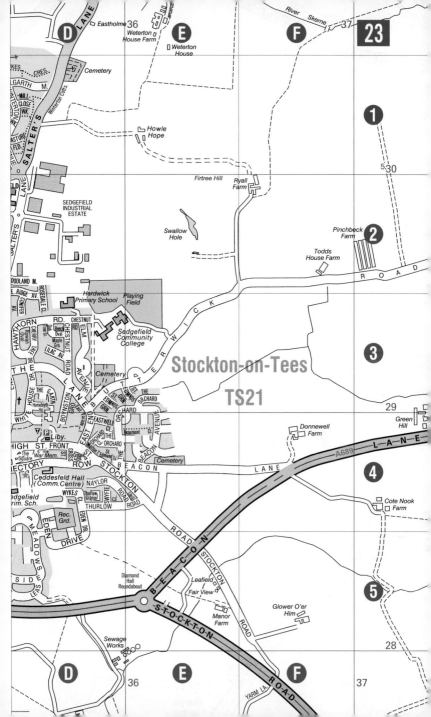

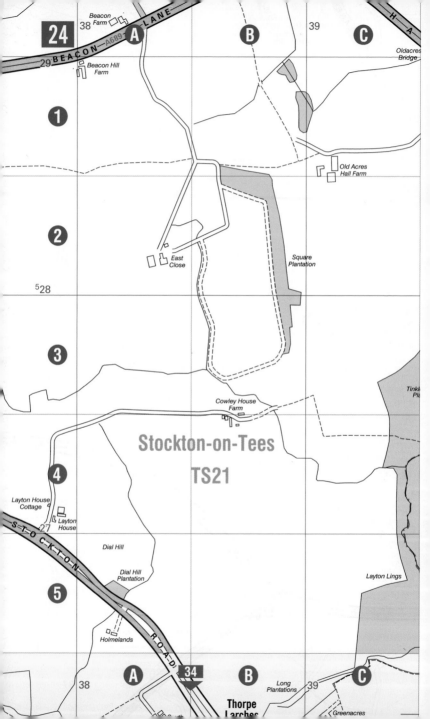

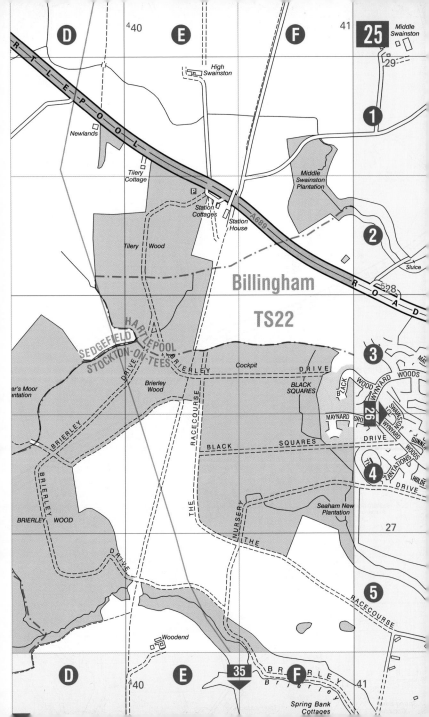

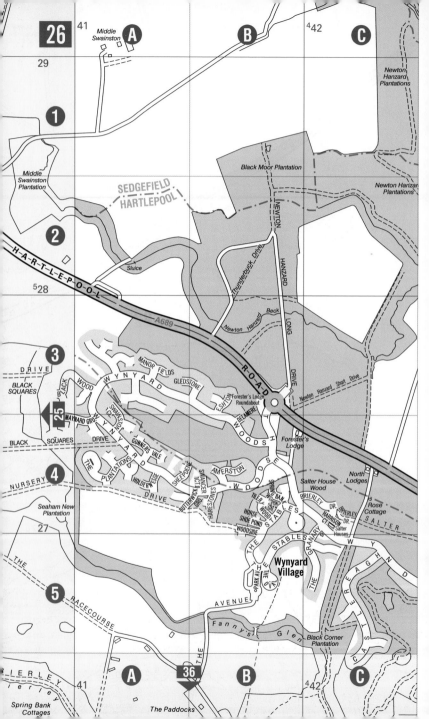

Middle Swainston **A**

B ⁴42 **C**

Newton Hanzard Plantations

1

Middle Swainston Plantation

Black Moor Plantation

Newton Hanzard Plantations

SEDGEFIELD
HARTLEPOOL

N E W T O N

H A R T L E P O O L

2

⁵28

Sluice

A689

H A N Z A R D

Thunderbuck Drive

Newton Hanzard Beck

L O N G

D R I V E

R O A D

3

DRIVE

BLACK SQUARES

BLACK WOOD

WYNYARD

MANOR FIELDS

GLEDSTONE

ESHTON

Forester's Lodge Roundabout

Newton Hanzard Short Drive

◄ **25**

MAYNARD GRO

SWAINSTON CL

DELAMERE

W O O D S

BLACK SQUARES

WYNYARD

DRIVE

GUNNERS VALE

Forester's Lodge

4

NURSERY

THE PLANTATIONS

HOLDERNESSE

BUTTERWICK CL

SHEPPENHALL

HARESTONES

AMERSTON

W O O D S E

SPRING BANK

Salter House Wood

North Lodges

Seaham New Plantation

27

DRIVE

HORSE SHOE POND

WOODSIDE

TILER WD

WENLOCK WD

STABLES

BRIERLEY DR

BRIERLEY DR

HARRISON CT

Salter Houses

Rose Cottage

SALTER

THE

SPRING BANK

W

GRANARY

Y

N

THE

S T A B L E S

Wynyard Village

PARK AVE

AVENUE

Fannys Glen

Black Corner Plantation

C A S T L E R E A G H

D R I V E

5

RACECOURSE

THE

BRIERLEY
ierley
41

A

▼ **36**

B ⁴42 **C**

Spring Bank Cottages

The Paddocks

A

B

C

29

1

Gunnersvale
Farm

16

45

Stotfold
Stables

d Gap
ttage

Sunderland
Lodge

Red
Gap

2

5 28

High
Burntoft

N O R T H

3

27

Whinny Moor
Plantation

Tofts
Farm

4

H A R T L E P O O L

S T O C K T O N - O N - T E E S

B U R N

Northbu
Bridge

27

5

Whinny Moor
Cottage

PEGASUS HO.

WYNYARD PARK

WYNYARD CE

WELLINGTON
HO.

COAL

LANE 44

A

WYNYARD

Annigate
(Samsung)
Roundabout

AVENUE

38

B

C

45

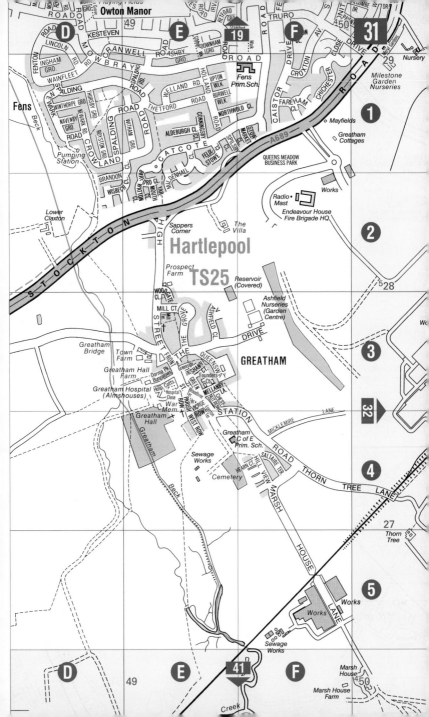

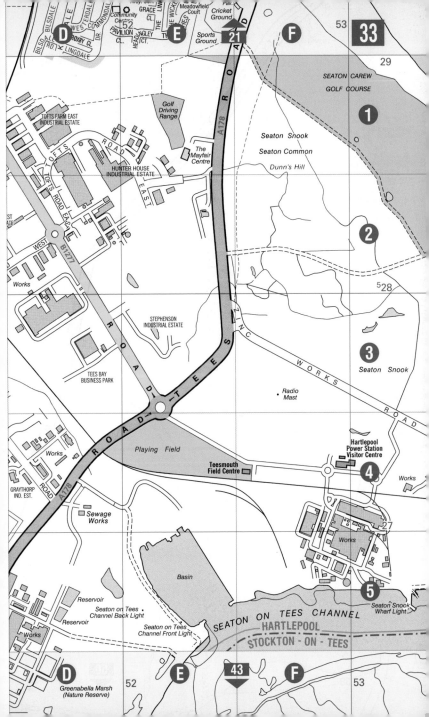

D
BILSDALE
WESTERDALE CL
COMMONDALE
ROXBY CL
LINGDALE
BILSDALE RD

Community
Pavilion
GRACE CL
THE LINKS
HEADINGLEY CT.
52

E
THE WICKETS
THE TEST

Meadowfield Court
Pav.
Cricket Ground

Sports Ground

F

21

53

29

SEATON CAREW
GOLF COURSE

1

TOFTS FARM EAST
INDUSTRIAL ESTATE

Golf Driving Range

The Mayfair Centre

Seaton Snook

Seaton Common

Dunn's Hill

TOFTS ROAD

HUNTER HOUSE
INDUSTRIAL ESTATE

TOFTS ROAD EAST

A178 ROAD

WEST

B1277

Works

STEPHENSON
INDUSTRIAL ESTATE

2

528

ROAD

TEES ZINC

3

Seaton Snook

WORKS

ROAD

TEES BAY
BUSINESS PARK

Radio Mast

ROAD A178

Works

GRAYTHORP
IND. EST.

Playing Field

Teesmouth
Field Centre

Hartlepool
Power Station
Visitor Centre

4

Works

27

Sewage Works

Works

Basin

Works

Reservoir

Seaton on Tees
Channel Back Light

Reservoir

Seaton on Tees
Channel Front Light

5

Seaton Snook
Wharf Light

SEATON ON TEES CHANNEL

HARTLEPOOL
STOCKTON - ON - TEES

D

52

E

43

F

53

Greenabella Marsh
(Nature Reserve)

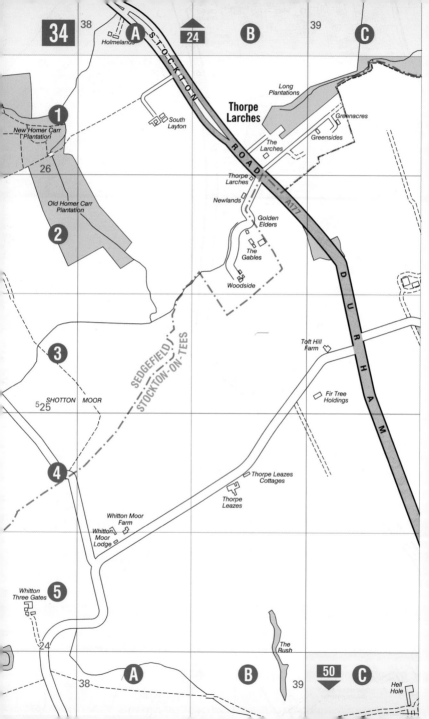

38

A

B

39

C

Holmelands

S·T·O·C·K·T·O·N

24

1

New Homer Carr Plantation

South Layton

Long Plantations

Thorpe Larches

Greenacres

Greensides

The Larches

26

R·O·A·D

Old Homer Carr Plantation

Thorpe Larches

Newlands

A177

2

Golden Elders

The Gables

Woodside

3

SEDGEFIELD

STOCKTON-ON-TEES

D·U·R·H·A·M

Toft Hill Farm

SHOTTON MOOR

25

Fir Tree Holdings

4

Thorpe Leazes Cottages

Thorpe Leazes

Whitton Moor Farm

Whitton Moor Lodge

Whitton Three Gates

5

The Rush

24

38

A

B

39

50

C

Hell Hole

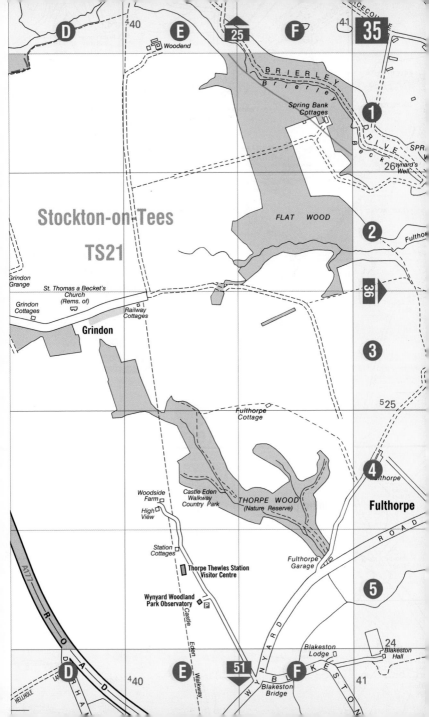

D ⁴40 **E** Woodend **25** **F** 41 **35**

BRIERLEY
Brierley
Spring Bank
Cottages
1
RIVE
SPR.
Beck
26 aynard's
Well

Stockton-on-Tees

TS21

FLAT WOOD
2
Fultho

Grindon
Grange
St. Thomas a Becket's
Church
(Rems. of)
Railway
Cottages
Grindon
Cottages
36
Grindon

3
⁵25

Fulthorpe
Cottage

4
ulthorpe

Woodside
Farm
Castle Eden
Walkway
Country Park
High
View
THORPE WOOD
(Nature Reserve)
Fulthorpe

ROAD
Station
Cottages
Fulthorpe
Garage
Thorpe Thewles Station
Visitor Centre
Wynard Woodland
Park Observatory
P
5
Castle

A177
R
O
A
D
U
R
H
A
M
Eden
Walkway
WYNYARD
Blakeston
Lodge
24
Blakeston
Hall
D HELLHOLE ⁴40 **E** **51** **F** BLAKESTON 41
Blakeston
Bridge

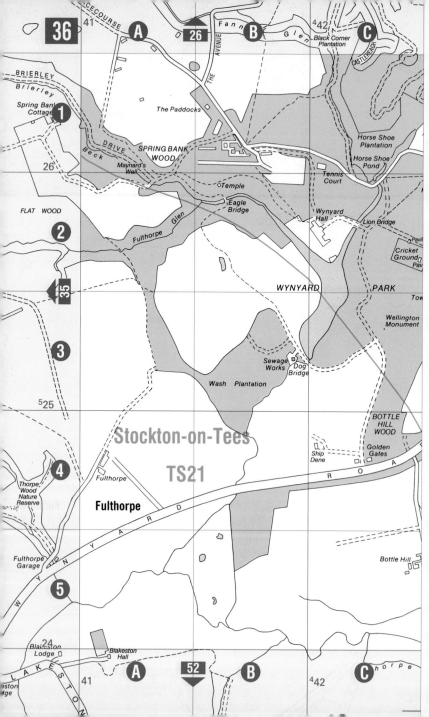

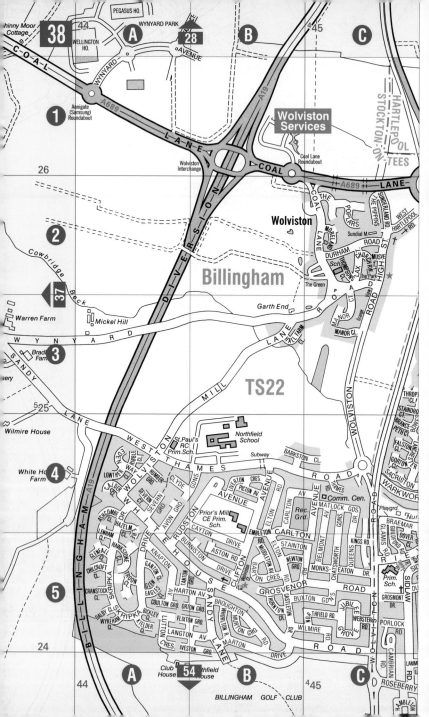

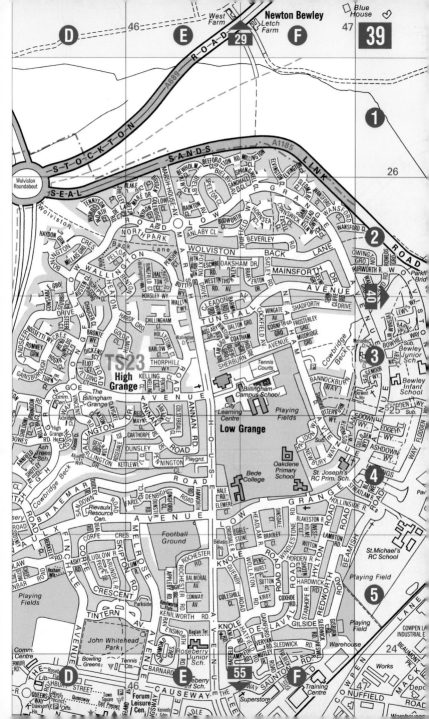

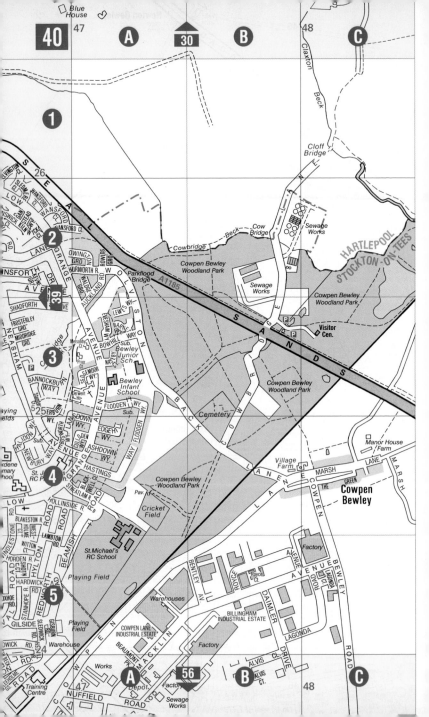

A ▲ 30 B 48 C

1

Blue House

Claxton Beck

Cloff Bridge

S E A L
26
LOW
KENTMERE
SWINDALE CL
SLEDMERE CL
WANSFORD CL
WANSFORD
WANSFORD CL
NSWICK CL
RD
LANE
2
GRANGE
OWINGTON GRO
NURWORTH R
ROWINS GRO
VILLAGE GRO
AUCKLAND RD
GREEN
DR
AVE
39
SHADFORTH
FROSTERLEY GRO
MIDDRIDGE GRO
NEASHAM
NSFORTH
cbridge
525
Cowbridge
Beck
Cowbridge
Cow Bridge
Parkflood Bridge
A1185
Cowpen Bewley Woodland Park
Sewage Works
Sewage Works
Cowpen Bewley Woodland Park
HARTLEPOOL
STOCKTON-ON-TEES
Sewage Works

P
Visitor Cen.
P

3
Bannockburn WAY
Bridge
Melsonby
Prior
LEWS
EVESHAM RD
BARNE
BOWHILL WAY
VISTON
BEWLEY
Bewley Junior Sch.
Sub.
AVENUE
SEAMOOR
Derwent
SANDS
Cowpen Bewley Woodland Park
BACK COWBR LANE
Cemetery

Manor House Farm

4
Playing Fields
NEWBURY WAY
JUNCTION
Sub.
GRANGE
STOCKTON
HASTINGS
FLODDEN
ASHDOWN WY
EDGEHILL WY
DOWN WY
Bewley Infant School
Sub.
FLODDEN WAY
Village Farm
MARSH
LANE
COWPEN
THE GREEN
Cowpen Bewley
St J RC P
ary ool
St J RC P
Cowpen Bewley Woodland Park
Pav.
Cricket Field
MARSH

5
LOW
BLAKESTON R
LAMBTON RD
WITTON CT
HYLTON
HARDWICK
HORDEN R
STANHOPE R
OXHOE R
GILSIDE
WICK RD
ROAD
REDWORTH
BEAMISH
HOLLINSIDE R
STOCKTON R
ROAD
St. Michael's RC School
Playing Field
Playing Field
Warehouses
BENTLEY AV
ROYCE
Rolls Royce Ct.
BILLINGHAM INDUSTRIAL ESTATE
DAIMLER
LAGONDA
AVENUE
ROAD
LAGONDA
BEWLEY
Factory
Factory
ROAD

Warehouse
COWPEN LANE INDUSTRIAL ESTATE
BEAUMONT
MACKLIN
Factory
Works
Training Centre
Depot.
▲ 56
NUFFIELD ROAD
Sewage Works
ALVIS CL
ALVIS CT
DRIVE

A 47 B 48 C

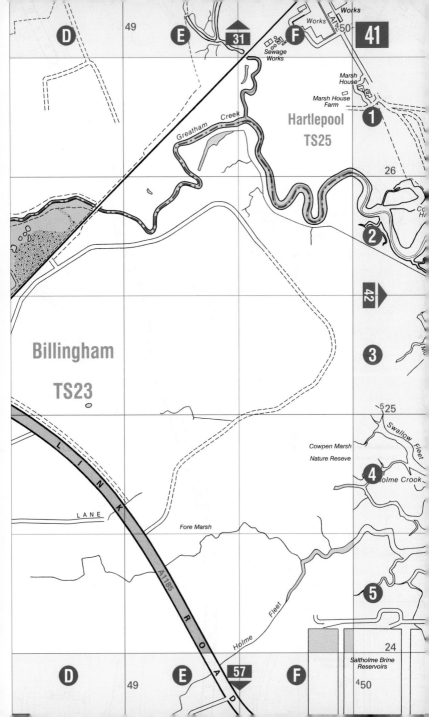

D 49 **E** **31** **F** **50** **41**

Works

Works

Sewage
Works

Marsh
House

Marsh House
Farm

1

**Hartlepool
TS25**

Greatham Creek

26

Co
H

2

42

3

M

525

Swallow Fleet

Cowpen Marsh
Nature Reseve

Billingham

TS23

4 olme Crook

LINK

LANE

Fore Marsh

5

A1185 ROAD

24

Holme Fleet

Saltholme Brine
Reservoirs

D 49 **E** **57** **F** ⁴50

42

450

Works

Works

A

32

B

51

C

ROAD

Marsh
House

Marsh House Farm

1

Hartlepool

TS25

A178

26

Cote Hill

2

Greatham Creek

TEES

41

Greatham Creek Bridge

3

Mucky Fleet

ROAD

Brine Field

525

P

Rough Marsh

Billingham

Swallow Fleet

Cowpen Marsh
Nature Reseve

4

Holme Crook

TS23

Holme Fleet

CAREW

5

A178

24

Saltholme Brine
Reservoirs

450

A

58

SEATON

B

51

C

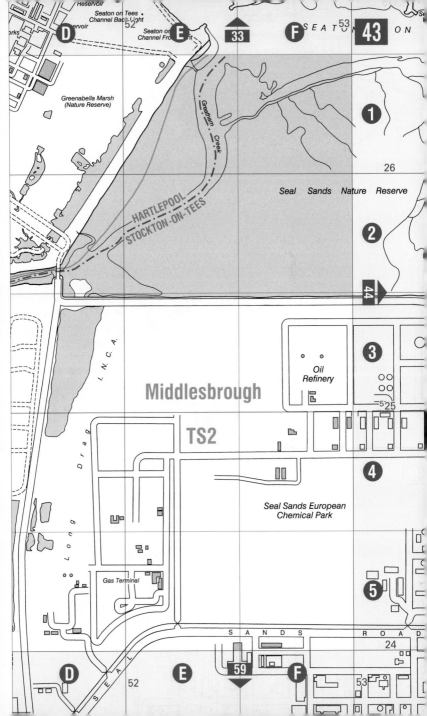

Seaton on Tees
Channel Back Light
52

Seaton on
Channel Front Light

Reservoir

Greenabella Marsh
(Nature Reserve)

Greatham Creek

1

26

Seal   Sands   Nature   Reserve

2

HARTLEPOOL
STOCKTON-ON-TEES

44

3

Oil
Refinery

I. N. C. A.

Middlesbrough

5 25

TS2

4

Seal Sands European
Chemical Park

Long   Drag

Gas Terminal

5

S   A   N   D   S   R   O   A   D

24

SEAL

D   52   **E**   **59**   **F**   53

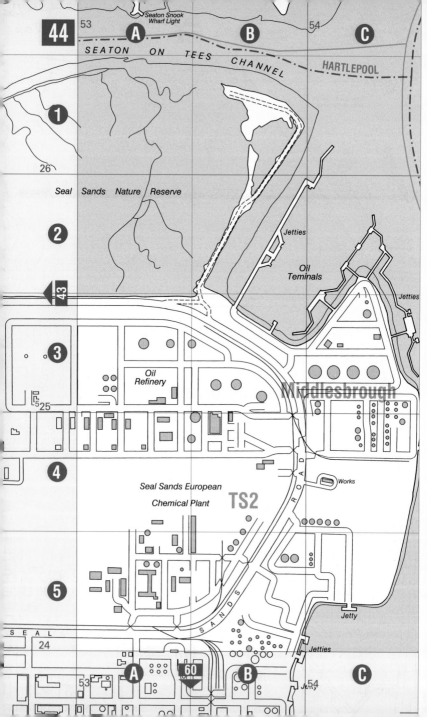

53   **A**   **B**   54   **C**

Seaton Snook
Wharf Light

S E A T O N   O N   T E E S   C H A N N E L   HARTLEPOOL

1

26

Seal   Sands   Nature   Reserve

2

Jetties

Oil
Teminals

◀ **43**

Jetties

3

Oil
Refinery

Middlesbrough

5
25

4

Works

Seal Sands European

Chemical Plant   **TS2**

5

Jetty

S E A L

24

Jetties

A   53   **60**   **B**   54   **C**

Je...y

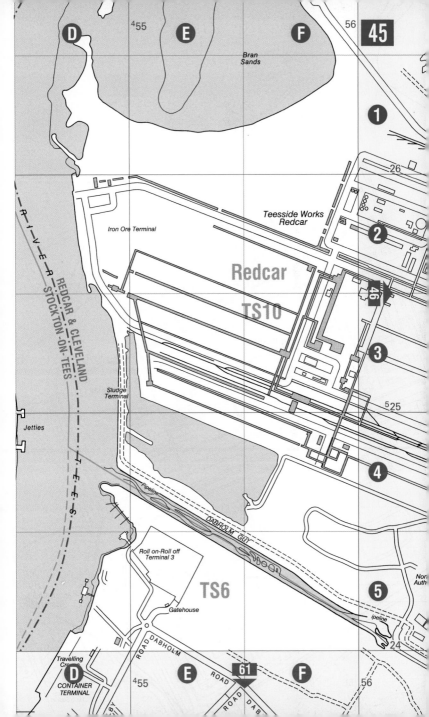

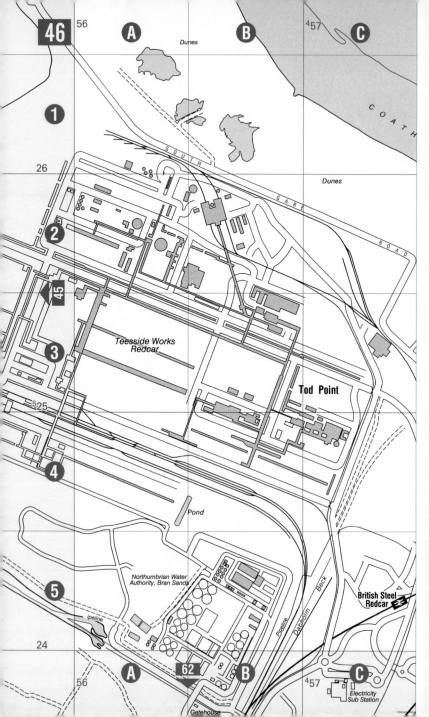

46 56

A   **B**   ⁴57   **C**

Dunes

1

C O A T H

26

S O U T H

G A R E

Dunes

R O A D

2

◄ **45**

3

*Teesside Works
Redcar*

⁵25

Tod Point

4

Pond

*Northumbrian Water
Authority, Bran Sands*

**British Steel
Redcar**

5

ipeline

Pipeline

Dabholm Beck

24

A   **62**   **B**   ⁴57   **C**

56

*Electricity
Sub Station*

Gatehouse

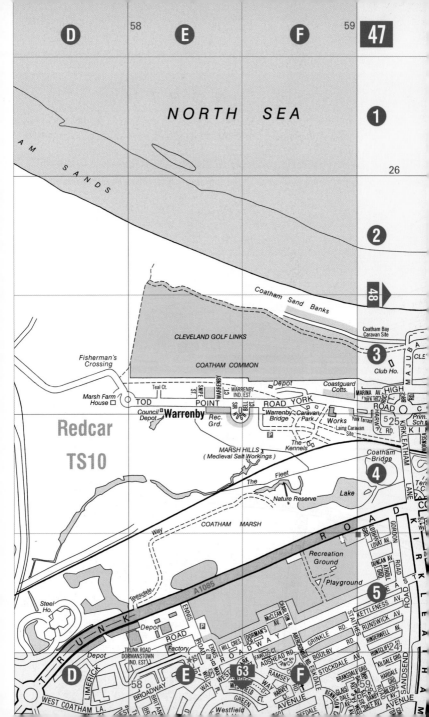

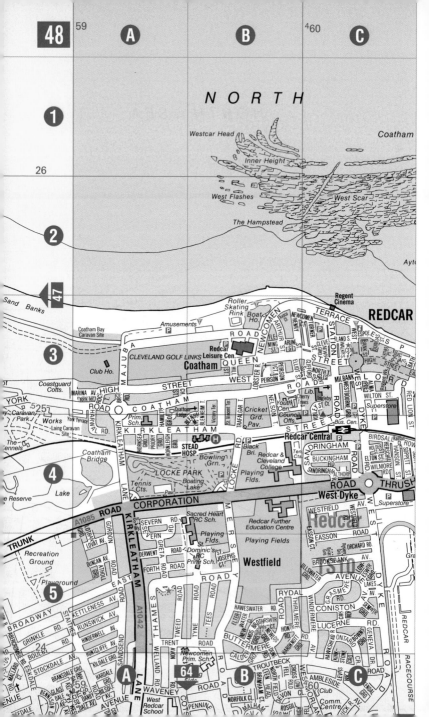

A   B   4 60   C

N O R T H

Coatham

Westcar Head

Inner Height

West Scar

West Flashes

The Hampstead

Sand Banks

Ayte

REDCAR

Regent Cinema

Roller Skating Rink

Boat Ho.

Amusements

Coatham Bay Caravan Site

Club Ho.

CLEVELAND GOLF LINKS

Redcar Leisure Cen.

Coatham

QUEEN   STREET   WEST

Coastguard Cotts.

YORK

Caravan Park

Works

Laing Caravan Site

The Kennels

Coatham Bridge

HIGH   ROAD

COATHAM

Prim. Sch.

Coatham Lodge

KIRKLEATHAM   STREET

Cricket Grd. Pav.

Youth Cen.

Council Offs.

Lib.

Cherry Trees

Superstore

BIRDSAL

Redcar Central

STEAD HOSP

Black Bri.

Redcar & Cleveland College

Playing Flds.

DRINGHAM

BUCKINGHAM RD

SANDRINGHAM

Bowling Grn.

LOCKE PARK

Tennis Cts.

Boating Lake

Lake

Reserve

ROAD   THRUSH

West Dyke

Superstore

CORPORATION   ROAD

KIRKLEATHAM   LANE

TRUNK

Recreation Ground

Playground

A1085

A1042

Sacred Heart RC Sch.

Playing Flds.

St. Dominic's RC Prim. Sch.

St. Josephs Ct.

Redcar Further Education Centre

Playing Fields

Westfield

WESTFIELD

Redcar

BROADWAY

STAITHES AV.

KETTLENESS AV.

RUNSWICK AV.

HINDERWELL AV.

HUNTCLIFFE AV.

KILDALE GRO.

GRINKLE RD.

STOCKDALE AV.

EASTSIDE

SANDSEND

THAMES ROAD

TWEED ROAD

TYNE ROAD

TEES ROAD

TRENT ROAD

Newcomen Prim. Sch.

64

WAVENEY ROAD

PENNINE

West Redcar School

A   B   C

NORFOLK CL.

TROUTBECK

AMBLESIDE

Club

Comm. Centre

REDCAR RACECOURSE

1

26

2

47

3

4

5

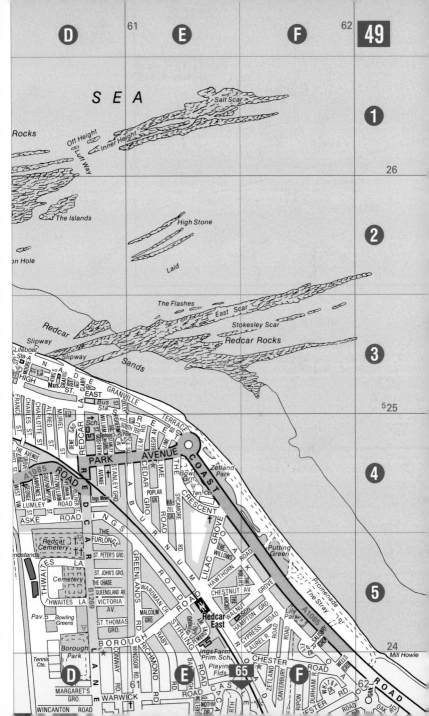

SEA

Salt Scar

1

Rocks

Off Height

Inner Height

Lun way

26

The Islands

2

High Stone

on Hole

Laid

The Flashes

East Scar

3

Redcar

Stokesley Scar

Redcar Rocks

Slipway

Lifeboat

Sta.

Slipway

Sands

5 25

HIGH

N

P

Mus.

ST.

GRANVILLE

CLARK

EAST

Bus

Sta.

CHARLOTTE ST

CHARLES ST

FRANCE ST

ALFRED ST

MURIEL ST

REDCAR LA

DENE GRO

Sch.

TERRACE

THE AVENUE

THE GROVE

PARK

AVENUE

COAST

Zetland

Park

4

A1085

SOUTHAMPTON

LAWRENCE'S

WEST VW

ST GEORGE'S

FITZWILLIAM S

STANLEY GRO

CEDAR GRO

Ings Mews

POPLAR GR

SYCAMORE

CRESCENT

Bowl.

Grn.

Ten. Cts.

ROAD

LUMLEY ST

ROAD

ABEL

ROAD

HAZEL GRO

THE WILLOWS

ASKE

ROAD

KING'S

GREENLANDS

LILAC GROVE

HAWTHORN ROAD

Putting

Green

Promenade

The Stray

5

Redcar

Cemetery

THE FURLONG

ST. PETER'S GRO.

THE CHASE

QUEENSLAND AV.

VICTORIA

AV.

ST. JOHN'S GRO.

ROAD

NUM

CHESTNUT

THE HOLLIES

GROVE

A1085

ndstands

B 1269

Cemetery

THWAITES LA.

THWAITES LA.

WARDMAN CR.

MALCOLM

GRO.

ST. THOMAS

AV.

STIRLING

THE WALNUT

Sch.

HAMPTON GRO

CYPRESS ROAD

LAUREL R

Lily

Park

SALISBURY ROAD

Pav.

Bowling

Greens

Borough

Park

BOROUGH

LANE

CONWAY

RD.

WINDSOR RD.

RICHMOND

RABY

Redcar

East

Ings Farm

Prim. Sch.

CHESTER

Playing

Flds.

65

ZETLAND ROAD

CANTERBURY R

RIPON

DURHAM R

WELLS

WHITBY R

OAK

ROAD

24

Mill Howle

ROAD

Tennis

Cts.

MARGARET'S

GRO.

WARWICK

WINCANTON ROAD

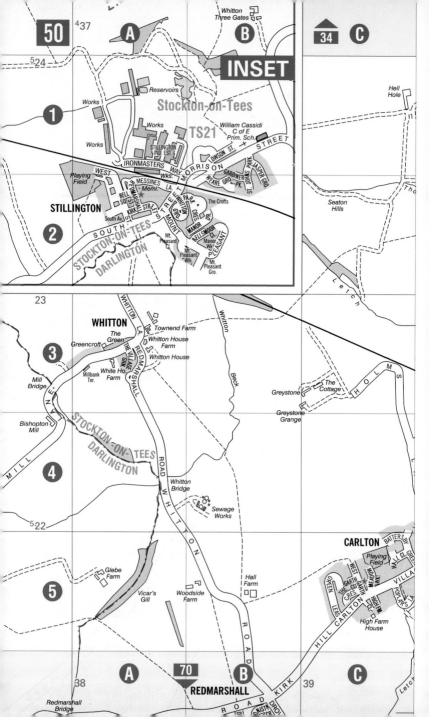

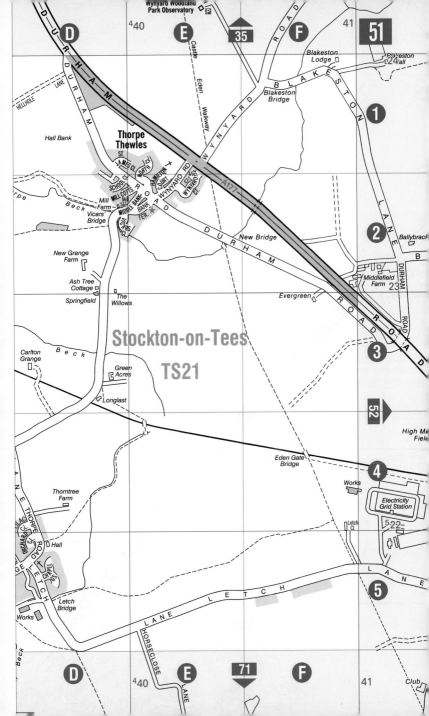

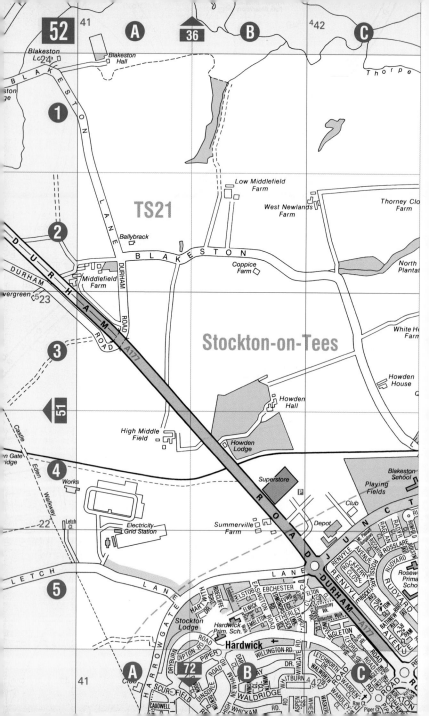

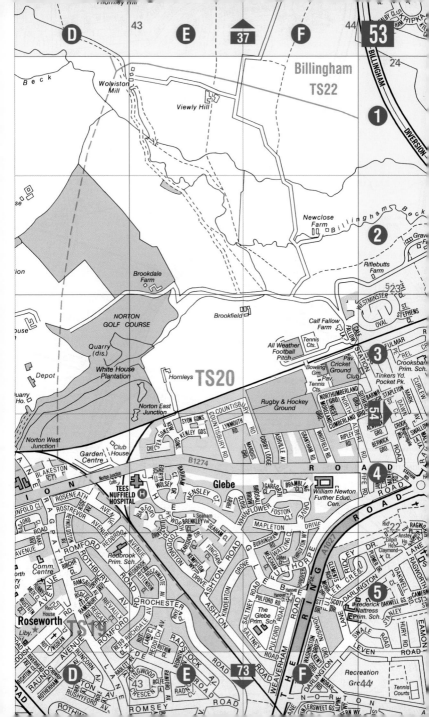

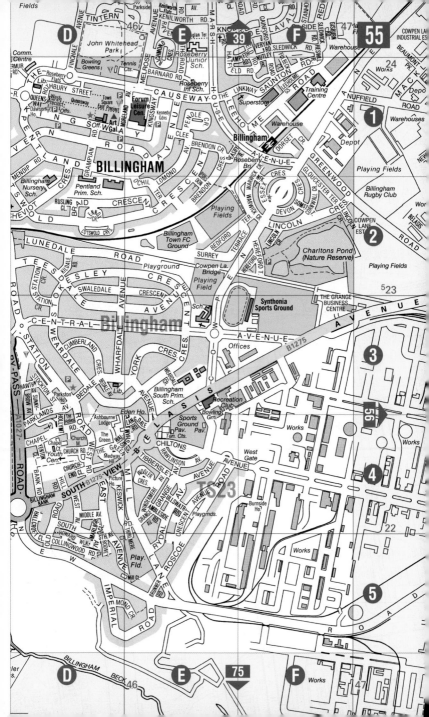

56

A **40** **B** **48** **C**

GILSIDE
STANHOPE RD.
RED
Pr47j Field
HARTSWICK RD.
Warehouse
NUFFIELD ROAD
Training Centre
Warehouse

1

Depot

2
Charltons Pond
(Nature Reserve)

3

55

4

22

5

NEW

A **76** **B** **48** **C**

BILLINGHAM
INDUSTRIAL ESTATE

DAMLER
LAGONDA
LANE

Factory

ALVIS
ALTS CT.
CLOSE
DRIVE

MACKLIN
BEAUMONT PK.
LANE

Depot
Factory
Sewage Works

Warehouses
Depot

Depot

Playing Fields

Billingham
Rugby Club

Works

NEWBURGH CT.
EARLS NOOK
THE
MOAT
WAY

BELASIS CT.
BELASIS
BUSINESS
CENTRE

COWPEN LANE ESTATE

Playing Fields

BRYLAND
ROAD

COXWOLD
WAY

MANOR
WAY

Billingham

TS23

BELASIS HALL
TECHNOLOGY PARK

FALCONBERG CT.

THE MOAT

COLMANS
NOOK

BELASIS
HALL TECH.
PARK

NELSON
AVENUE

Pipe Line
Belasis

Beck

Works

BEWLEY

COWPEN

THE GRANGE
BUSINESS
CENTRE

B1275

BELASIS AVENUE

BELASIS AVENUE

AVENUE

Warehouses

PROCESS
PLANT
PARK

Cemy.

Works

FERMENTER RD.

Works

Works

A1046

HILL

BAMLETTS WHARF
INDUSTRIAL ESTATE

Slipw

Works

Works

Works

A1046

Tees Salt
Bridge

BAMLETTS WHARF RD.

Bamlett's
Wharf

Bamlett's Bight

RIVER

Brighouse
Ct.

BRIGHOUSE
RD.

BRIGHOUSE
BUSINESS
VILLAGE

COLLINGWOOD CT.

MICKLE

RIVERSIDE

HIGH FORCE

ROAD

HAVERTON

BILLINGHAM
REACH
DUSTRIAL ESTATE

47

48

BARTON

Aurora
Ct.

STARTFORT

BART

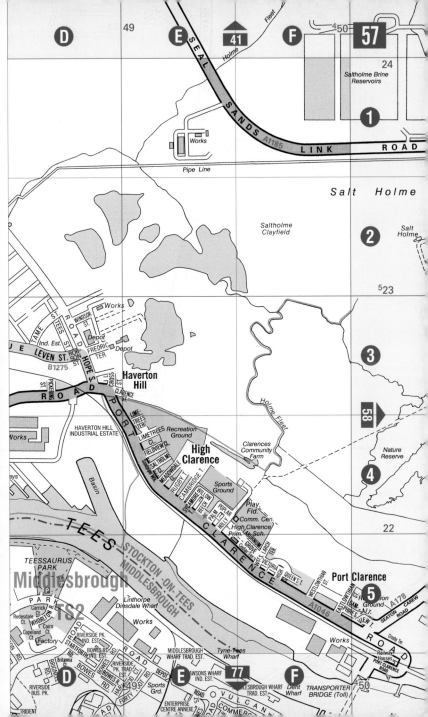

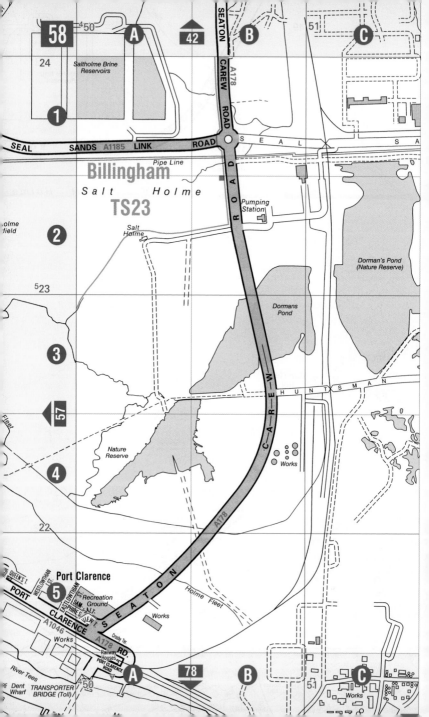

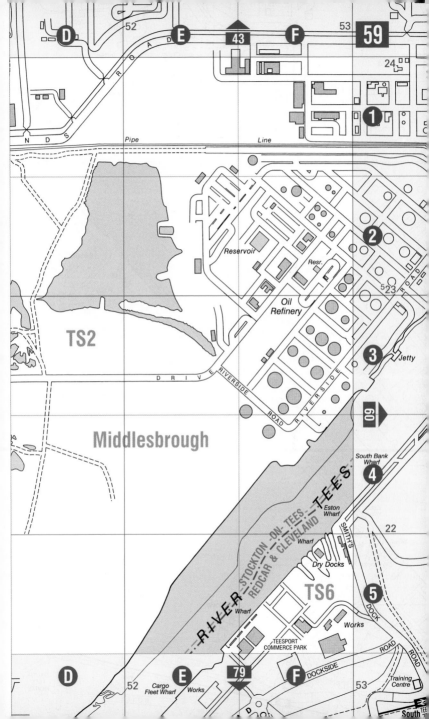

52

D

E

43

F

24

1

Pipe   Line

N   S

2

Reservoir

Resr.

52 23

Oil
Refinery

TS2

3   Jetty

D   R   I   V   E   RIVERSIDE   ROAD   RIVERSIDE

Middlesbrough

60

South Bank
Wharf

4

22

Eston
Wharf

SMITH'S

Wharf

Dry Docks

TS6

RIVER STOCKTON -ON- TEES
REDCAR & CLEVELAND   T E E S

5

DOCK

Wharf

Works

Works

TEESPORT
COMMERCE PARK

ROAD

ROAD

D

E

79

F   DOCKSIDE

Training
Centre

52   Cargo
Fleet Wharf   Works

53

South TE

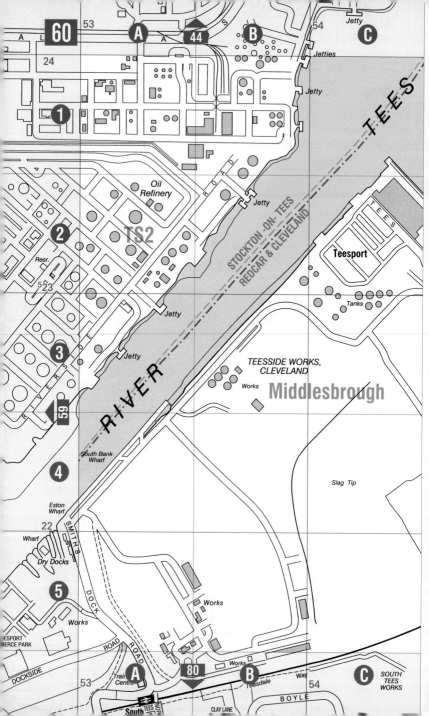

60 53

A

A

A

44

B

54

Jetty

C

24

Jetties

1

Jetty

TEES

ROAD

Jetty

STOCKTON -ON- TEES

REDCAR & CLEVELAND

Oil Refinery

2

TS2

Teesport

Resr.

523

Tanks

Jetty

RIVERSIDE

Jetty

3

TEESSIDE WORKS, CLEVELAND

RIVER

Jetty

Middlesbrough

Works

59

South Bank Wharf

4

Slag Tip

Eston Wharf

22

SMITH'S

Wharf

Dry Docks

DOCK   ROAD

5

Works

ROAD

Works

ESPORT COMMERCE PARK

Works

DOCKSIDE

A

53

Train Centre

80

TEES

Works

B

54

Teesdale   *Way*

C

SOUTH TEES WORKS

South TEES NOP

BOYLE

CLAY LANE

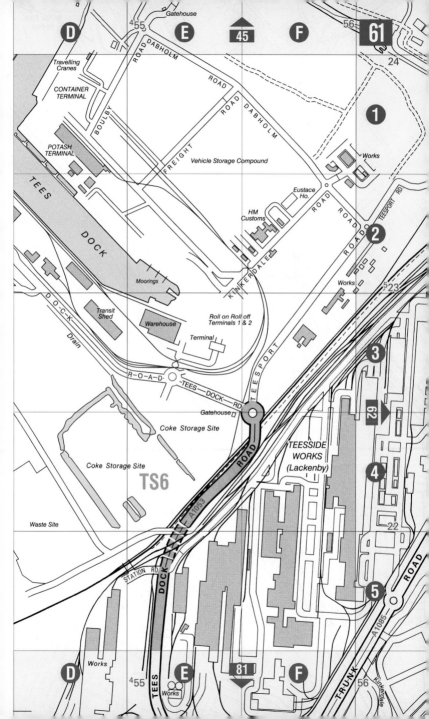

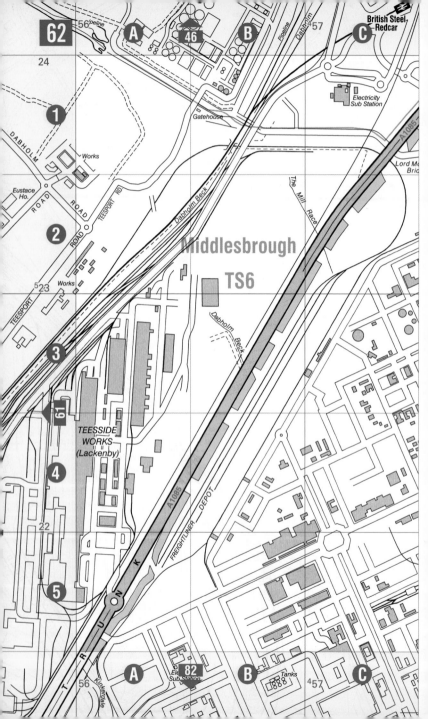

62

24

56 Pipeline

A

46

B

Pipeline   Dabholm 457

C British Steel
Redcar

Electricity
Sub Station

Gatehouse

1

DABHOLM

Works

Eustace
Ho.

ROAD   ROAD

TEESPORT   RD

2

Dabholm Beck

ROAD

Lord Me
Brid

A1085

The Mill Race

Middlesbrough

TS6

56 23   Works

TEESPORT

Dabholm   Beck

3

61

*TEESSIDE
WORKS
(Lackenby)*

4

A1085

FREIGHTLINER   DEPOT

22

5

T   R   U   N   K

A

El
Sub Station

82

Tanks

B

C

56   Runtercale

457

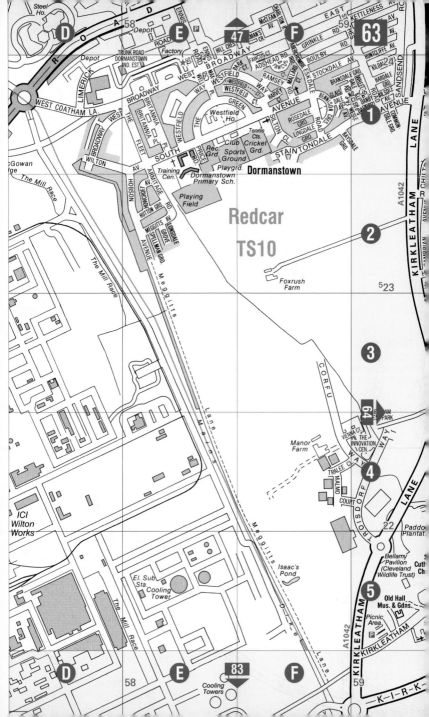

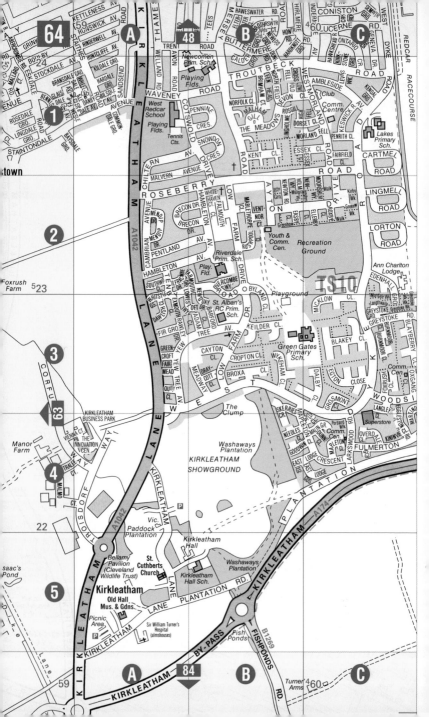

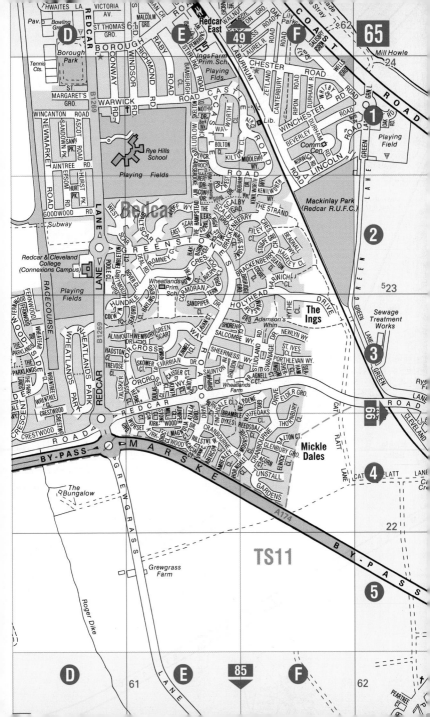

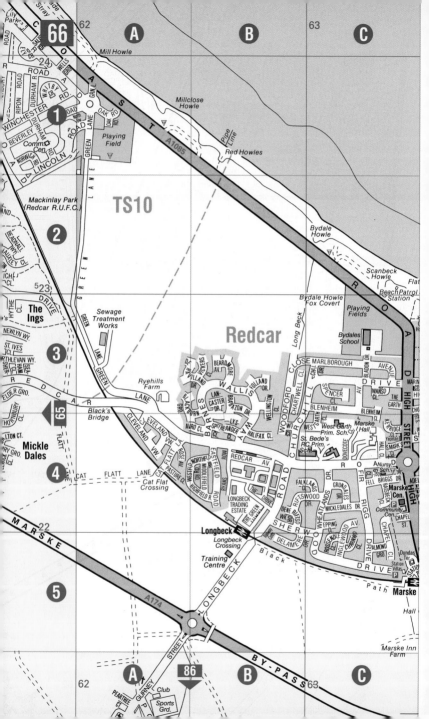

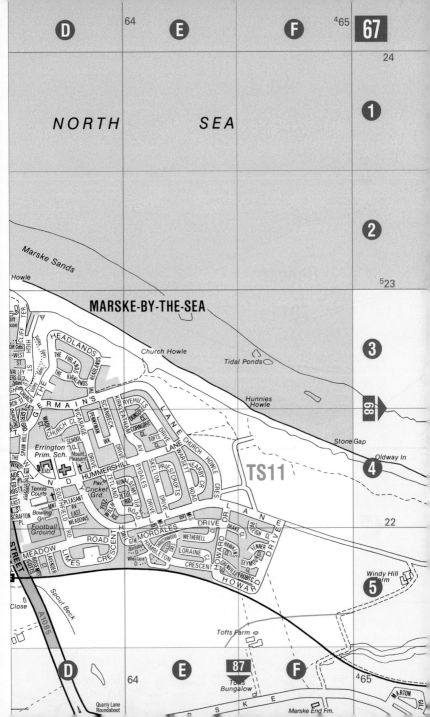

NORTH   SEA

Marske Sands

Howle

MARSKE-BY-THE-SEA

Church Howle

Tidal Ponds

Hunnies
Howle

Stone Gap

Oldway In

TS11

Errington
Prim. Sch.

Tennis
Courts

Bowling
Grn.

Football
Ground

Pav.
Cricket
Grd.

Windy Hill
Farm

Tofts Farm

Tofts
Bungalow

Marske End Fm.

Quarry Lane
Roundabout

Spout Beck

Close

STREET

A1085

MEADOW

⁴65 **A** **B** 66 **C**

23

❶

◀67

Stone Gap

Oldway ln

❷

Agar's Gap

NORTH

⁵22

Redcar

TS11

Windy Hill
Farm

❸

Grove

Hazel

Caravan Park

MARSKE

MARTON

❹

Marske End
Riding School

21 ◀87

THE PARKWAY

IRVIN

MARSHALL

JOHNSTON

THE CHINE

AVENUE

NORTH RD

AVENUE WEST

RIFTS AV.

RUSKIN RD.

ROAD

MARSKE

MARSKE MILL LANE

LIVERTON

WHIN

WILTON

BANK

QUEENSWAY

WOODROW AV.

Ten.
Cts.

Cemetery

ELM
GTE
FROST

WILTON WY.

SYCAMORE AV

CHESTNUT

RENWOOD DR

LILAC CL

WILLOW CL

BANK

**SALTBURN-
BY-THE-
SEA**

Recreation
Ground

Playing
Fields

Pav.
Ckt. Grnd.

Pav. P

**Saltburn
Leisure Cen.**

Huntcliffe
School

Saltburn
Prim.
Sch.

WINDSOR

Gresley

PRINCES

RD

UPLEATHAM ST.

CAMBRIDGE ST

OXFORD ST.

MONTROSE
ST.

RANDOLPH STREET

LAUREL CL.
CLOSE

BECKWOOD

RUBY

CRESCENT

Saltburn
Prim.
Sch.

EDEN ST

LEVEN ST

LUNE

AVON

GRETA

ROSE

ROAD

Langbaurgh De Brus
PARADE
GARNET

BACK GARNET
STREET

CORAL

Marine
Ct.

EMERALD

DIAMOND

RUBY ST

Hanover

†

Saltburn
⪼ P

MILTON

DUNDAS STREET WEST STA.SQ.DUNDAS
HILDA PLACE
BRISTOL ST.
EXETER ST.
BATH ST.

TWEED ST
Glenbrook Grove

ALBION TERRACE

WINDSOR

STREET

ROAD

Supermarket

Lib.

PEARL

❺

GUISBOROUGH

P

LANE

THE FAIRWAY

Club
Ho.

HOB HILL

THE
GREEN

HOB HILL

MARSKE MILL LANE

HILL TOP

VICTORIA
ST.

MARSKE MILL LA.

N.E. RIDGE

Cottages

MARSKE

Rockdaw Sq.

VICTORIA

ROAD

Meldreth
House

Youth
Hostel

Rifts
Wood

Rush
Hall

Ri

Th

⁴65 **A** HOB ◀88▼ **B** 66 **C**

HILL SALTBURN
GOLF COURSE

HOB

HILL

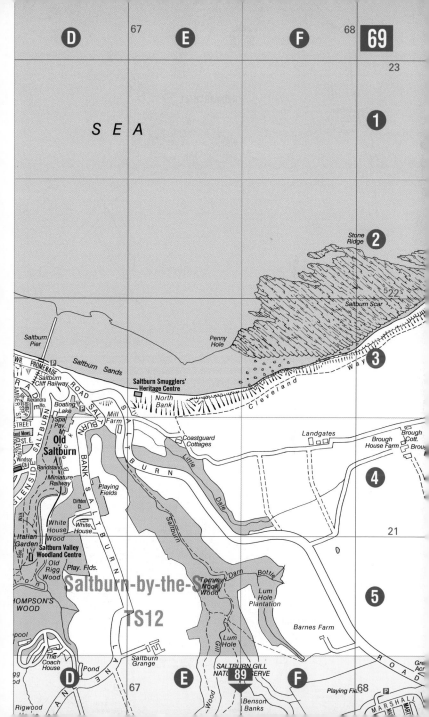

23

S E A

1

Stone
Ridge

2

Saltburn Scar
522

Penny
Hole

Cleveland Way

3

Saltburn
Pier

WR. PROMENADE   Saltburn Sands

Saltburn
Cliff Railway

Alexandra
Ho.

Boating
Lake

Spa
Pav.

ROAD   SAL

**Saltburn Smugglers'
Heritage Centre**

*North
Bank*

Mill
Farm

STREET

Windsor
Ct.

**Old
Saltburn**

Bandstand

Miniature
Railway

Cliffden
Ct.

Playing
Fields

**White
House**

White
House

Italian
Garden

**Saltburn Valley
Woodland Centre**

Old
Rigg
Wood

Play. Flds.

**THOMPSON'S
WOOD**

Saltburn-by-the-S

TS12

Wood

SALTBURN

BANK

B   U   R   N

Saltburn

Little
Dale

BURN

*Coastguard
Cottages*

Landgates

Brough
House Farm

Brough
Cott.

Brou

4

21

Darn

Tommy
Nook
Wood

Bottle

Lum
Hole
Plantation

Barnes Farm

5

Gre
Acr

The
Coach
House

Pond

Saltburn
Grange

Lum
Gill

Lum
Hole

**SALTBURN GILL
NAT. RESERVE**

ROAD

Rigwood

LANE

D   67   E   **89**   F   68

Benson
Banks

Playing Fie   P

MARSHALL

MART

70

38

A

50

B

39

C

High Farm
House

Vicar's
Gill

Woodside
Farm

HIGH FM.

HILL CARLTON

WHITTON RD.

KIRK

REDMARSHALL

Redmarshall
Bridge

1

Karamea

REDMARSHALL

HALL

ROAD

DROVERS

CHURCH

RYDAL

CONISTN.
CR.

DERWENT
CL.

FERGUSON
WY.

WINDERMERE
AV.

LANE

High
Farm

Mainside

Church
Farm Flats

The
Mains

Letch

High
View

Hill House
Farm

The
Garth

21

2

Gately Moer
Reservoir

Reservoir

3

STOCKTON-ON-TEES
DARLINGTON

520

4

TS21

Ox Eye
Farm

Whispers

Hill
View

Longhirst

LANE

Delholme
Farm

5

Whinny Hill

DARLINGTON

SANDY LEAS LA.

BACK

Gooseberry
Farm

Sunnyfield
Stud

Ox Hill
Farm

19

A

94

Cindolowen

B

Sandyleas
Plantation Farm

39

C

38ine Acres
Nurseries

The
Bungalow

Depot

Sandyleas
Plantations

Elton Moor

CARLTON **D**

E

51

F

41

1

21

Letch Bridge

Works

LANE

HORSECLOSE

⁴40

LANE

Club

Club

California

Bishopsgarth School

2

Comm. Cen.

Bishopsgarth

72

Stockton-on-Tees

DALE

DAL

TOVIL CL.

MOWBR

WIDDRIGT

MITF

WH. LEAM

HARROWGATE LANE

DRIVE

POWBN CL.

BONONE GRO.

3

THE WYNDE

MALTON

MALTO

East View Reservoir (Covered)

TS19

Bishopsgarth

Bishopsgarth Cottages

20

East View

Coalgarth House

REDMARSHALL

WIMPOLE

ROAD

THE CLOISTERS

CATHEDRAL WY.

CL.

CARDINAL GRO.

TYRONE RD.

Two Mile House Farm

BISHOPTON

BACK

ABBOTS WY.

WIMPOLE ROAD

MARIA

SHA

Ouston Moor House

Grassy Nook Farm

ROAD

ABBEY WY.

SAND

MARIA

KENWIL GRO.

DR.

Elton Lane Farm

ARMSIDE CL.

BARRHEAD

S.

4

WEST

Ouston Moor Farm

DARLINGTON

KIRKWALL CL.

ROPNER

LEONARD

CL.

ORVILLE

FAIRSTNE RD.

FAIRTHORN AV.

FARTHORN

CL.

Ox Eye Fox Covert

YARM

LERWICK CL.

ULLAPOOL CL.

STORMO

GRANGEVILLE AV.

BROOKFIELD RD.

GUNNER

LIMBRI

RD.

CL.

ROSS

GRO.

ELSTANE

Elton Lane Gdns.

BACK

CULROSS GRO.

CLIXTON CL.

5

GRO.

ASLAN

CL.

19

SADBERGE

Elton Park

LANE

LYNDON

WY.

GREENFIELDS WY.

M. CLI TON

SCALBY GRO.

KNAYTON GRO.

KILDAL

MUKER

D

⁴40

E

95

Betty Farm

F

HAYLING

SIMONS CL.

⁴41

D

MERRI

GRO.

KILDALE

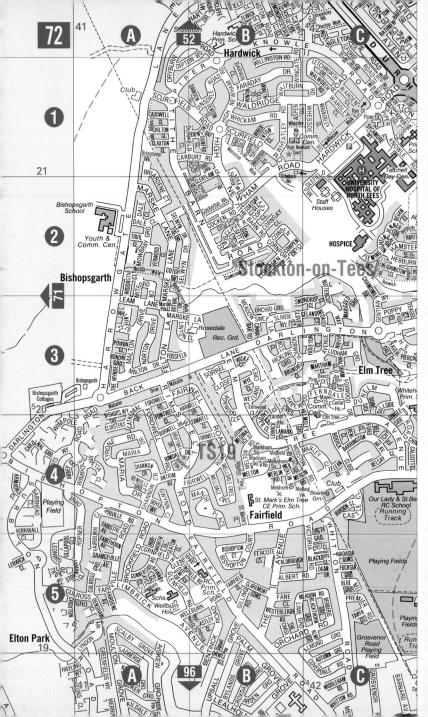

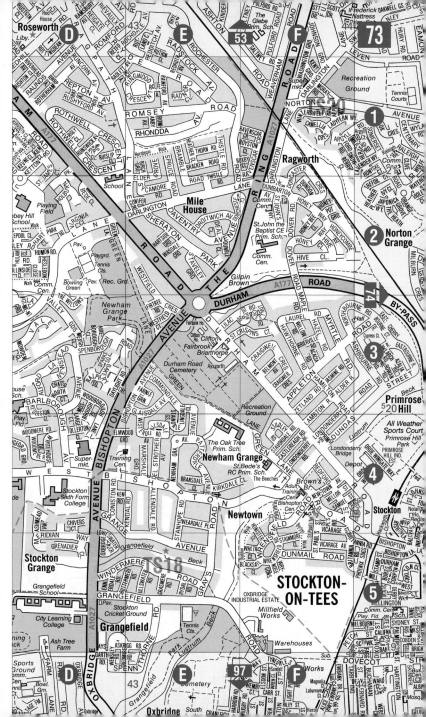

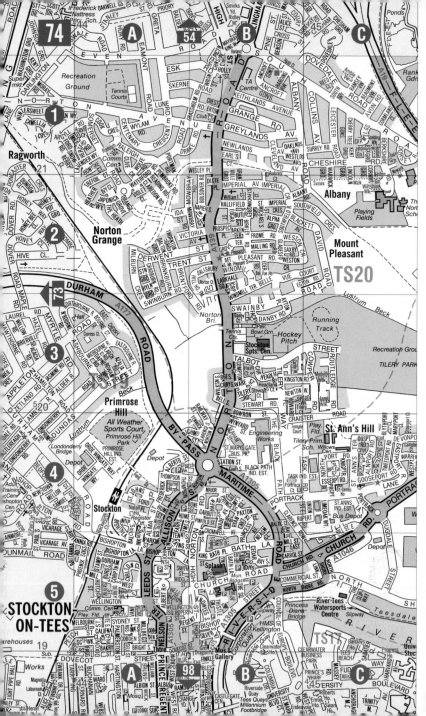

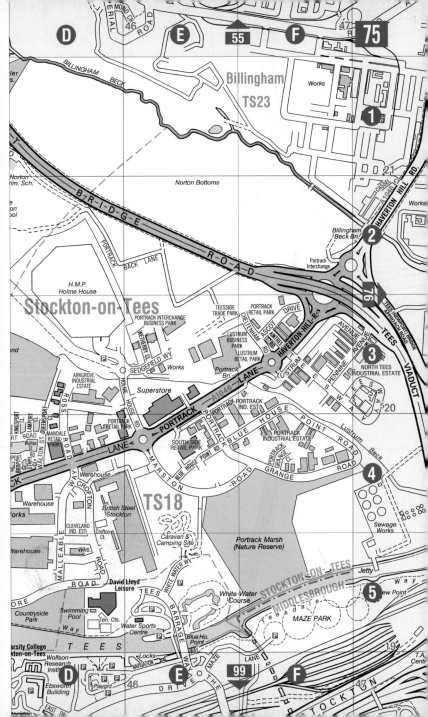

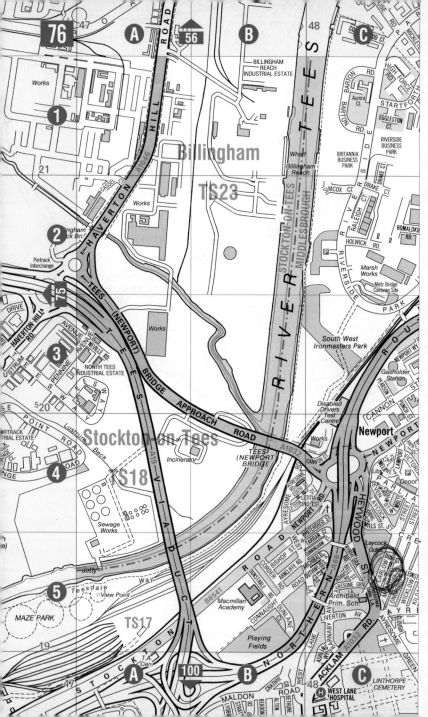

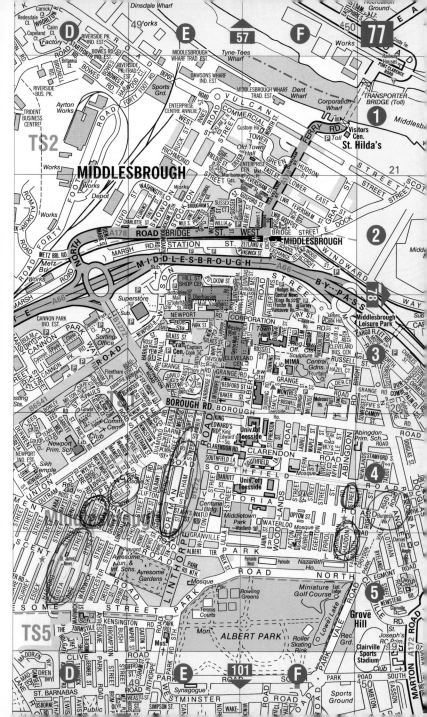

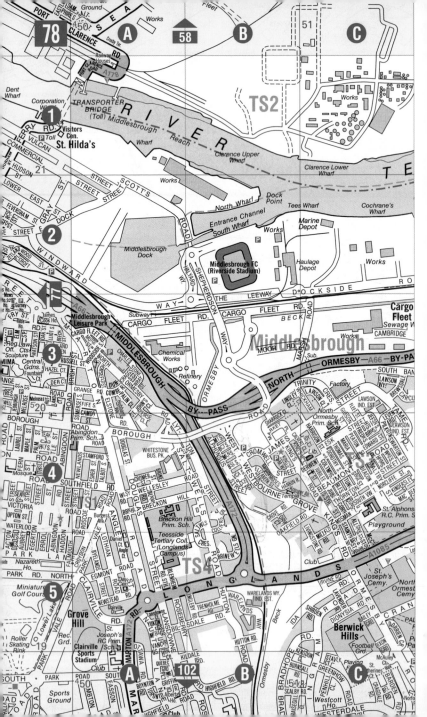

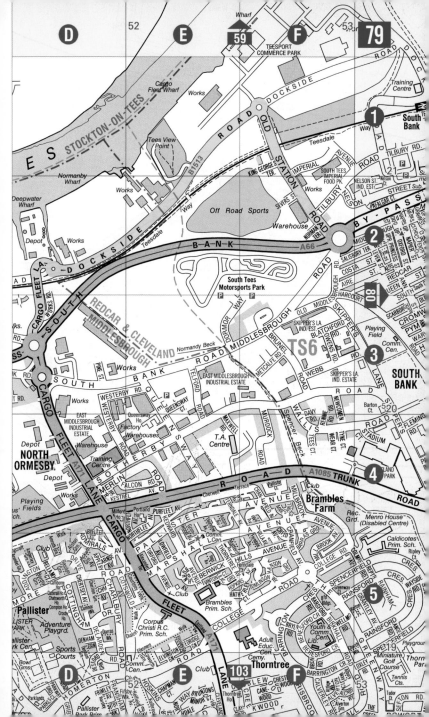

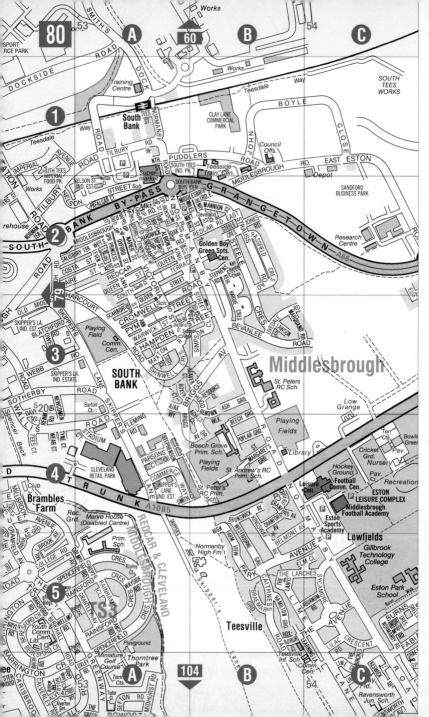

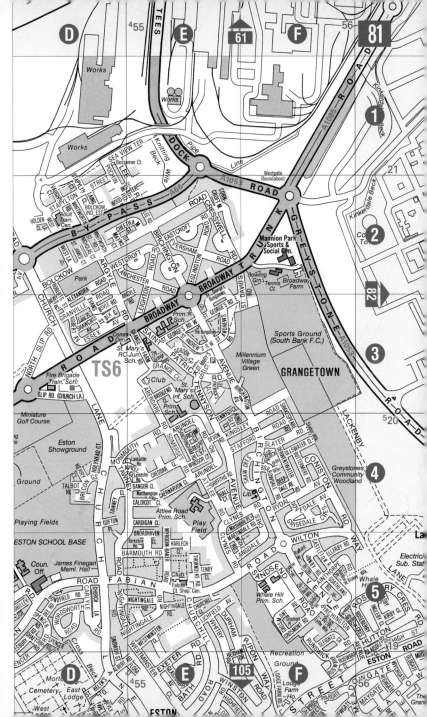

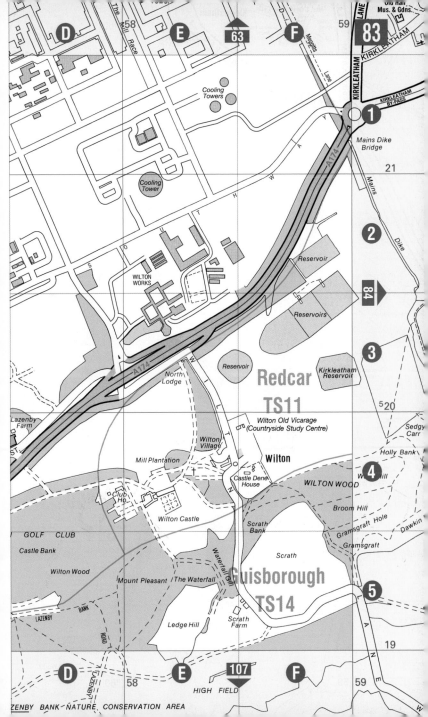

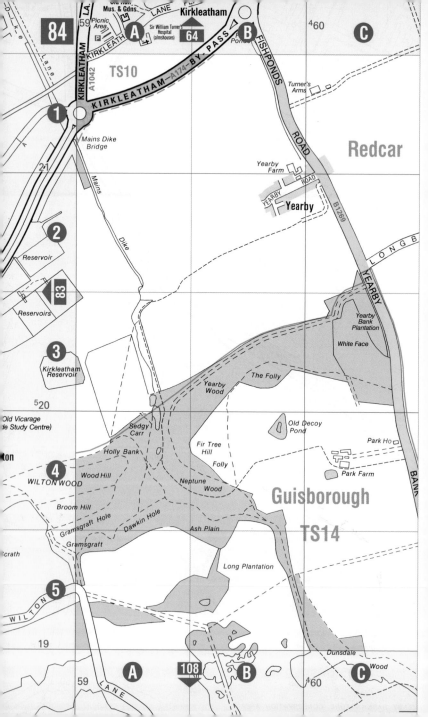

85

D · 61 · E · ▲ 65 · F · 62

Roger Dike

GREWGRASS LANE

Fell Briggs Farm

Thrushwood Farm

LONGBECK LANE

GREWGRASS LANE

BECK

TS11

Reservoir

Barr's Plantation

Reservoir

New Buildings Farm

SANDY LANE

REDCAR ROAD

The Stripe

B1269

Dunsdale

NEW ROW

Dunsdale Farm

Dunsdale Beck

How Close Plant.

D · 61 · E · 109 · F · 62

Sparrow Park Farm

PEARTREE CT

GURNEY

DALE

VICTORIA

LANE

GLENESK RD

EAGLES

ST ANDREWS

Charles Cliff Way

ANNES RD

TONGE RD

KILLBRIDGE CL

ROAD

SUNNINGDALE ROAD

BIRKDALE

OAKDALE RD

MERION DR

HARTSBOURNE

FULFORD GRO

NOPE CT

HUNSTN GRO

MOORTOWN

SANDMOOR ROAD

NEW Marske Prim Sch

GEORGE'S CR

HIGHCLIFFE GRO

ROAD

ASHRIDGE CT

RYDER

SELACY

GREEN CK CL

WALMER CR

PRESWICK RD

PINEHURST

ABRIDGE CL

ABRIDGE CT

COXMOOR WY

ALLENDALE TEE

ROAD

ROSEMT RD

DOWNFIELD DR

WOODBRK CL

TURNBERRY

HILLSIDE

TANKERSLEY RD

Football Ground

Playing Field

Reservoir (covered)

Picnic Area

86

1

2

3 · Erring Woo

Patterson's Bank

20

Falkland

4

SANDY LANE

Soap Well Walk Wood

5

19

Fl

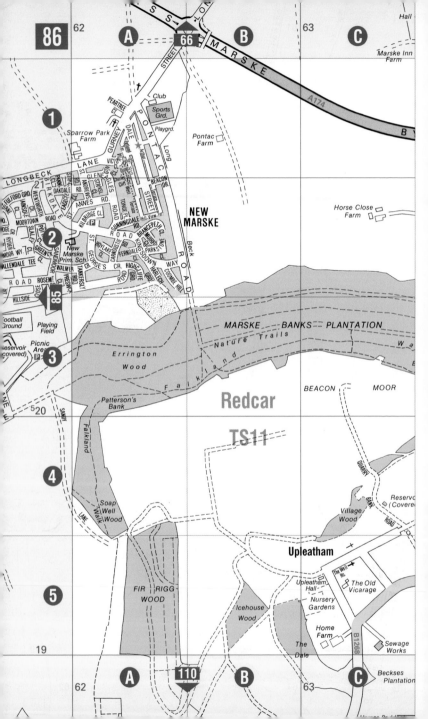

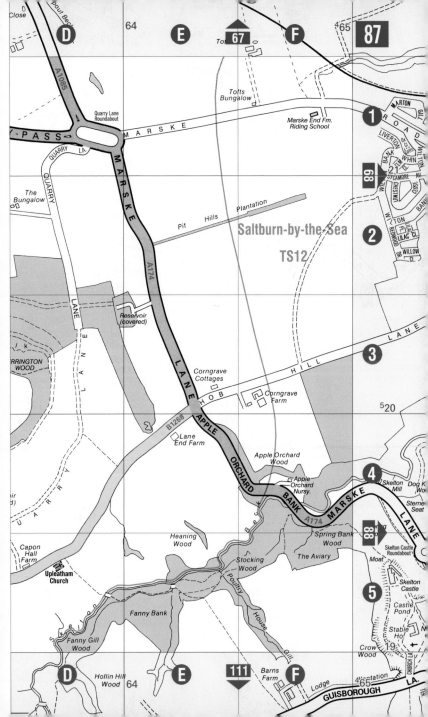

88

SALTBURN-BY-THE-SEA

SALTBURN GOLF COURSE

Recreation Ground

Club Ho.

Meldreth House

Youth Hostel

Chards Cottages

Rifts Wood

Rush Hall

VICTORIA RD.

MARSKE MILL LA.

N.E. RIDGE

HOB HILL

THE LINKS

THE GREEN

THE FARWAY

GUISBOROUGH RD.

HOB HILL WOOD

Beck

Crow Wood

Jackdaw Scar

Gill

Mill Gill

Thorney Close Wood

Saltburn Lane

MARSKE MILL LA.

Railway Cottages

SALTBURN BY-PASS

A174

Skelton

Mary Dale Leap

Pav.

Cricket Ground

Skelton Mill

Dog Kennel Wood

Sterne's Seat

Spring Wood

Skelton Bank

The Aviary

MARSKE

A174

Fish Pond

SKELTON / BROTTON

STONEDALE

BOWLAND DALE

NIDDERDALE

THORNTHWAITE CL.

GRINSIDE CL.

PENDLE CL.

BRAITHWAITE CL.

APPLETHWAITE GDNS.

KENTMERE AV.

ROSTHWAITE DR.

LONGTHWAITE

HAMSTERLEY

TYNEDALE CL.

CALDERDALE

WHARFDA

EDEN

ROAD

LONGSCAR CL.

V. ORCHARD

Resr. (Cov.)

STAT

Apple Orchard Nursy.

ORCHARD BANK

Skelton Mill

Skelton Castle Roundabout

Saw Mill

Playing Fields

Moat

Skelton Castle

Castle Pond

De Brus School

ROAD

ROS... CL.

MARLBOROUGH RD.

GRAMPIAN RD.

COTSWOLD DR.

HAMBLEDON CR.

PENNINE WY.

SIDLAW

CHEVIOT DR.

MENDIP AV.

MALVN. AV.

PENTLD

Bowl. Gm.

Playing Fields

BAD... AV.

Stable Ho.

Nursery Grnd.

Crow Wood

Plantation

Lodge

GUISBOROUGH

CHURCH LA.

LANE

North Terrace

North Terrace

West South Ter.

TOWN GRN.

SOMERSET RD.

WILTSHIRE RD.

DEVON CK.

DORSET RD.

NORFOLK RD.

LAWNS

GILL

EMERALDALE

ULLSWATER DR.

RIDGE

NORTH RIVAL

WINDERMERE

THIRLMERE DR.

GRASMERE

HIGH

WINDERMERE RD.

CONISTON

DRIVE

DERWENT RD.

DERWENT RD.

Home Farm

WOODS Cen.

South RD.

Carlick's Yd.

REAR HIGH ST.

Egg-Cup Farm

Chapels

Cemetery

STREET

Lane Ho.

Tce.

The Hills

SKELTON

Saltburn-by-the-Sea

TS12

New Wood

Bowman Hill

BACK

LANE

Back Lane Farm

Back Lane Cotts.

CASTLE LANE

BOOSBECK

GREEN LANE

Comm. Cen.

Throston Place

GRANGE

Green Farm

Chapel

Comm. Cen.

HALL

TROUT LANE

ELLIOT ST.

Newbrook

Tro

Skelton Green

Manless Green Farm

THOMPSON'S RD.

CLEVELAND VIEW

NEWLANDS RD.

MANLESS TER.

NEW... DURY

Skelton High Green

BOOSBECK RD.

Cold Keld Spring

Cleve...

Caravan Park

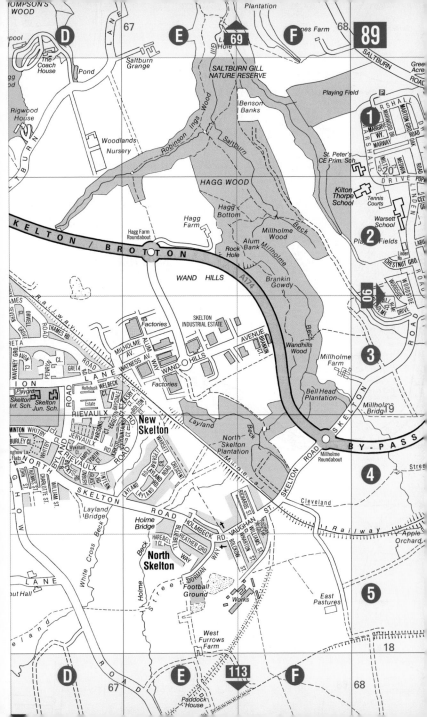

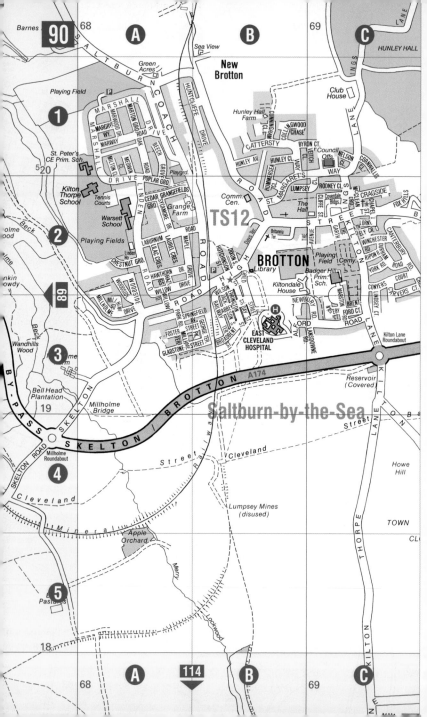

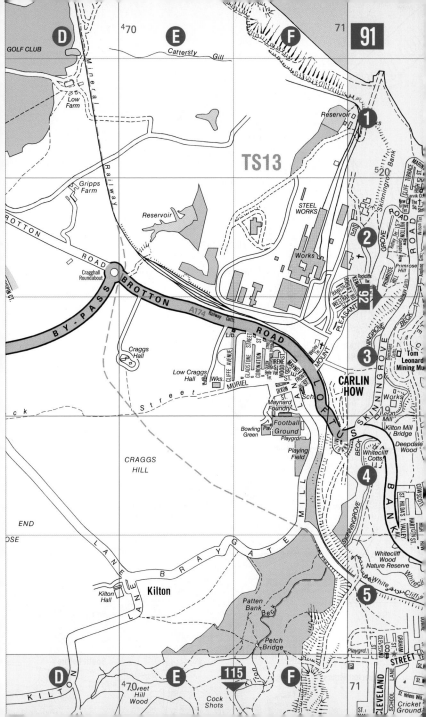

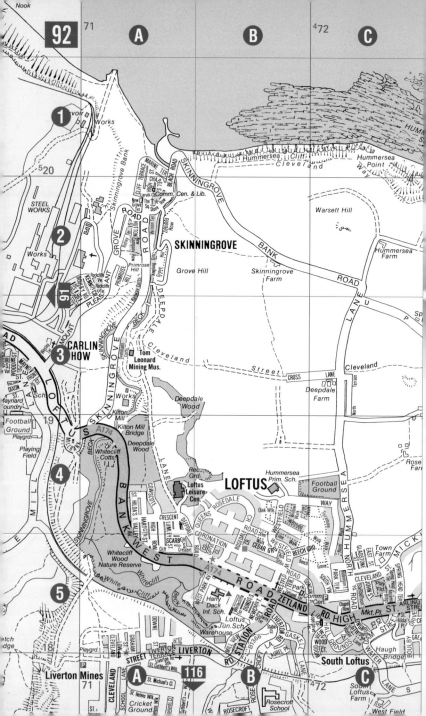

71   **A**   **B**   472   **C**

Nook

Reservoir
Works

1

520

STEEL
WORKS

Works

2

MARINE TERRACE
CLIFF TERRACE
BEACH ROAD
SKINNINGROVE ROAD
CHA
Larick
New Grove
The Stones
Comm. Cen. & Lib.
ZIGZAG Row
Wilson Ter.
NOLLING
Primrose Hill
PRIMROSE
Watson Ter.

SKINNINGROVE

Grove Hill

GROVE ROAD

Rockcliffe Vw.
Rockcliffe
KENNEDY GDNS.
IRENE ST.
PLEASANT
MOUNT PLEASANT

19 61

CARLIN HOW

3

IRENE ST.
ST.
DIXON ST.
FRONT ST.
Maynard Foundry

DEEPDALE BECK

Tom Leonard Mining Mus.

Cleveland Street

Works

Kilton Mill
Kilton Mill Bridge

LOFTUS BANK A174

Football Ground
Playgrds.

19

Playing Field

SKINNINGROVE ROAD

Whitecliff Cotts.

Deepdale Wood

4

Deepdale Wood

BECK

BANK WEST ROAD

Whitecliff Wood Nature Reserve

White Cliffs

COWSCOTE

ST HILDA'S
TALLEY
HARTIN ST.
HIGH ROW
LUMLEY ROW
Cliff Crescent
CRESCENT
SCARBO CRESCENT
CORONATION
NEPTUNE

QUEENS

ROSEDALE

ROAD

ROSEDALE CR.
CEDAR GRO.
WESTFIELD AV.

Rec. Grd.

Loftus Leisure Cen.

LOFTUS

Hummersea Prim. Sch.

Oak Wlk.

WESTFIELD

Warsett
Walk
Walk

Football Ground

WAY

BEECH GRO.
Grove

HUMMERSEA

Cleveland Street CROSS LANE

Deepdale Farm

Cleveland

North Terrace

Warsett Hill

Skinningrove Farm

Hummersea Farm

Hummersea Point

HUMMERSEA

Cleveland Way

SKINNINGROVE BANK ROAD

LANE

Spr.

5

Whitecliff

White Cliffs

BECK

DOWNE

GRAHAM

STEWART

West Park Av.

Harry Dack Inf. Sch.

Loftus Jun. Sch.
Warehouse

EDWARDS
NEWTON

Stable

Liverton Ter.

LIVERTON GASKELL

WEST RD.
ROAD DUNCAN
ZETLAND

Park
Comm. Cen.
Chapel Row

DUNCAN

SOUTH TER.

PARK TER.

Cleveland
JOHN ST.
Play Fld.

GLADSTONE ST.
EAST ST.

Town Farm

MICKLE

SPRING HEAD RD.

Mkt. Pl.
Hilda La.

ARLING STREET

HIGH ST.

RD.

WOOD CT.

Haugh Bridge

South Loftus

18

Playgrd.

Liverton Mines

71

A

CLEVELAND

SCHOOL

St. Michael's Cl.
St. Helens Wlk.
Cricket Ground

STREET TERRACE **LIVERTON**

St. Cuthbert's Wlk.
Liverton Ter.

116

ROSE

STATION RD.

B1366

LAUREL LA.

LANE

ROSECROFT

B

472

C

South Loftus Farm

BOULBY GRN.

WATER LANE

Rosecroft School

West Field

ROSECROFT

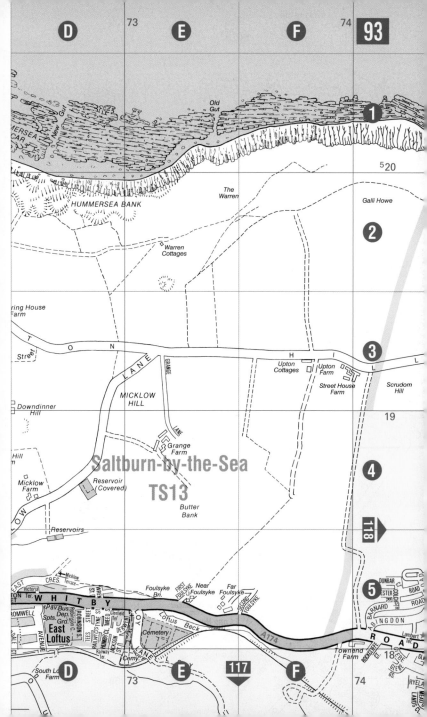

Old Gut

1

⁵20

The Warren

Galli Howe

HUMMERSEA BANK

2

Warren Cottages

ring House Farm

T O N

Stre-

3

H

Upton Cottages

Upton Farm

L

L

L A N E

GRANGE

Downdinner Hill

MICKLOW HILL

Street House Farm

Scrudom Hill

19

LANE

Grange Farm

Saltburn-by-the-Sea

TS13

Hill

Micklow Farm

Reservoir (Covered)

4

Butter Bank

LOW

Reservoirs

118

Micklow Terrace

CRES.

5

DUNBAR CL COLCHSTR ROAD

CHESTER ROAD

Victoria Ter.

W H I T B Y

Foulsyke Bri.

FIRST FOULSYKE

Near Foulsyke

Far Foulsyke

SECOND FOULSYKE

BARNARD

-ON Ter.

Pav Bus Dep. Grd.

Spts.

Robinson's

NHRN ST

RAILWY

TEES STREET

THE WD

Glenfield Ter.

HUMBLE CL WED

JACKSON

Loftus Beck

LOY

CROMWELL

East Loftus

AVENUE

ST

Railway Ter.

Cemetery

Cemy.

L A N E

A174

R O A D

A B I N G D O N

Lambert Ter.

GLEBE

ROCKCLIFFE CT.

18

Townend Farm

South Lo Farm

CREW

RYELA MEAD LANDS

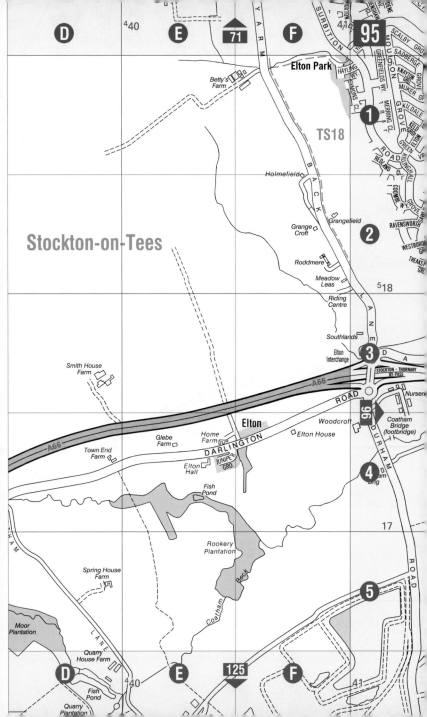

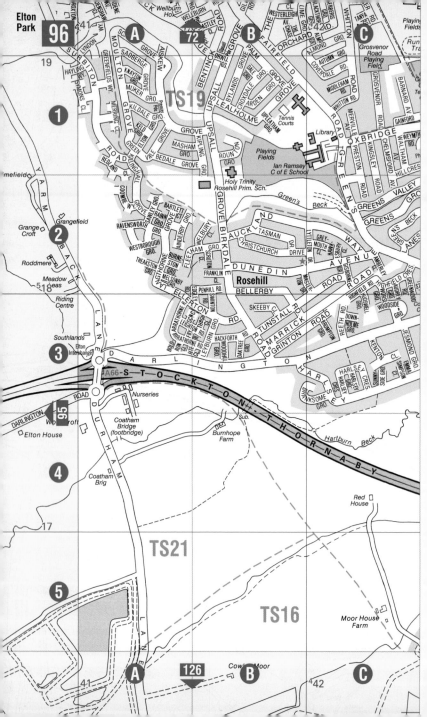

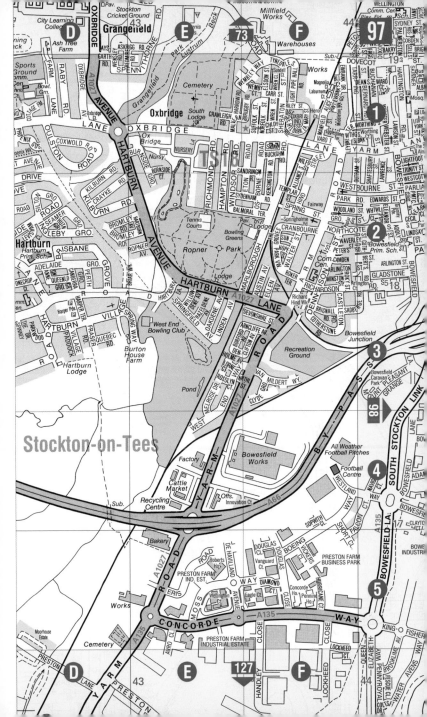

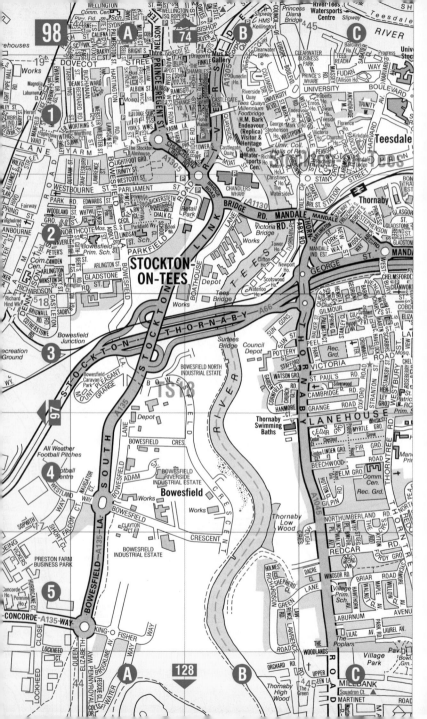

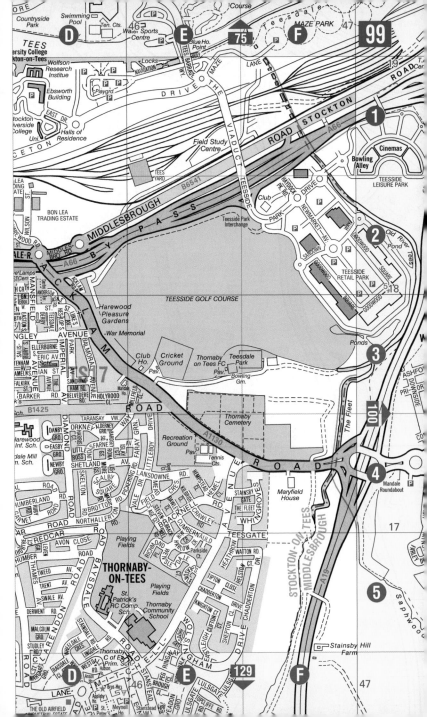

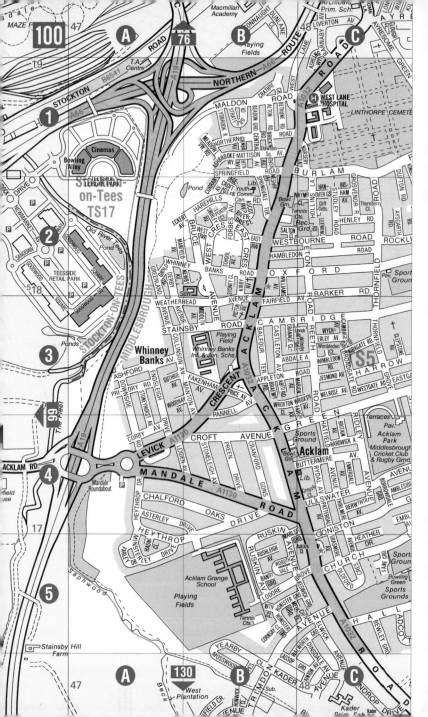

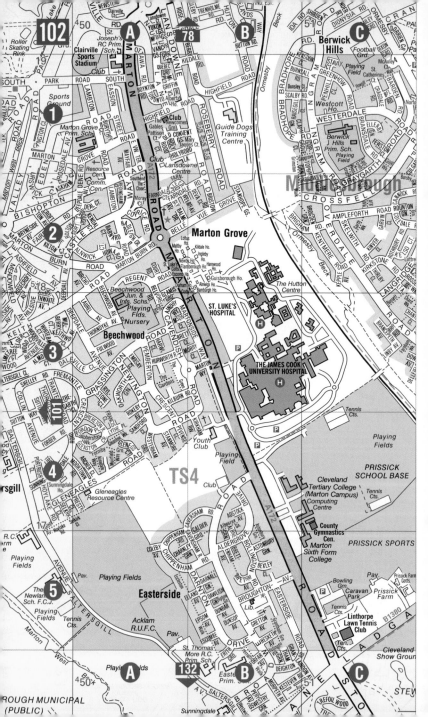

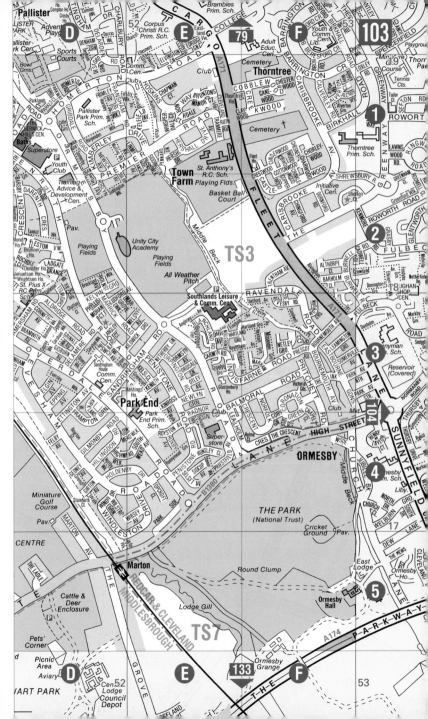

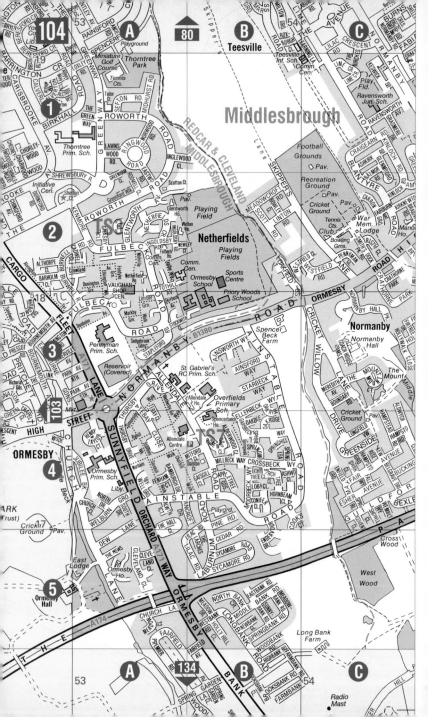

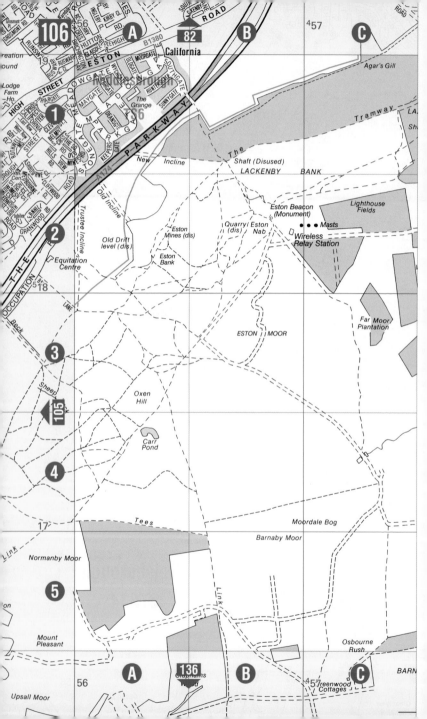

106 **A** 82 **B** 457 **C**

California

STREET

Middlesbrough

The Grange

Sunnygate

California

PARKWAY

New Incline

Old Incline

Trustee Incline

Equitation Centre

518

OCCUPATION

Eston Mines (dis)

Old Drift level (dis)

Eston Bank

Eston Beacon (Monument)

Quarry (dis)

Eston Nab

The Shaft (Disused)

LACKENBY BANK

• • • Masts

Wireless Relay Station

Lighthouse Fields

Agar's Gill

Tramway

Far Moor Plantation

ESTON MOOR

Oxen Hill

Carr Pond

Sheep

105

Moordale Bog

Barnaby Moor

Tees

17

Link

Normanby Moor

Mount Pleasant

Upsall Moor

Osbourne Rush

Greenwood Cottages

BARN

A 136 **B** 457 **C**

56

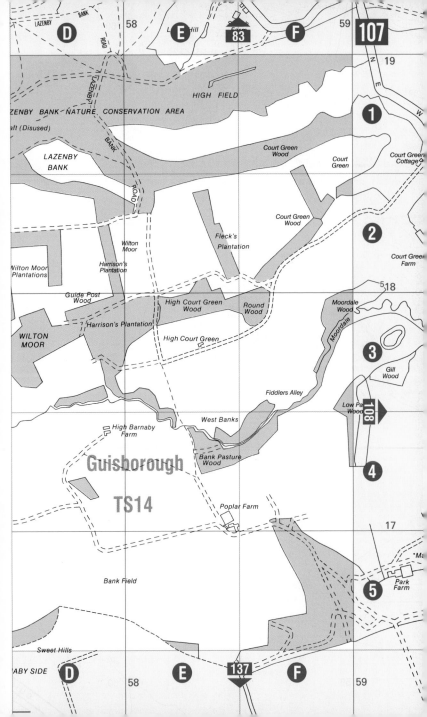

LAZENBY BANK

58

LAZENBY
ROAD
BANK

L__ Hill

83

59

107

N

19

HIGH FIELD

ZENBY BANK NATURE CONSERVATION AREA

aft (Disused)

LAZENBY
BANK

ROAD

Court Green
Wood

Court
Green

Court Green
Cottage

1

W

Wilton Moor
Plantations

Wilton
Moor

Harrison's
Plantation

Fleck's
Plantation

Court Green
Wood

Court Green
Farm

2

Guide Post
Wood

Harrison's Plantation

High Court Green
Wood

Round
Wood

5 18

Moordale
Wood

Moordale

Gill
Wood

3

WILTON
MOOR

High Court Green

Fiddlers Alley

Low Park
Wood

108

West Banks

High Barnaby
Farm

Bank Pasture
Wood

4

Guisborough

TS14

Poplar Farm

17

Ma

Bank Field

Park
Farm

5

Sweet Hills

ABY SIDE

D

58

E

137

F

59

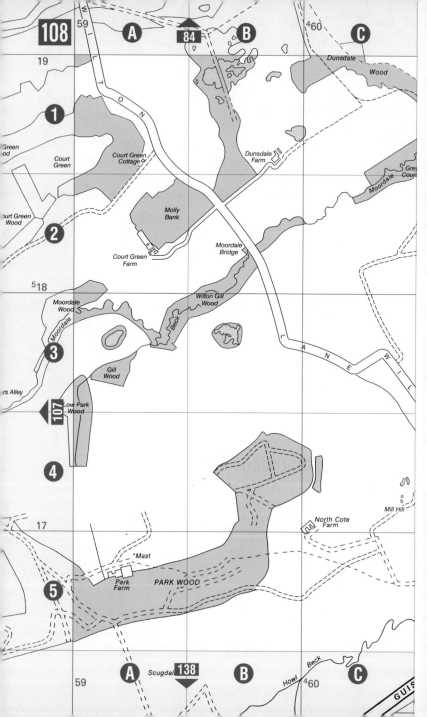

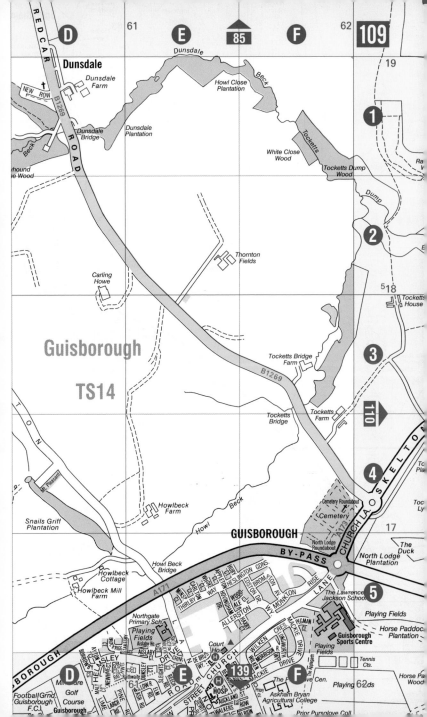

REDCAR

19

Dunsdale

Dunsdale

NEW ROW

B1269

Dunsdale Farm

Howl Close Plantation

Beck

Dunsdale Bridge

Dunsdale Plantation

Beck

1

Tocketts

White Close Wood

Tocketts Dump Wood

Ra

hound e Wood

Dump

2

Thornton Fields

5 18

Tocketts House

Carling Howe

Guisborough

TS14

Tocketts Bridge Farm

3

B1269

Tocketts Bridge

Tocketts Farm

110

SKELTON

To Pla

Mt. Pleasant

4

To Ly

Snails Griff Plantation

Howlbeck Farm

Howl Beck

Cemetery Roundabout

Cemetery

GUISBOROUGH

North Lodge Roundabout

CHURCH LA.

A173

17

The Duck

North Lodge Plantation

BY-PASS

Howl Beck Bridge

Howlbeck Cottage

A171

Howlbeck Mill Farm

Northgate Primary Sch.

Playing Fields

HIRD

HESLINGTON GDNS.

APPLETON WAY

HOVINGHAM DR.

WOOD

ALT CL.

EDSTON DR.

BROMPTON AV.

WY. MONKSON

RISE

PEGMAN CL.

The Lawrence Jackson School

LANE

5

Playing Fields

Aislaby Ho.

Court Ho.

H

CHURCH

WILKEN

CRES.

MACKIE DRIVE

Playing Fields

MORRISON R.

LINGWORTH DR.

Guisborough Sports Centre

Horse Paddock Plantation

Tennis Cts.

D

61

E

F

62

Mill re

Football Grnd (Guisborough F.C.)

Golf Course

Guisborough

STREET

139

HOSP

AUCKLAND ST.

The

Priory

Askham Bryan Agricultural College

ve Cen.

Playing ds

Prior Pursglove Coll

Horse Pa Wood

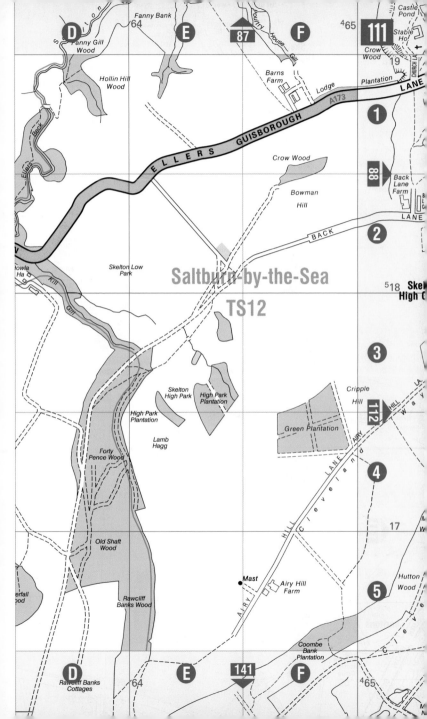

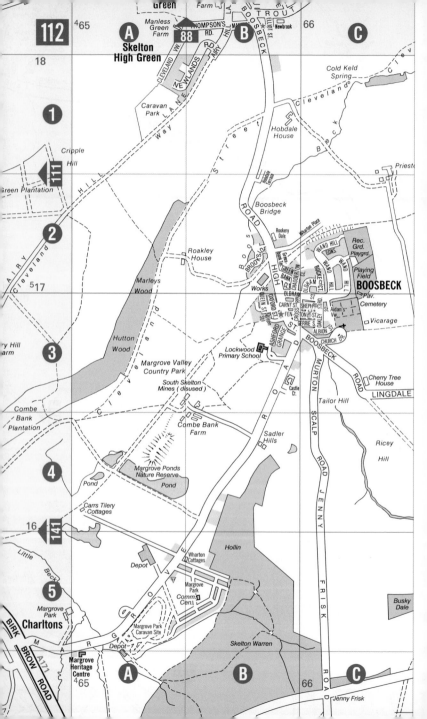

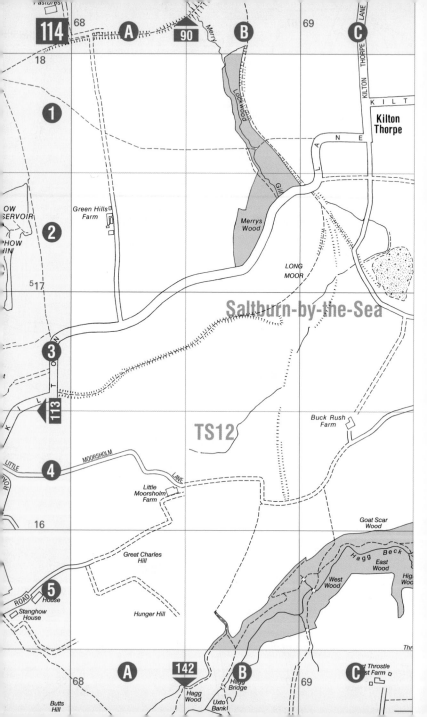

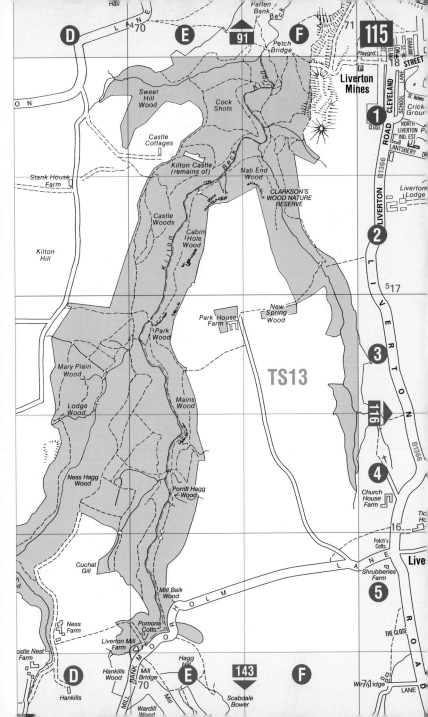

D **E** **91** **F** 71 **115**

Hall

LANE 70

Patten Bank

Petch Bridge

Beck

Kilton

Playgrd.

STREET

GRAHAM

18

P

Liverton Mines

CLEVELAND

SCHOOL LANE

St. Helens

Crick
Grou

ROAD

1

CLOSE

NORTH
LIVERTON
IND. EST.

LANTSBERY

Sweet Hill Wood

Cock Shots

Castle Cottages

Kilton Castle (remains of)

Nab End Wood

Stank House Farm

CLARKSON'S
WOOD NATURE
RESERVE

LIVERTON

Liverton
Lodge

B1366

Castle Woods

Kilton Hill

Castle Woods

Cabin Hole Wood

Beck

Kilton

2

5 17

Park House Farm

New Spring Wood

LIVERTON

3

TS13

116

Park Wood

Mary Plain Wood

Lodge Wood

Mains Wood

B1366

4

Church House Farm

Ness Hagg Wood

Porritt Hagg Wood

16

Petch's Cotts.

LANE

Live

Cuchat Gill

Shrubberies Farm

5

Mill Balk Wood

HOLM

MOOR

THE CLOSE

ROAD

Ness Farm

Pomona Cotts.

Liverton Mill Farm

stle Nest Farm

Hankills Wood

Mill Bridge

Hagg Hill

143

F

Tic
Ho

†

Wir Ridge

7 ¼idge

LANE

D **E** 70

Hankills

BANK

MILL

MOOR

MILL

Scabdale Bower

Wardill
Wood

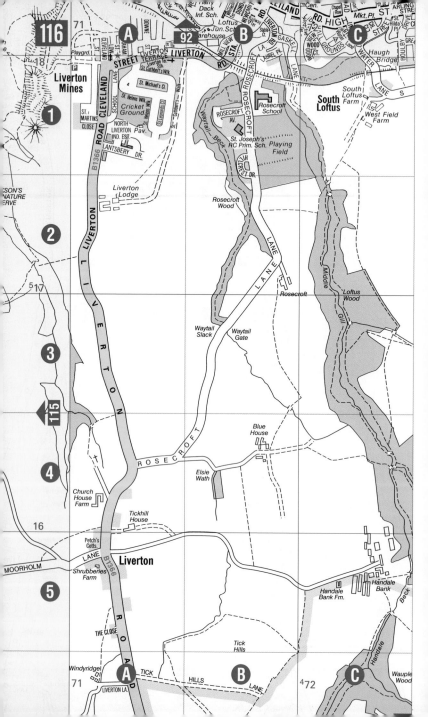

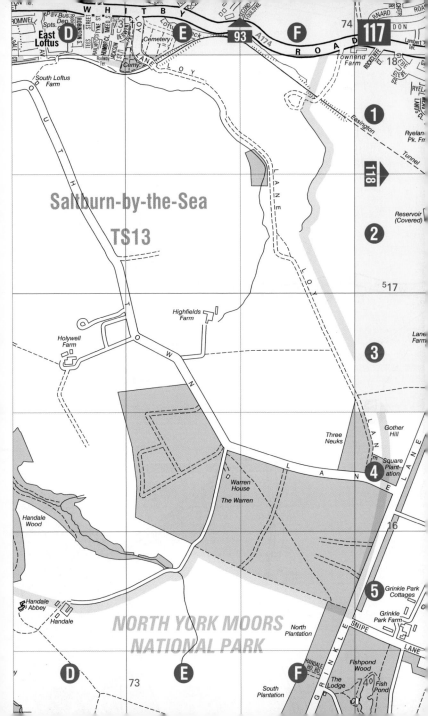

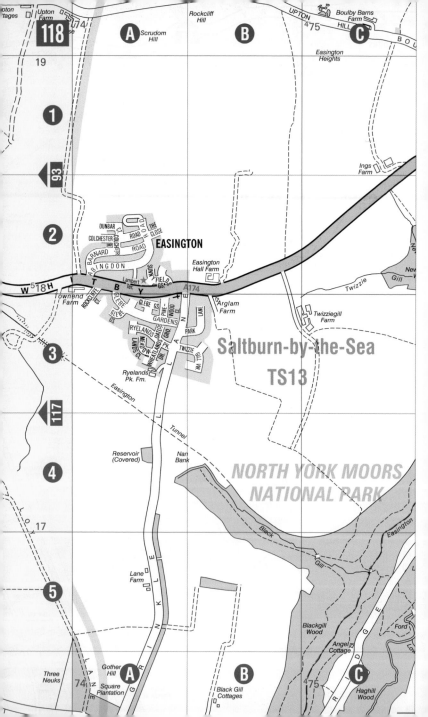

A Scrudom Hill

B

Rockcliff Hill

UPTON 475 HILL **C**

Boulby Barns Farm

BO

Upton Cottages

Upton Farm

74

19

Easington Heights

1

93

Ings Farm

2

DUNBAR ROAD

COLCHESTER RD

ST COLGHSTR RD

THE CLOSE

BARNARD

ABINGDON ROAD

EASINGTON

NUNS FIELD

Easington Hall Farm

New V

Twizzie Gill

Ze

W 518 H

Townend Farm

ROCKCLIFFE CT

GLEBE

Lambert Terr

B

GLEBE GS

Y

A174

Arglam Farm

Twizzie

Twizziegill Farm

3

GLEBE GS

GLEBE GDNS

PINE CL

WOOD GRO

GARDENS

OATES

FORD

LANE

PARK

RYELANDS

WHITLANDS PK

MEADOW

LANDS CL

LANE

TWIZZIE

W TWIZ

Saltburn-by-the-Sea

117

Ryelands Pk. Fm.

TS13

Easington

Tunnel

4

Reservoir (Covered)

Nan Bank

NORTH YORK MOORS NATIONAL PARK

17

L O X

Black Gill

Easington

GRIN KLE

LANE

5

Lane Farm

Blackgill Wood

Ford

Low

Three Neuks

74

GRIN KLE LA

Gother Hill

A

Square Plantation

B

Black Gill Cottages

475

Angel Cottage

RIDGE

C

Haghill Wood

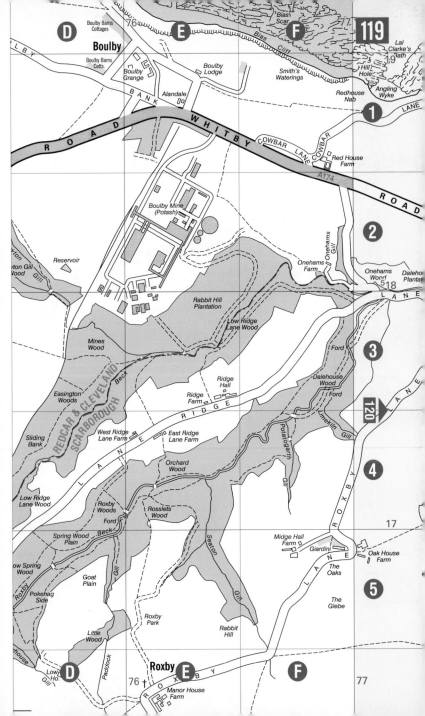

Boulby

Boulby Barns Cottages

Boulby Barns Cotts.

Boulby Grange

Alandale

Boulby Lodge

Smith's Waterings

Bias Scar

Lal Clarke's Bath

Hill Hole

Redhouse Nab

Angling Wyke

ROAD

BANK

WHITBY

ROAD

COWBAR LANE

COWBAR LANE

Red House Farm

A174

1

ROAD

Boulby Mine (Potash)

Reservoir

newton Gill Wood

Gill

Onehams Farm

Onehams Gill

Onehams Gill

Onehams Wood

Daleho Planta

518

2

Rabbit Hill Plantation

Low Ridge Lane Wood

Mines Wood

Ford

3

Dalehouse Wood

Ridge Hall

Ford

REDCAR & CLEVELAND

SCARBOROUGH

Beck

Easington Woods

Ridge Farm

RIDGE

Potababarth Gill

Limekiln Gill

120

Sliding Bank

West Ridge Lane Farm

East Ridge Lane Farm

LANE

4

ROXBY

LANE

17

Low Ridge Lane Wood

Orchard Wood

Roxby Woods

Ford

Rosslets Wood

Midge Hall Farm

Giardini

Oak House Farm

The Oaks

Spring Wood Plain

Beck

Gill

Seaton

Gill

Low Spring Wood

Roxby

Goat Plain

Pokehag Side

Roxby Park

Rabbit Hill

The Glebe

5

Little Wood

Paddock

Roxby

ROXBY

Manor House Farm

76 †

77

Low Ho.

Gill

D

E

F

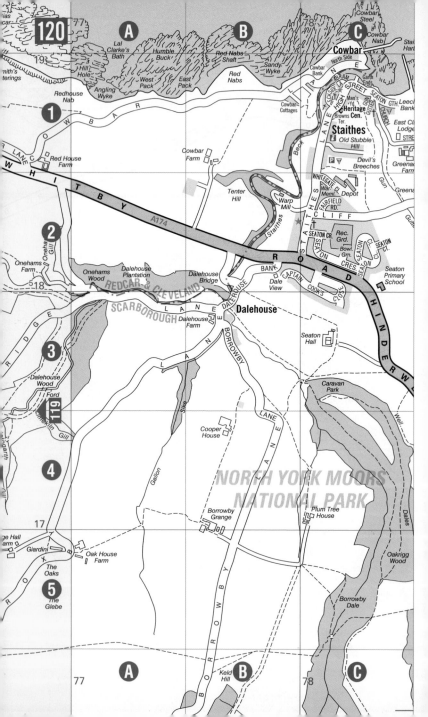

A   **B**   **C**

19

Lal Clarke's Bath

Humble Buck

Red Nabs Shaft

Sandy Wyke

Cowbar Steel

Cowbar Nab

Cowbar

North Side

Hill Hole

West Pack

East Pack

Red Nabs

Cowbar Bank

Cowbar Cottages

Garth Ends

Man's Yd.

Heritage Cen.

Browns Ter.

East Cli Lodge

1

Redhouse Nab

Angling Wyke

Staithes

Old Stubble Hill

Devil's Breeches

Greenac Farm

Red House Farm

Cowbar Farm

Beck

Depot

Greena

Tenter Hill

WHITEGATE CL.

War. Meml.

FAIRFIELD RD.

Gun

2

Oneha Gill

Onehams Farm

Warp Mill

Staithes

CLIFF

SEATON CR.

Rec. Grd.

Bowl. Gn.

SEATON CT.

518

Onehams Wood

Dalehouse Plantation

A174

ROAD

Seaton Primary School

REDCAR & CLEVELAND

Dalehouse Bridge

BANK

Dale View

CAPTAIN COOK'S

SCARBOROUGH

Dalehouse Farm

Dalehouse

COOK'S CLOSE

3

RIDGE

Dalehouse Wood

Ford

BORROWBY LANE

Seaton Hall

HINDERW

119

Gill

Caravan Park

Well

4

Slike

LANE

Cooper House

NORTH YORK MOORS
NATIONAL PARK

Dales

17

ge Hall rm

Giardini

Oak House Farm

Borrowby Grange

Plum Tree House

Oakrigg Wood

The Oaks

5

The Glebe

BORROWBY LANE

Borrowby Dale

A   Keld Hill   **B**   78   **C**

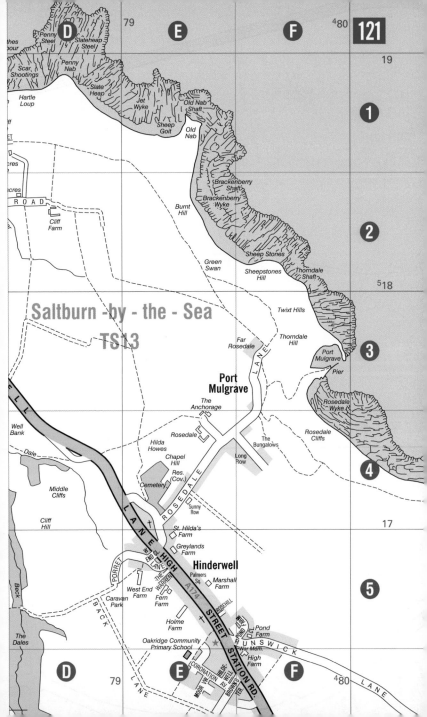

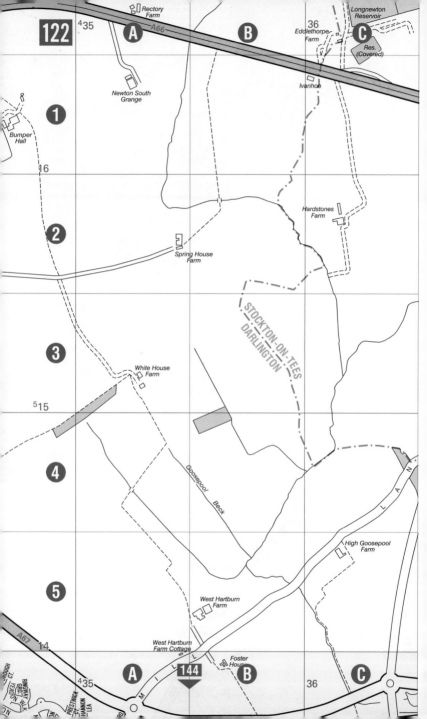

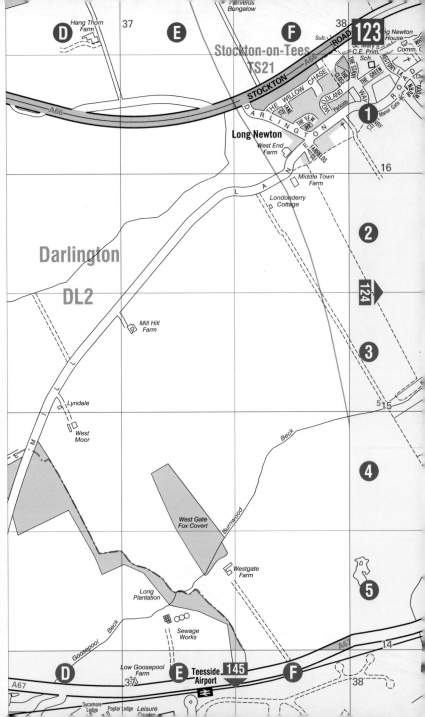

Hang Thorn Farm

D

37

E

Fairfields Bungalow

F

38

Sub.Sta.

ROAD

123

ig Newton House

Comm.

St. Mary's C.E. Prim. Sch.

Stockton-on-Tees

TS21

THE WILLOW CHASE

STOCKTON

THE YEW

OODLAND

THE STRAY

THE GREEN

RECTORY LANE

WAY

Parkside

NEW

ROAD

Manor Gate

 ENBY

CL

1

DARLINGTON

A66

Long Newton

West End Farm

THE VINE WK

FAIRFIELDS CL

16

Middle Town Farm

Londonderry Cottage

LANE

2

Darlington

124

DL2

3

Mill Hill Farm

5 **15**

Lyndale

Beck

West Moor

4

West Gate Fox Covert

Burnwood

Westgate Farm

5

Long Plantation

Goosepool Beck

Sewage Works

A67

14

D

Low Goosepool Farm

37

E **Teesside Airport**

145

F

38

Sycamore Lodge

Poplar Lodge

Leisure Centre

A67

Moor
Plantation

D

COATHAM LANE

⁴40

E

Coatham

▲ 95

F

41

Quarry
House Farm

Fish
Pond

Quarry
Plantation

Coatham
Stob

1

16

Beck

N

Red Roofs

Ponds

2

126

Stockton-on-Tees

Admiralty Ecology Park
(Carter Moor Nature Reserve)

3

Red
Gro

Pav.

Carter
Moor

WHITEH
ROAD
ROAD

CEYLON
SQUARE

SINGAPORE
SQUARE

515

Urlay Nook
Bridge

Works

Works

L
A
N
E

LANCASTER

GIBRALTAR RD.

HONG KONG RD.
MALTA RD.

PORTSMOUTH

CHATHAM

ROAD

Works

ROAD
ROAD

Eaglescliffe
Logistics
Centre

4

Low
Crook Farm

URLAY

Playing
Field

Police
Training
Centre

South Urlay
Nook Farm

Urlay Nook

TS16

NOOK

GRASSHOLME

NEWBIGGIN
CL.

COTHERSTONE
CT.

MIDDLE-
TON
CL.

GRASSHOLM
WY.

ROAD

Allens

Sports
Ground

**Orchard
Estate**

5

EMSWORTH

MICKLE-
TON
CL.

HUNTERS
A RN.

MAYFIELD
RD.

MAYFIELD

A67

E MERGE
CL.
EASTW. WY.
NEWTON DR.

HUNTERS
A'RN.

URLAY

NOOK RD.

The
Grange

VALLEY GDNS.

COATH-
VALE

D

⁴40

E

▼ 147

F

41

Hunter's
Rest

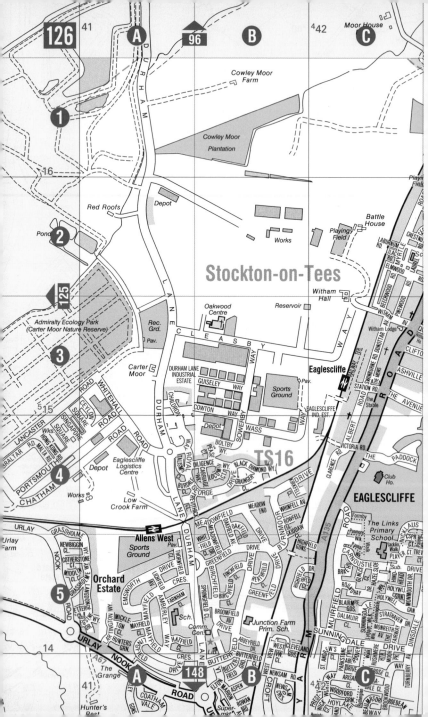

126 41   Ⓐ   ▲96   Ⓑ   ⁴42   Moor House   Ⓒ

❶

Cowley Moor Farm

Cowley Moor Plantation

16

Red Roofs

Depot

Pond ❷

Battle House

Playing Field

Works

Stockton-on-Tees

▲125

Admiralty Ecology Park
(Carter Moor Nature Reserve)

❸

Rec. Grd.
Pav.

Oakwood Centre

Reservoir

Witham Hall

Witham Lodge

WITHAM

WAY

Carter Moor

CLEASBY

WAY

Eaglescliffe

DURHAM LANE INDUSTRIAL ESTATE

GUISELEY WAY

Sports Ground

Pav.

EAGLESCLIFFE IND. EST.

STATION RD.

The Stable

15

LANCASTER

WHITEHALL ROAD

CEYLON SQUARE

SINGAPORE SQUARE

HONG KONG CL.

MALTA RD.

CHAUDRON

ROAD

COWTON WAY

SOWERBY WAY

WASS

ASHVILLE

THE AVENUE

GIBRALTAR

PORTSMOUTH RD.

Wks

Depot

Eaglescliffe Logistics Centre

❹

DURHAM

BOLTBY WY.

Depot

Pav.

VICTORIA RD.

ALBERT ROAD

THE PADDOCK

CHATHAM

Works

Low Crook Farm

ROYAL

TALUS

PEASE WY.

DILIGENCE

CARRIAGE

GRAINGER

BLACK DIAMOND WY.

DRIVE

TS16

BURDALE

GEORGE

PETTING

CLARENCE RD.

Club Ho.

EAGLESCLIFFE

URLAY

GRASSHOLME

Urlay Farm

NEWBIGGIN CL.

COTHERSTONE CT.

MIDDLIN CL.

NOOK

❺

Orchard Estate

EMSWORTH

MAYFIELD DRIVE

LICHFIELD CRES.

FARNHAM CL.

MEADOWFIELD

OAKFIELD DR.

WHIT

WOODFIELD DR.

GREENFIELD

FINCHFIELD CL.

WESTFIELD CL.

GREENFIELD

MEADOW END

WHINFELL AV.

BOWFELL

SKIRDAW CL.

HIGHFIELD GDNS.

BURNMOOR DRIVE

DRIVE

Formby

The Links Primary School

Panmure Wk.

Panar

Jackling Walk

PLAYER

CSPR

AUS

CT. TREV

DRIVE

Allens West

Sports Ground

Pav.

THORNFIELD CL.

BIRCHFIELD

SPRINGFIELD CL.

BROOMFIELD DRIVE

HIGHFIELD DR.

ROAD

MUIRFIELD

CARNOUSTIE CL.

GLENCOE RD.

HAZELSLADE

HOLYWELL

HOLYWELL GRN.

MONMOUTH GRN.

HOYLAKE

Sub.

DRIVE

14

URLAY NOOK ROAD

A67

The Grange

Hunter's Rest

MICKLE TON CL.

ARTINGTON WY.

MAYFIELD CL.

AMBERLEY WAY

HATFIELD CL.

HUNTERS GRN.

MAYFIELD CRES.

FESTIVE WY.

GRASSHOLME WY.

ETTERGILL DR.

NETTLE CL.

Sch.

Comm. Cen.

ABBEYFIELD DR.

BROOMFIELD DR.

BUTTERFIELD

BUTTERFIELD GRO.

BUTTER FIELD

ELTON

ASPEN

ROWAN RD.

Super-mkt.

COATHAM VALE

Ⓐ **▲148** ROAD Ⓑ

Junction Farm Prim. Sch.

ABBEYFIELD DR.

NEWSAM RD.

NEWSAM RD.

CROFT

YARM

ROAD

WEST CLEVELAND GDNS.

ST. ANDREW'S CL.

PARKSTONE

RUSHMERE

SUNNINGDALE DRIVE

BLAIRMORE GDNS.

DALMUIR CL.

STRATHAVEN DR.

MONREITH AV.

CL.

INNSDALE

A135

ROAD

CLIFTON

DURHAM

PRESTY

WICK

WAY

ARISAIG WAY

ROSE CL.

WOODFORD GRN.

HOYLAKE

BELLAMORE GRN.

ROEDEAN

TORBAY

CL.

TREV

41 41 ⁴4 Ⓒ

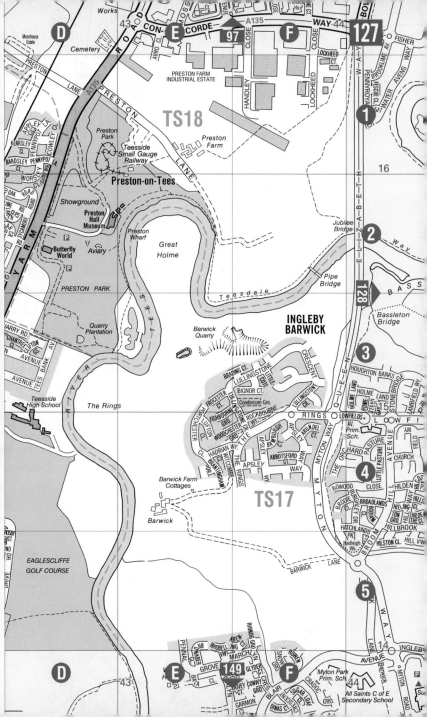

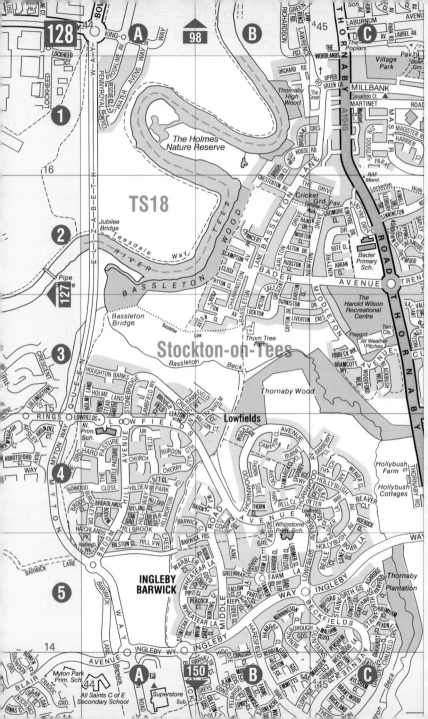

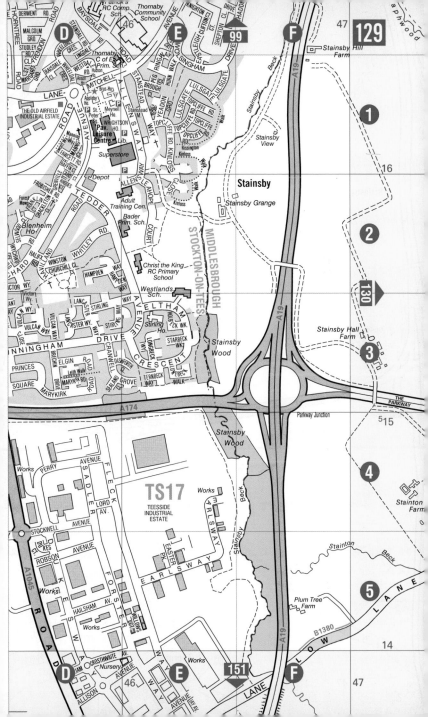

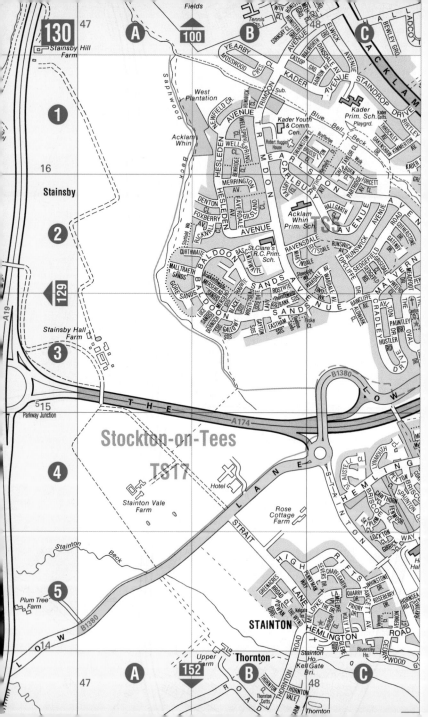

130 47

Stainsby Hill Farm

A **B** 100 **C**

Fields

Tennis Ct.

HALL

BEWLEY GRO.

ALDCOT

WIN. CL. HOMSIDE

RUNSTEAD

CORNSAY CL.

AVENUE

48

ELWICK

CASSOP GRO.

HAXWORTH

DINSDALE AV.

PLANTON AV.

STAINDROP DRIVE

BIRTLEY

BROCKLEY

DARENHAM

KIMMERTON

YEARBY CL.

MOSSWOOD CRES. CL.

KADER

AVENUE

Sub.

Blue Bell

Kader Prim. Sch. Playgrd.

Kader Cotts.

Beck

DAKENHAM

KADER

GRE

NEWFIELD CR.

WELLSPRING CL.

TRIMDON

Kader Youth & Comm. Cen.

Brafferton

HANKLEY

BRUSSEL CL.

SHERBURN

PARTRIDGE CL.

FORCETT CL.

1

West Plantation

Acklam Whin

HESLEDEN AVENUE

RIMDON

Robert Hugill House

CARLSDON

AVENUE

16

Stainsby

MERRINGTON AV.

CARLBURY

Hallgarth Road

ROTHERSTONE

GATENBY

Saphwood

Beck

DENTON CL.

HESLEDEN

FOXBERRY AV.

FAVERDALE

GILSLAND

RICKNALL

AVENUE

Acklam Whin Prim. Sch.

TS5

AVENUE

AVENUE

MEADFOOT

2

Stainsby Hall Farm

129

Stanford Wk.

CORTHWAITE

St. Clare's R.C. Prim. Sch.

RUNSWICK AV.

SDALE

RUNSWICK

SEDGEFIELD

TOPCLIFFE DR.

MARDALE

CRADLEY

MALVERN

A19

MALLTRAETH SANDS

BALDOON

BAS.

HINTHWAITE

BRACKENHEATH

MERSEHEAD

DANWIKE

SANDS

MISTY SEAL

ROSTWTE

Thornthwaite

BANK SDS.

RAVENSDALE

VDALE

MARDALE AV.

Stonebridge

TINTXE

RANCLIFFE

CRAYTON

RONWIK

THE

OVAL

PAUNTLEY DR.

HUSTLER RD.

DRIVE

GORE SANDS

SANTON SDS.

DERMNON SDS.

BLACK SDS.

GALLOW SDS.

GAYTON SDS.

EASTHAM SDS.

Fiske Ct.

Century

3

Stainby Hall Farm

5 15

Parkway Junction

THE

B1380

A174

LOW

Stockton-on-Tees
TS17

AUSTELL CL.

LYNMOUTH CL.

HEMLINGTON

Hotel

STRAIT

Stainton Vale Farm

LANE

Rose Cottage Farm

HEMLINGTON

ST. STAINTON

CAWTHORN

FENWOR

SPAINTON

BRISCOE

PLUM

LOCKTON CL.

GIRRICK CL.

WAY

Hi Hal

4

Stainton Beck

RIFTS

WHINSTONE DR.

ROSEBERRY DR.

HORNSE

CEDARWOOD

HIGH LANE

CHARLGARTH

SEVERS DR.

GREENACRES

BROAD GRO.

MANNHAM

QUARRY DR.

PRIORY DR.

LANCETT AV.

Plum Tree Farm

B1380

5

STAINTON

THE WYND

Kelgate

MELDYKE

LA. MELDYKE

THE ORCHARD

HOLLY LA.

ROAD

Riversley Ho.

STAINTON

HEMLINGTON

GLEBE

LOW

014

Upper Farm

Thornton

Stainton Ho.

Kell Gate Bri.

A 152 **B** 48 **C**

47

ROAD

THORNTON Cotts.

THORNTON VALE

Thornton FARM

Thornton

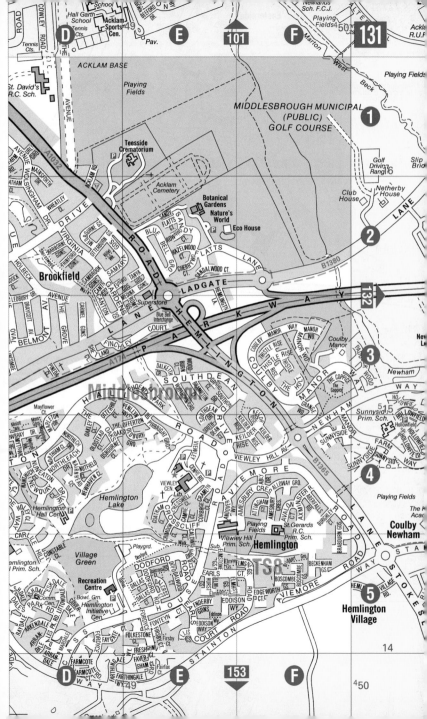

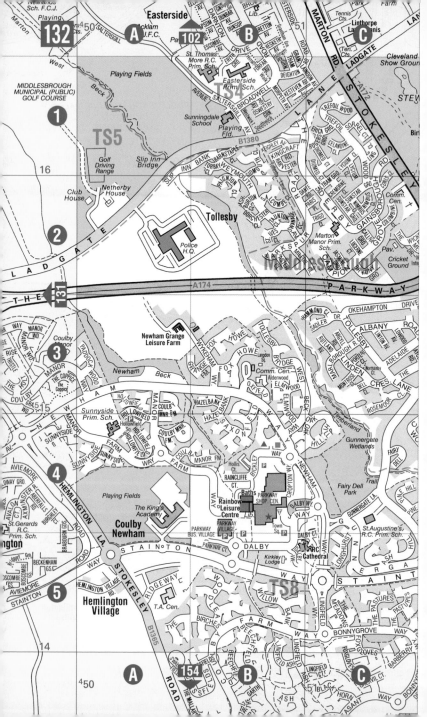

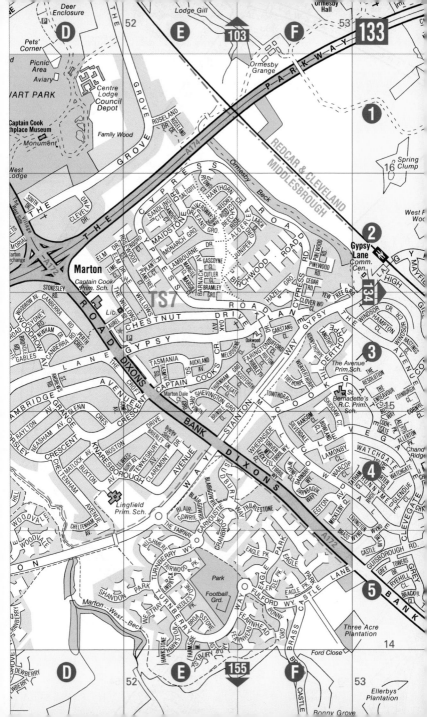

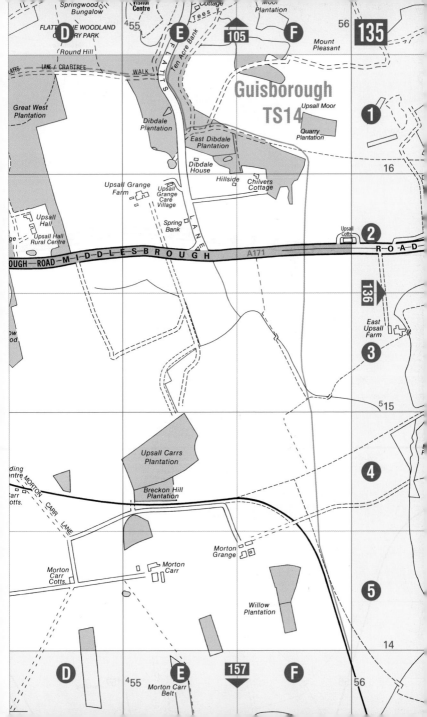

on

Pleasant

56

A

106

B

57

C

Osbourne
Rush

BARN

Upsall Moor

1

Quarry
Plantation

Claphams
Wood

Greenwood
Cottages

16

Cross Keys
Plantation

Mill
Farm

Barnaby Side
Farm

Sewage
Works

MIDDLESBROUGH

Upsall
Cotts

2

A171

Wayside

Hamble
Hill Farm

Hamble Hill
Cottages

135

East
Upsall
Farm

Main

3

515

The Long
Belt

Boundary
Plantation

Low
Farm

4

Thomas's
Clump

Middlesbrough

Spite Hall
Farm

TS7

5

14

56

A

158

B

457 Green Hills

C

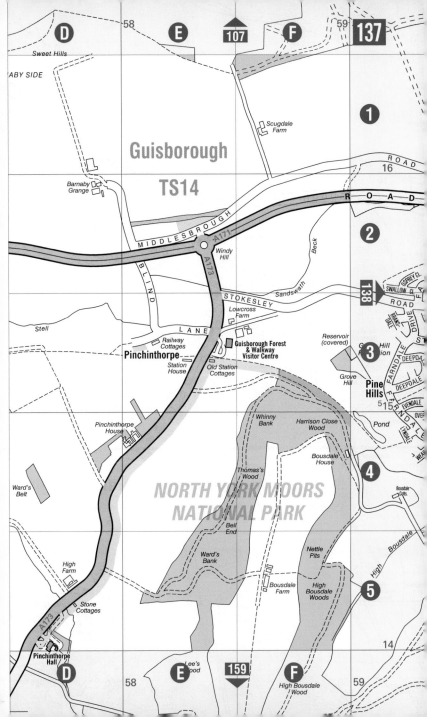

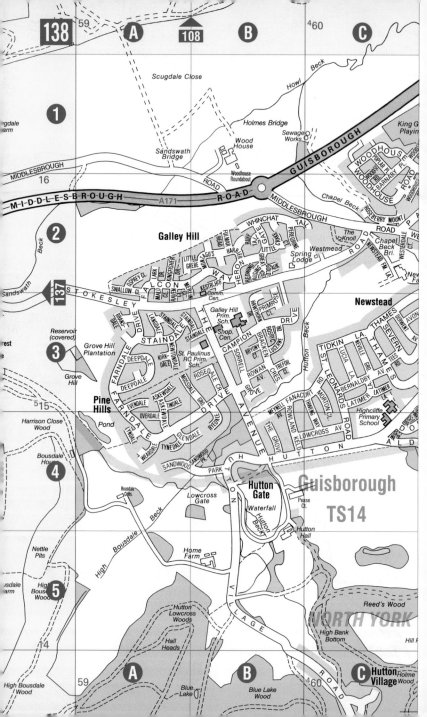

138 59 **A** **108** **B** 460 **C**

1

Scugdale Close

...gdale Farm

Holmes Bridge

Wood House

Sandswath Bridge

Woodhouse Roundabout

Sewage Works

GUISBOROUGH

King G...
Playi...

WOODHOUSE

WOODHOUSE

BARNABY PL.

ROSEBERRY MOUNT

ROAD

MIDDLESBROUGH 16

M-I-D-D-L-E-S-B-R-O-U-G-H A171 ROAD

MIDDLESBROUGH

Chapel Beck

ROAD

Chapel Beck Bri.

WESTERDALE CT.

Ne...
F...

2

Beck

Galley Hill

Sandswath

137 STOKESLEY

SWALLOW CL.

OSPREY CL.

FALCON

LARK

MALLOW

KINGFISHER

RAVENSWORTH

WREN

LITTLE GREBE

LAPWING

MARTIN

JAY'S

HARRIER

HERON

WAY

WHINCHAT

FULMAR

BUFF

TEAL

REDWING

FIELDING

GREAT

KESTREL ROW

Comm. Cen.

HAWTHORN

GREAT

PRIMROSE

TIT

GATE

LITTLE

PEREGRINE

HAUK

DRIVE

Westmead

Spring Lodge

The Knoll

Newstead

ROAD

3

Reservoir (covered)

Grove Hill Plantation

Grove Hill

...rest

BRANS DYKE

DRIVE

LANGDALE

STAINDALE

STAINDALE

STAINDALE

STAINDALE

STAINDALE

NEWTONDALE

KIRK-DALE

Galley Hill Prim. Sch.

Shop. Cen.

St. Paulinus RC Prim. Sch.

CAMPION

SORRELL

BRYONY CT.

ROSEDALE CRES.

ROWAN AV.

BRACKEN CT.

ROSSCO CT.

LISERWE

TREFOIL CL.

CHES.

HUTTON

Beck

TIDKIN

ST. LEONARDS

LUCIA LA.

NEVILLE GRO.

BERNALDBY

AV.

THAMES

THAMES

SEVERN

BURNIM RD.

LATIMER

AVON

LA.

LATIMER LA.

LATIMER LA.

DEEPDALE

DEEPDALE

FARNDALE

FARNDALE

ASKEWDALE

ASKEWDALE

MISSONDALE

TINDALE

ROSEDALE

BRO...

DRIVE

MEYNELL

FANACURT

ROWLAND KELD

MORTON CL.

THING WAY

LOWCROSS AV.

Highcliffe Primary School

DO...

ALD

4

Harrison Close Wood

Bousdale Hous...

5 15

Pine Hills

Pond

EVENDALE

OVERDALE

WEARDALE

TYNEDALE

GLENDALE

RYEDALE

TY...DALE

SANDWOOD

SANDWOOD

PARK

THE GROVE

AVENUE

HUTTON

Hutton Gate

Waterfall

Pease Ct.

Guisborough

TS14

5

Nettle Pits

...usdale arm

High Bousdale Wood

Bousdale Cotts.

Beck

Bousdale

High

Lowcross Gate

Home Farm

Hutton Beck

Hutton Hall

Reed's Wood

NORTH YORK

14

High Bousdale Wood

59 **A**

Hutton Lowcross Woods

Hall Heads

Blue Lake

B

Blue Lake Wood

460 **C**

V-I-L-L-A-G-E

ROAD

High Bank Bottom

Hill ...

Hutton Village Holme Wood

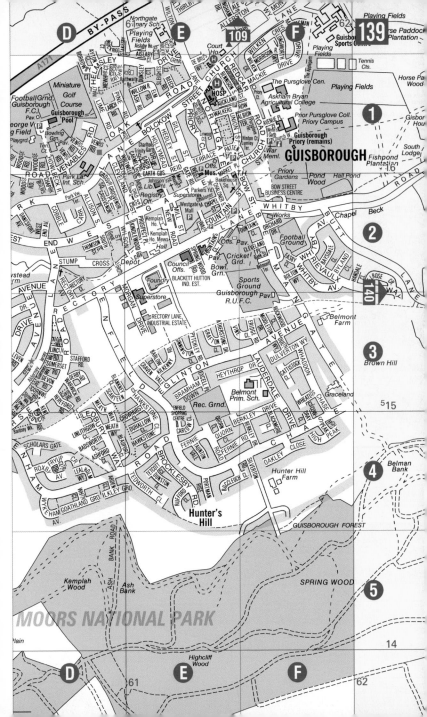

140
62
A
110
B
63
C

Playing Fields
PEGMAN...
MACKIE DRIVE
...WORTH
...borough
...Sports Centre
Horse Parks
Plant...
Plantation
MUCKY
LANE
A171
WHITBY

Playing Fields
Tennis Cts.
Pursglove Cen.
Playing Fields
Horse Parks Wood
Gisborough Hall
ROAD
Waterfall Cottages

...am Bryan
...tural College
Prior Purse... Coll.
Priory Cam...us
1
Gisborough House
Gisborough Priory (remains)

GUISBOROUGH
16
South Lodge
Priory
Gardens
Pond Wood
Hall Pond
Fishpond Plantation

STREET
...SS CENTRE
WHITBY
Chapel Beck

...orks
AV
...BY
2
Football Ground
BAISDALE
RIEVAULX
BYLAND
MANDALE
MELROSE CR.
WAY
Foxdale Farm

...ASBY
BOLTON
WHITBY
139
Belmont Farm

...NUE
GATE
3
...ERTON WY.
WHADDON
...TTISTOCK
WHEATL...
Brown Hill
Guisborough
TS14

DRIVE
...A...
HIGH PEAK
CLOSE
Graceland
15

Cow Pasture Hill

4
...ter Hill
Farm
Belman Bank
West Banks

GUISBOROUGH FOREST
GUISBOROUGH WOODS

SPRING WOOD
5

14

A
62
B
63
C
Westworth Wood

ROAD FANCY BA...
Little Waterfall Farm
Waterfall Farm
LANE

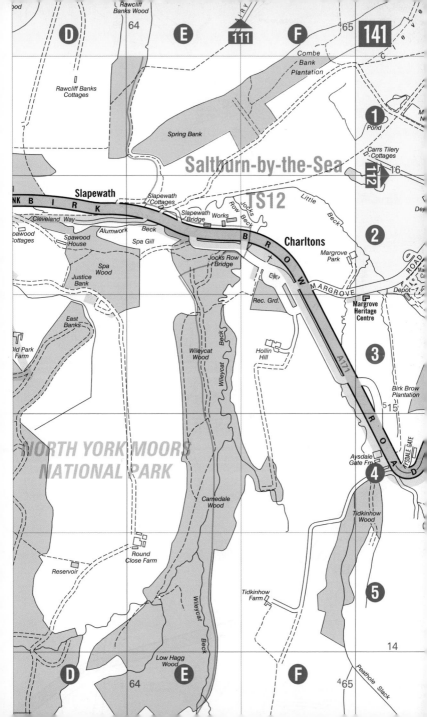

D

E

111

F

465

Rawcliff
Banks Wood

64

Combe
Bank
Plantation

Rawcliff Banks
Cottages

1

Pond

Spring Bank

Carrs Tilery
Cottages

Salthurn-by-the-Sea

12

16

Slapewath

TS12

Little

NK B I R K

Cleveland Way

Slapewath
Cottages

Row Beck

Jocks

Beck

2

Spawood
Cottages

Spawood
House

Alumwork

Slapewath
Bridge

Works

Beck

B

Charltons

Margrove
Park

Spa Gill

Justice
Bank

Spa
Wood

Jocks Row
Bridge

R

MARGROVE

ROAD

Depot

East
Banks

Rec. Grd.

O

Margrove
Heritage
Centre

3

Old Park
Farm

Wileycat
Wood

Beck

Hollin
Hill

W

A171

Wileycat

R

O

Birk Brow
Plantation

515

NORTH YORK MOORS
NATIONAL PARK

Camedale
Wood

A

YSDALE GATE

Aysdale
Gate Fm

4

D

Round
Close Farm

Reservoir

Tidkinhow
Wood

Wileycat

Beck

Tidkinhow
Farm

5

14

D

64

E

Low Hagg
Wood

F

465

Peathole Slack

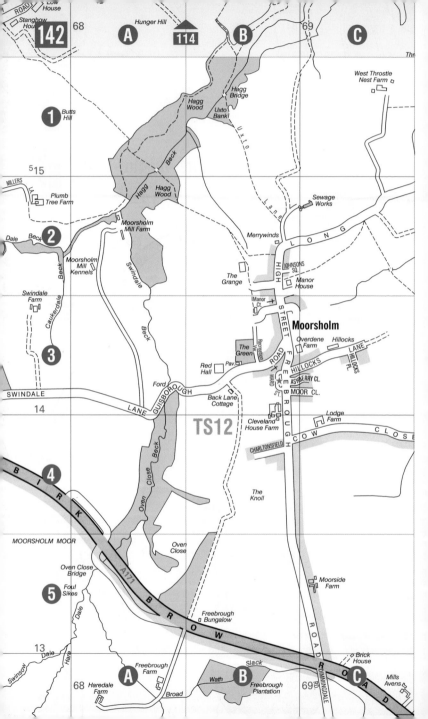

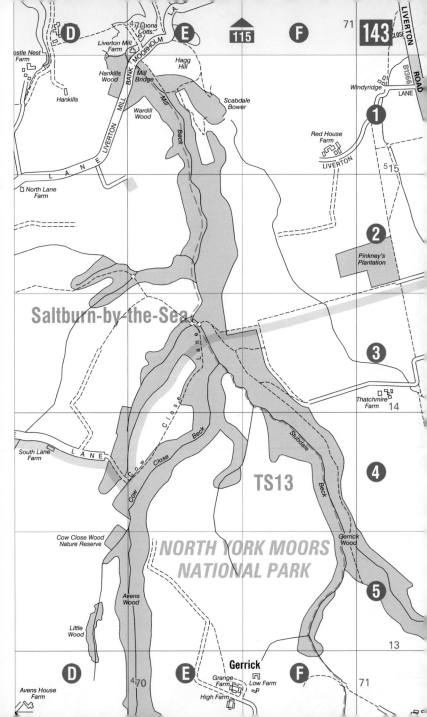

D **E** **115** **F** 71

LIVERTON ROAD
CLOSE
B1366
LANE

Windyridge

1

Liverton Mill Farm
Liverton Mill Farm
Hagg Hill
Hankills Wood
Mill Bridge
BANK
MILL
MOORHOLM
LA

Castle Nest Farm
Hankills
Wardill Wood
Scabdale Bower
Mill Beck
LIVERTON LANE
North Lane Farm

Red House Farm
LIVERTON
5 15

2

Pinkney's Plantation

Saltburn-by-the-Sea

3

Thatchmire Farm
14

Cow Close Lane
COW Close Beck
LANE
Stubdale Beck

South Lane Farm

TS13

4

Cow Close Wood
Nature Reserve

**NORTH YORK MOORS
NATIONAL PARK**

Gerrick Wood

5

Avens Wood

Little Wood

13

D **E** **F** 71

Avens House Farm
4 70
Gerrick
Grange Farm
Low Farm
High Farm

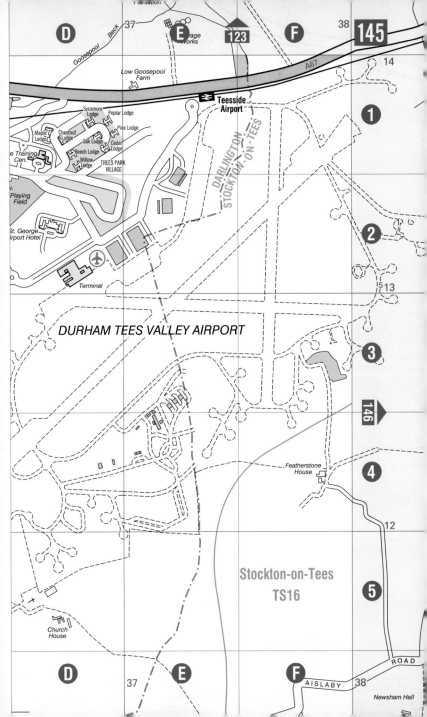

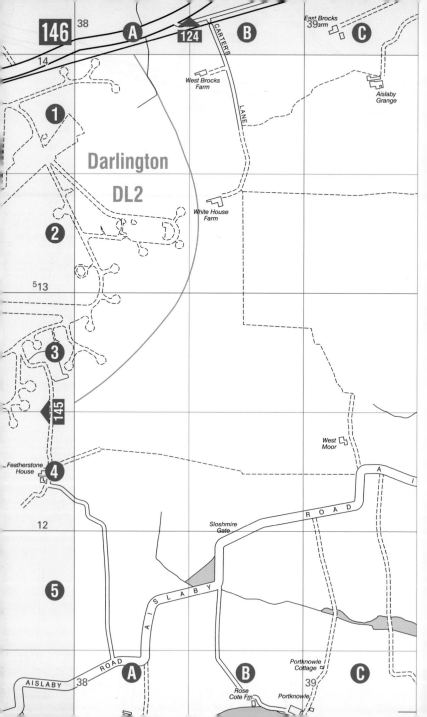

A

124

B

East Brocks
39 arm

C

West Brocks
Farm

CARTERS

LANE

Aislaby
Grange

14

1

Darlington

DL2

White House
Farm

2

5 13

3

145

West
Moor

Featherstone
House

4

A l

ROAD

Sloshmire
Gate

12

5

A
I
S
L
A
B
Y

R O A D

Portknowle
Cottage

C

ROAD

A 38

AISLABY

B

Rose
Cote Fm

Portknowle

39

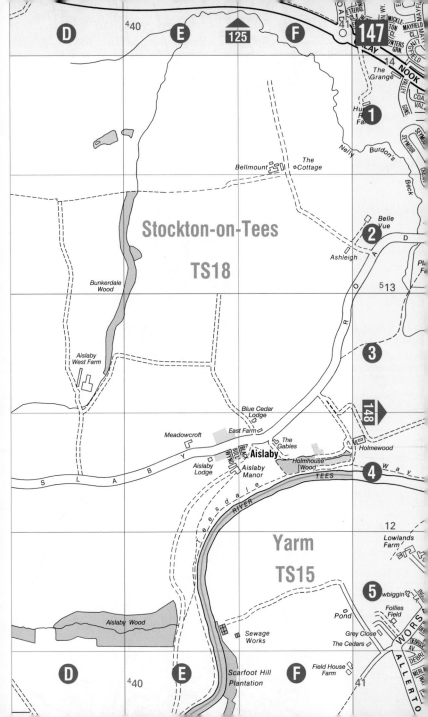

D ⁴40 **E** ▲ 125 **F** 147

ROAD

LAY NOOK

The Grange

14

1

Nelly Burdon's Beck

Bellmount The Cottage

Stockton-on-Tees

Belle Vue

TS18 Ashleigh **2**

⁵13

Bunkerdale Wood

3

Aislaby West Farm

148

Blue Cedar Lodge

Meadowcroft East Farm

Holmewood

The Gables

Aislaby Holmhouse Wood Way

Aislaby Lodge Aislaby Manor

TEES **4**

S L A B Y

RIVER

12

Lowlands Farm

Yarm

TS15

5

Follies Field

Pond

Grey Close

Aislaby Wood The Cedars

WORS

Sewage Works

ALLERTO

D ⁴40 **E** Scarfoot Hill Plantation **F** Field House Farm 41

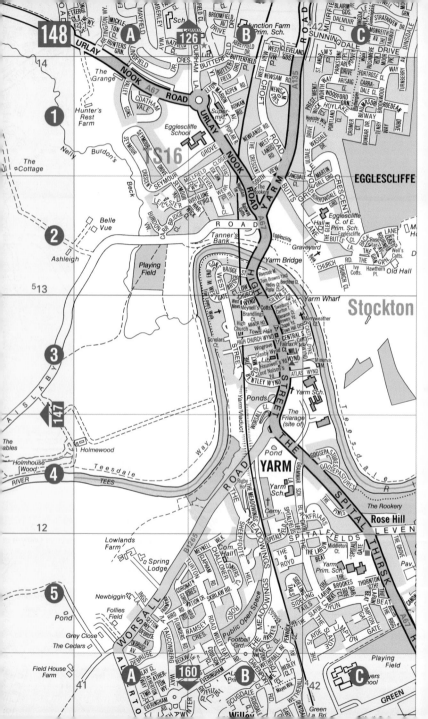

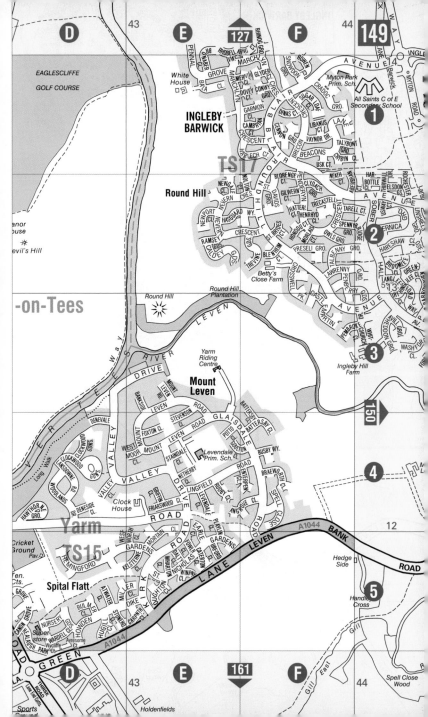

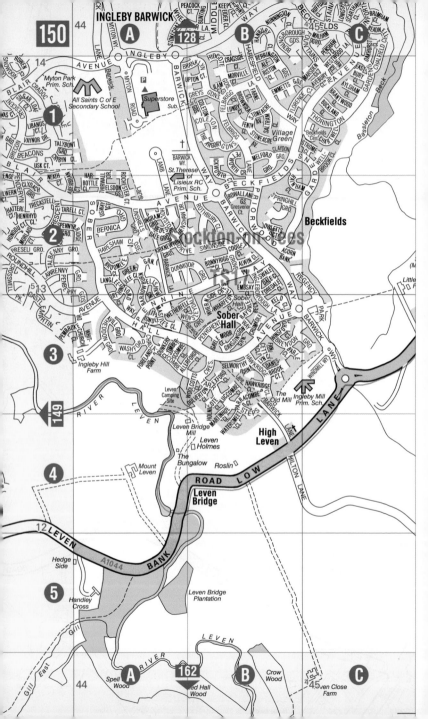

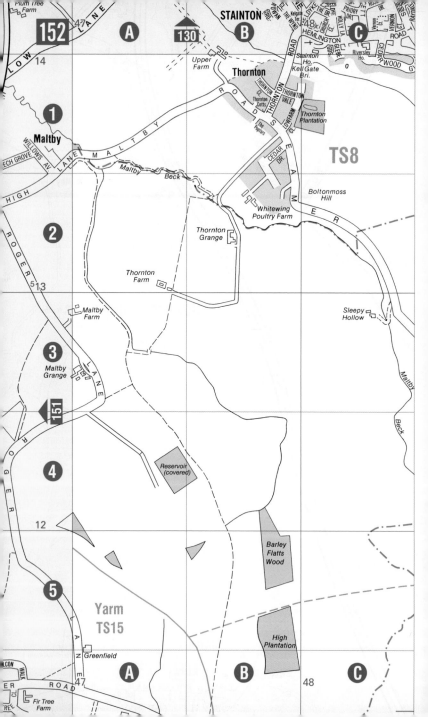

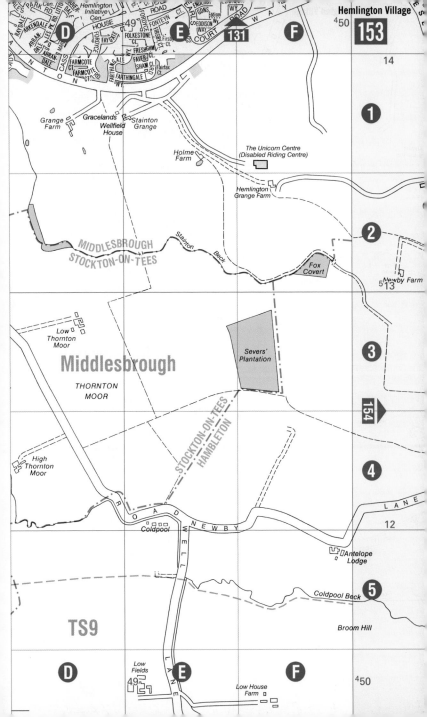

PARK
RD. RD. LTTO DALE
Hemlington
Initiative
Cen.
HOUSE
FORDYCE
49
ROAD
ENDLFIOT
GDNS.
Eddison
WY
ROAD
CARLS
CT.
FONTEYN
FORDYCE
WY.
FOLKESTONE
CL.
FRESHGHM
First
FRISBY
CT.
Edison
(WAY)
WAY

D
E
131
F

BAYDALE
ARKENDALE
ABRAN-
NES. PK. RD. DALE
DALE
FAYRE
CL.
FARMCOTE
CT.
FARMCOTE
CT.
ARRAN
DALE
CASS
CT.
FARTHINGALE
DALE
FAVER
SHAM
CL.
FARTHINGALE
WY.
FARTHINGALE
CRO
Fairfax
Ct.

14

1

Grange
Farm

Gracelands
Wellfield
House

Stainton
Grange

Holme
Farm

The Unicorn Centre
(Disabled Riding Centre)

Hemlington
Grange Farm

MIDDLESBROUGH
STOCKTON-ON-TEES

Stainton
Beck

2

Fox
Covert

Newby Farm

⁵13

Low
Thornton
Moor

Middlesbrough

Severs'
Plantation

3

THORNTON
MOOR

154

STOCKTON-ON-TEES
HAMBLETON

High
Thornton
Moor

4

ROAD WELL

NEWBY

LANE

12

Coldpool

Antelope
Lodge

Coldpool Beck

5

Broom Hill

TS9

D

Low
Fields

E

Low House
Farm

F

⁴50

49

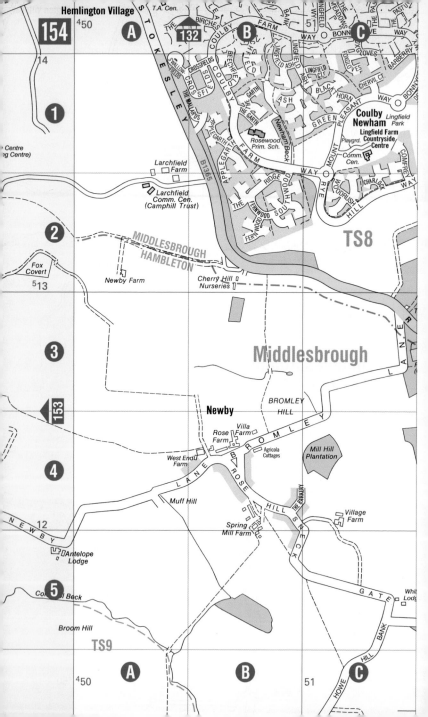

D 52 **E** 133 **F** 53 **155** 14

Marton — West — Beck

Grd.

WESTRAY

HAWKSTONE

HANKS

BROA DSTONE PK.

FARNSIDE

WOODHOUSE

ASTBURY

WL

KEDLE

BRASS CASTLE LANE

GROVE

CONN

Ford Close

Three Plan

Ellerbys Plantation

1

Bonny Grove Plantation

MIDDLESBROUGH GOLF COURSE

Newham Whin

Newham Hall Farm

Oak Wood

Club House

Rye Hill

Ryehill House

Fishpond Plantation

W CI

2

Newham Hall

Ryehill Farm

Cleveland Cottage

Jubilee Plantation

13

The Lodge

DE BRUS PARK

BRASS

CASTLE LANE

STOKESLEY

ROAD

Reservoir (Covered)

Arcadia Nurseries

Birch Hill

Moor Close

Spion Kop

South Ryehill

3

igh Tunstall Farm

156

4

Long Plantation

B1365

Sunny Cross Plantation

TUNSTALL LANE

LANE

Tunstall Farm

TS7

12

GREEN

Newby Grange

Tunstall Cottage

5

River Tame

ROAD

LANE

Castle Hill

D 52 **E** **164** **F** 53

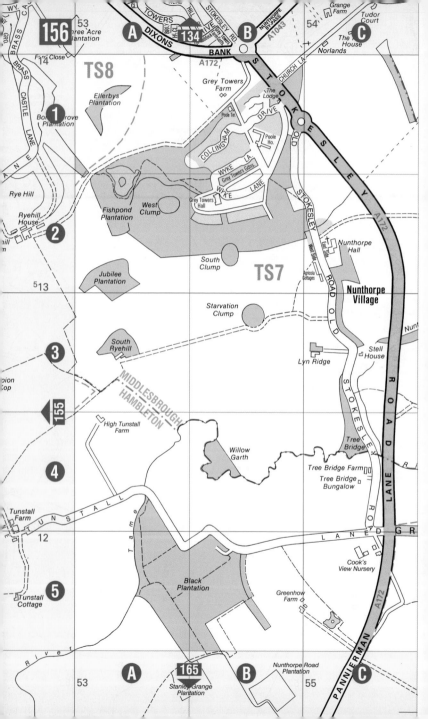

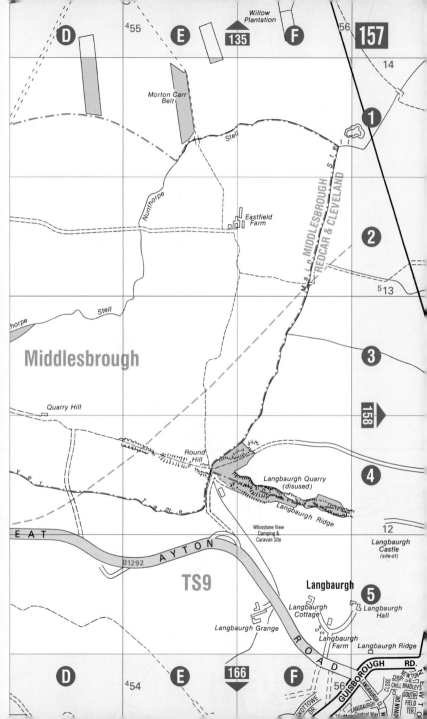

D ⁴55 **E** 135 **F** 56 **157** 14

Willow Plantation

1

Morton Carr Belt

Stell

MIDDLESBROUGH

REDCAR & CLEVELAND

2

⁵13

Nunthorpe

Eastfield Farm

3

thorpe Stell

Middlesbrough

158 ▶

Quarry Hill

4

Round Hill

Langbaurgh Quarry (disused)

Langbaurgh Ridge

12

Whinstone View Camping & Caravan Site

Langbaurgh Castle (site of)

EAT AYTON

B1292

TS9

Langbaurgh

5 Langbaurgh Hall

Langbaurgh Cottage

Langbaurgh Grange

Langbaurgh Farm

Langbaurgh Ridge

D ⁴54 **E** 166 ▽ **F** 56 GUISBOROUGH RD.

NEWTON

CHUR CHILL BRADLEYS

CLOSE

SOUTH FIELD TER

ROAD

KOTTOWE DR

Langbaurgh Central Way

OWAN DR

56 14

A

136

B

57

C

1

Green Hills

Snow Hall Farm

Steel

Main

2

513

CHURCH LANE

Hall Hill

Old Hall

Newton Grange

Newton Hall

BACK LANE

The Grn.

Danespark

Newton under Roseberry

Whitegate Hill

Sewage Works

ROSEBERRY LANE

3

Whitegate Farm

P

157

ROAD

Middlesbrough

Depot

TS9

baurgh Quarry (disused)

4

angbaurgh Ridge

12

Ne W

Langbaurgh Castle (site of)

Quarry House

Chapel Well Plantation

Cliff Rigg Q (Whinston

5

Langbaurgh Cottage

Langbaurgh Hall

Cliffe House

Patsholme

Cliff Rigg Wood

AYTON

Langbaurgh Farm

Langbaurgh

Langbaurgh Ridge

ROSEBERRY

Cliff Ridge Wood

ROAD

GUISBOROUGH

WHEATLAND

ORCHARD CL

CRESCENT

ROSEBERRY AV

CRESCENT

California

Cliff Rigg Cottage

A

56

SKOTTOWE DR

LANGBAURGH CL

COWAN DR

SOUTH FIELD TER.

CHILL

DUDLEY'S

CALIFORNIA GRO

Central Way

167

ROSEBERRY CRT

B

57

C

A173

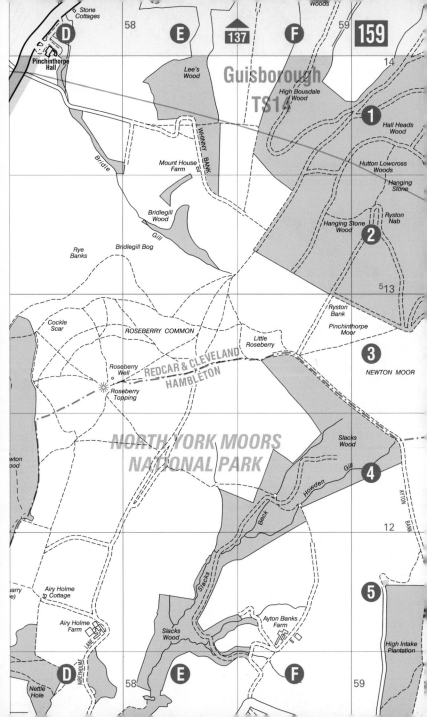

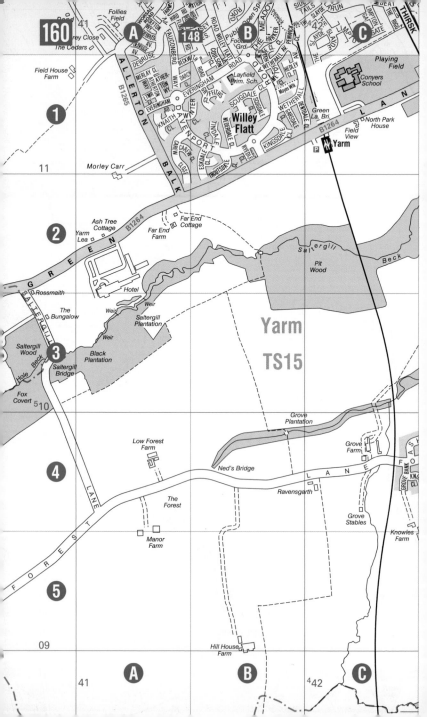

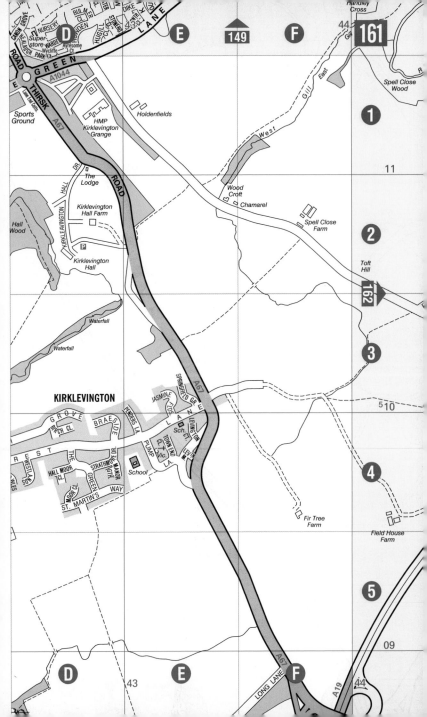

CANON GROVE
NURSERY
BULM...
WARDE...
HUGILL
STONG...
DIKE LANE
Handley Cross

D **E** ▲ 149 **F** 44 161

GREEN
A1044
Superstore
CLAUGH PARK
Wycliffe
Ct
Ayresome Ct

Spell Close Wood

THIRSK

East Gill

Sports Ground

Holdenfields

West Gill

1

HMP Kirklevington Grange

11

HALL DR

The Lodge

ROAD

Wood Croft

Chamarel

KIRKLEVINGTON

Kirklevington Hall Farm

Spell Close Farm

2

Hall Wood

P

Kirklevington Hall

Toft Hill

162 ►

3

Waterfall

Waterfall

5 10

SPRINGFIELD GR

JASMINE CL

A67

KIRKLEVINGTON

GROVE
BRCH CL
BRAESIDE
PENDERS LA
Sch
FOSS LA
TOWN END CT
LEVINGTON CL
Vic.
PUMP LA
LEVINGTON M
CREST
WESTLA...
WLES
THE
HALL MOOR CL
MOOR CT
STRATHMORE
GREEN
MANOR GTH
WAY
ST. MARTIN'S

School

Fir Tree Farm

4

Field House Farm

5

09

D **E** **F**

43

LONG LANE

A67

A19 44

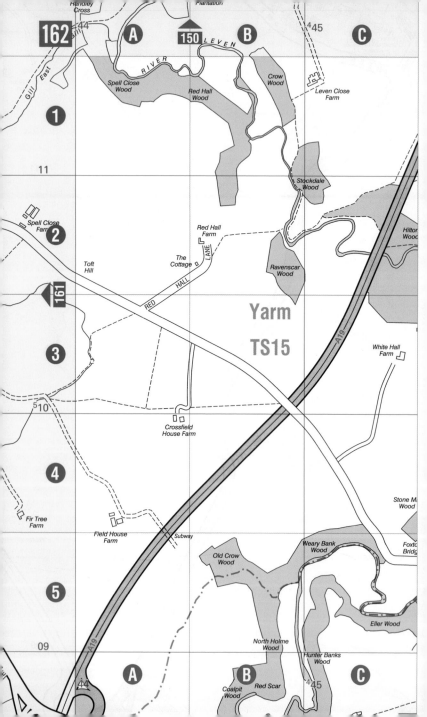

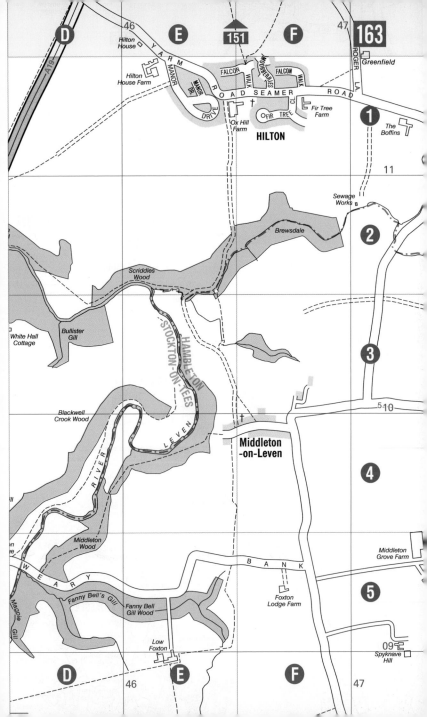

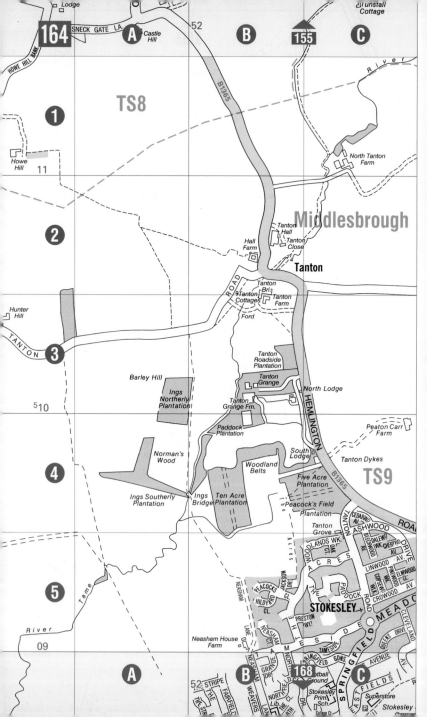

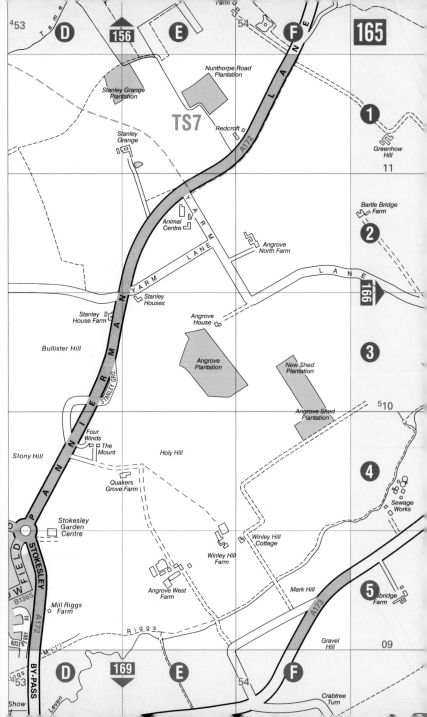

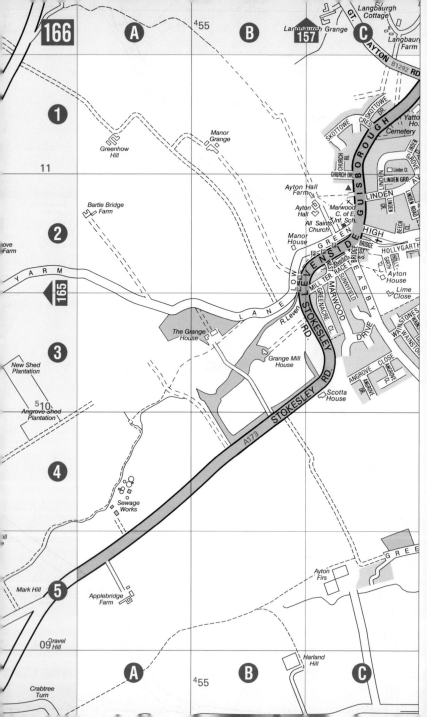

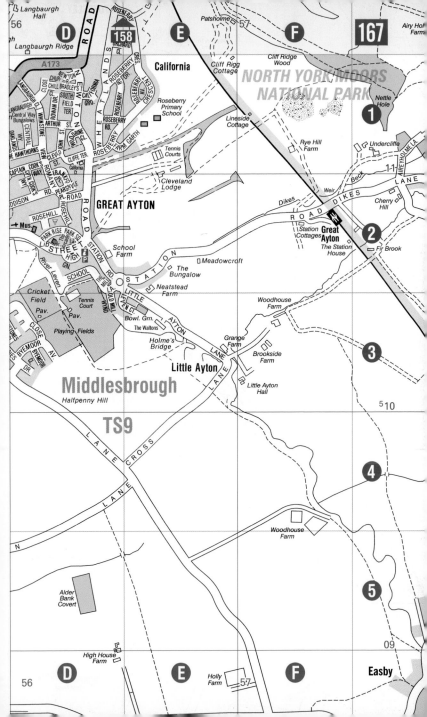

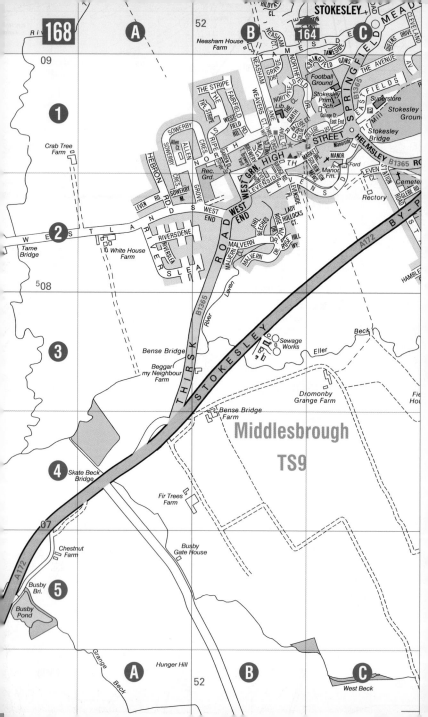

168

STOKESLEY

164

Ri... 52 09

A Neasham House Farm **B** **C**

HILDY... CL.
NEASHAM
TAMESIDE
CLEVELAND
QUEENS DRIVE
DRIVE
CLEVELAND AV
THE AVENUE
SPRINGFIELD GDNS
SPRINGFIELD
EASTFIELDS
B1365

THE STRIPE
FAIRFIELD
WEAVERS CT
NORTHFIELD
GRANGE DR
NEASHAM LANE
Football Ground
Stokesley Prim. Sch.
Superstore
Stokesley Ground
P

Crab Tree Farm

1

HEBRON ROAD
SOWERBY
SOWERBY CRES
ALLEN CRES
ALLEN GROVE
SOWERBY M.
LEVEN RD

THE STRIPE
THE STRIPE
WEST FIELD RD
THE STRIPE

NORTY...
Lib.
College Ct
East End
TM III
Stokesley Bridge
B1365
R...

STREET

HIGH STREET
BREWERY
BALLIOL CT
TEW...
MARKET PL
THE GARTH
GOLDEN LION
MANORING...

MANOR
Manor Fm.
Ford
LEVEN CL.
Cemetery
HELMSLEY B1365
LEVEN STATION RD
GLEBE RD

2 W E S T L A N D

Tame Bridge
White House Farm
RIVERSDENE
RIVERSLEA
PRIVERSLEA

WEST END
WEST END
WEST GRN
LEVENSIDE
LEVENSIDE
LEVENSIDE CT
Rec. Grd.
THE BEECHES
LADY HULLOCKS CT
DR. TH
DR. ROSE HILL WY.

Rectory

MALVERN
MALVERN
Leven
MALVERN
River

3

Bense Bridge
Beggar my Neighbour Farm

B1365
THIRSK ROAD STOKESLEY

Sewage Works
Beck
Eller

Dromonby Grange Farm
Bense Bridge Farm

Middlesbrough

TS9

Fie...
Ho...

4 Skate Beck Bridge
Fir Trees Farm

07
A172
Chestnut Farm
Busby Gate House

5 Busby Bri.
Busby Pond

A172
A172

A Hunger Hill 52 **B** **C** West Beck

Grange Beck

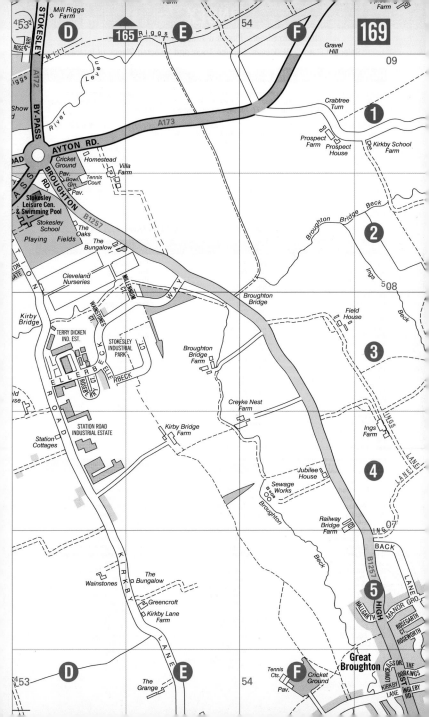

INDEX

Including Streets, Places & Areas, Industrial Estates,
Selected Flats & Walkways, Service Areas and Selected Places of Interest.

HOW TO USE THIS INDEX

1. Each street name is followed by its Postcode District and then by its Locality abbreviation(s) and then by its map reference; e.g. **Abingdon Rd.** TS1: Midd . . . .5F **77** is in the TS1 Postcode District and the Middlesbrough Locality and is to be found in square 5F on page **77**. The page number is shown in bold type.

2. A strict alphabetical order is followed in which Av., Rd., St., etc. (though abbreviated) are read in full and as part of the street name; e.g. **Ash Rd.** appears after **Ashridge Cl.** but before **Ashton Rd.**

3. Streets and a selection of flats and walkways too small to be shown on the maps, appear in the index with the thoroughfare to which it is connected shown in brackets; e.g. **Admiral Ho.** TS24: H'pool . . . .3D **15** (off Admiral Way)

4. Addresses that are in more than one part are referred to as not continuous.

5. Places and areas are shown in the index in **BLUE TYPE** and the map reference is to the actual map square in which the town centre or area is located and not to the place name shown on the map; e.g. BOOSBECK 3B 112

6. An example of a selected place of interest is Captain Cook Birthplace Mus. 1D 133

7. Service Areas are shown in the index in **BOLD CAPITAL TYPE**; e.g. **WOLVISTON SERVICES 1B 38**

GENERAL ABBREVIATIONS

All. : Alley	**Flds.** : Fields	**Nth.** : North
App. : Approach	**Gdn.** : Garden	**Pde.** : Parade
Arc. : Arcade	**Gdns.** : Gardens	**Pk.** : Park
Av. : Avenue	**Gth.** : Garth	**Pl.** : Place
Bk. : Back	**Ga.** : Gate	**Pct.** : Precinct
Blvd. : Boulevard	**Gt.** : Great	**Prom.** : Promenade
Bri. : Bridge	**Grn.** : Green	**Ri.** : Rise
Bldgs. : Buildings	**Gro.** : Grove	**Rd.** : Road
Bungs. : Bungalows	**Hgts.** : Heights	**Rdbt.** : Roundabout
Bus. : Business	**Ho.** : House	**Shop.** : Shopping
Cvn. : Caravan	**Ho's.** : Houses	**Sth.** : South
Cen. : Centre	**Ind.** : Industrial	**Sq.** : Square
Chu. : Church	**Info.** : Information	**St.** : Street
Cl. : Close	**Intl.** : International	**Ter.** : Terrace
Cnr. : Corner	**Junc.** : Junction	**Trad.** : Trading
Cotts. : Cottages	**La.** : Lane	**Up.** : Upper
Ct. : Court	**Lit.** : Little	**Va.** : Vale
Cres. : Crescent	**Lwr.** : Lower	**Vw.** : View
Cft. : Croft	**Mnr.** : Manor	**Vs.** : Villas
Dr. : Drive	**Mdw.** : Meadow	**Vis.** : Visitors
E. : East	**Mdws.** : Meadows	**Wlk.** : Walk
Ent. : Enterprise	**M.** : Mews	**W.** : West
Est. : Estate	**Mt.** : Mount	**Yd.** : Yard
Fld. : Field	**Mus.** : Museum	

LOCALITY ABBREVIATIONS

Ais : **Aislaby**	Gran : **Grangetown**	Midd : **Middlesbrough**
Bill : **Billingham**	G Ayt : **Great Ayton**	M Row : **Middleton One Row**
Bis : **Bishopton**	G Bro : **Great Broughton**	M Lev : **Middleton-on-Leven**
Boo : **Boosbeck**	Grea : **Greatham**	M Geo : **Middleton St George**
Boul : **Boulby**	Guis : **Guisborough**	Moor : **Moorsholm**
Bri : **Brierton**	Hart : **Hart**	Newb : **Newby**
Brot : **Brotton**	H'pool : **Hartlepool**	N Mar : **New Marske**
C How : **Carlin How**	Hem : **Hemlington**	News : **Newsham**
Car : **Carlton**	H Lev : **High Leven**	N Bew : **Newton Bewley**
C Ede : **Castle Eden**	Hilt : **Hilton**	N Ros : **Newton under Roseberry**
Cast : **Castlelevington**	Hind : **Hinderwell**	Norm : **Normanby**
Char : **Charltons**	I Bar : **Ingleby Barwick**	N Orm : **North Ormesby**
Clax : **Claxton**	Kirk : **Kirkby**	Nort : **Norton**
C New : **Coulby Newham**	K'ham : **Kirkleatham**	Nun : **Nunthorpe**
C Bew : **Cowpen Bewley**	K'ton : **Kirklevington**	O Lac : **Old Lackenby**
D Pie : **Dalton Piercy**	Laze : **Lazenby**	Orm : **Ormesby**
Dun : **Dunsdale**	Ling : **Lingdale**	Pin : **Pinchinthorpe**
Eag : **Eaglescliffe**	L Ayt : **Little Ayton**	P Cla : **Port Clarence**
Eas : **Easington**	Live : **Liverton**	P Mul : **Port Mulgrave**
Egg : **Egglescliffe**	Loft : **Loftus**	P Tee : **Preston-on-Tees**
Elt : **Elton**	L New : **Long Newton**	Redc : **Redcar**
Elw : **Elwick**	Malt : **Maltby**	Redm : **Redmarshall**
Est : **Eston**	M Sea : **Marske-by-the-Sea**	Runs : **Runswick**
Fish : **Fishburn**	Mart : **Marton**	Sadb : **Sadberge**

Salt : **Saltburn-by-the-Sea**
S San : **Seal Sands**
Seam : **Seamer**
S Car : **Seaton Carew**
Sed : **Sedgefield**
Sher : **Sheraton**
Skel : **Skelton**
Skin : **Skinningrove**
Slape : **Slapewath**

S Ban : **South Bank**
Stain : **Stainton**
Stait : **Staithes**
Stil : **Stillington**
S Tee : **Stockton-on-Tees**
Stok : **Stokesley**
T Tee : **Thornaby-on-Tees**
Thor : **Thornton**
T Lar : **Thorpe Larches**

T The : **Thorpe Thewles**
Uple : **Upleatham**
W Hill : **Whinney Hill**
Whit : **Whitton**
Wilt : **Wilton**
Wolv : **Wolviston**
Wyn : **Wynyard**
Yarm : **Yarm**
Year : **Yearby**

A

Abberley Dr. TS8: Hem 4F **131**
Abberston Wlk.
    TS4: Midd 4A **102**
Abbey Cl. TS19: S Tee. 4F **71**
Abbey Ct. TS6: Norm 1D **105**
Abbeyfield Dr. TS16: Eag 5B **126**
Abbey St. TS12: Brot 3B **90**
    TS24: H'pool 1F **15**
Abbotsford Ct. TS17: I Bar . . . 4F **127**
Abbotsford Rd. TS5: Midd . . . 3B **100**
Abbots Lea TS27: D Pie 1E **17**
Abbots Way TS19: S Tee 4F **71**
Abdale Av. TS5: Midd 3B **100**
Abdiel Ct. TS24: H'pool 5C **8**
Abdiel Ho. TS24: H'pool 2D **15**
Aberbran Ct. TS17: I Bar 2F **149**
Abercrombie Rd.
    TS10: Redc 5F **47**
Aberdare Rd. TS6: Gran 3E **81**
Aberdeen Rd. TS25: H'pool . . 3A **20**
Aberdovey Dr. TS16: Eag . . . 1C **148**
Aberfalls Rd. TS8: Hem 4F **131**
Abigail Wlk. TS24: H'pool . . . 2B **14**
Abingdon Rd. TS1: Midd. 5F **77**
    TS13: Eas 2A **118**
Abram La. TS13: Stait 1C **120**
Abrams Bldgs. TS13: Loft 5C **92**
Abridge Cl. TS11: N Mar 2F **85**
Acacia Ct. TS10: Redc 4E **65**
Acacia Rd. TS19: S Tee 3F **73**
Acclom St. TS24: H'pool 1A **14**
Achilles Cl. TS6: S Ban 4B **80**
ACKLAM 4C **100**
Acklam Ct. TS5: Midd 5C **100**
Acklam Hall Cotts.
    TS5: Midd 5D **101**
Acklam Rd. TS5: Midd 3B **100**
    TS17: T Tee 2D **99**
Acklam Sports Cen. 5D **101**
Acklam St. Nth. TS2: Midd. . . 1E **77**
Acklam St. Sth. TS2: Midd. . . 2E **77**
Ackworth Grn. TS3: Midd. . . . 5D **79**
Acorn Bank TS17: I Bar 2B **150**
Acorn Cl. DL2: M Geo 1A **144**
Acorn Ct. TS10: Redc 4F **65**
Acres, The TS9: Stok 4B **164**
    (not continuous)
Acton St. TS1: Midd 5F **77**
Adam Cl. TS10: Redc 3B **64**
Adam St. TS18: S Tee. 4A **98**
Adcott Rd. TS5: Midd 5C **100**
Adderley St. TS18: S Tee 2A **98**
Addington Dr. TS3: Midd 5D **79**
Addison Rd. TS5: Midd 1D **101**
    TS9: G Ayt. 2D **167**
    TS24: H'pool 2B **14**
Adelaide Gro. TS18: S Tee . . . 2D **97**
Adelaide Pl. TS11: M Sea 4C **66**
Adelaide Rd. TS7: Mart 3C **132**
Aden St. TS5: Midd 5C **76**
Admiral Ho. *TS24: H'pool* *3D* **15**
    (off Admiral Way)
Admirals Av. TS3: Midd 5D **79**

Admiralty Ecology Pk.
  (Carter Moor Nature Reserve)
    . . . . 3F **125**
Admiral Way TS24: H'pool . . . 3D **15**
Adshead Rd. TS10: Redc 1F **63**
Adstock Av. TS4: Midd 4B **102**
Agecroft Gdns. TS5: Midd . . 2B **100**
Agricola Cotts. TS7: Nun 2C **156**
    TS8: Newb. 4B **154**
Ainderby Gro. TS18: S Tee . . . 2A **96**
Ainderby Wlk. TS24: H'pool . . 5B **8**
Ainderby Way TS4: Midd 3A **102**
Ainsdale Cl. TS11: N Mar 2F **85**
Ainsdale Way TS4: Midd 4A **102**
Ainsford Way TS7: Orm 3B **104**
Ainsley St. TS25: H'pool 5D **15**
Ainstable Rd. TS7: Orm 4A **104**
Ainsworth Way TS7: Orm . . . 3B **104**
Ainthorpe Pl. TS6: Est 5F **81**
Ainthorpe Rd. TS6: Est 5F **81**
Aintree Rd. TS10: Redc 1D **65**
    TS18: S Tee 3F **75**
Airdrie Gro. TS25: H'pool . . . 3F **19**
Aireborough Cl.
    TS19: S Tee. 3D **73**
Aire St. TS1: Midd 5D **77**
    TS6: S Ban. 2F **79**
Aireyholme La.
    TS9: G Ayt. 5D **159**
Airy Hill La. TS12: Boo 5F **111**
Aiskew Gro. TS18: S Tee 5A **72**
AISLABY 4F **147**
Aislaby Gro. TS23: Bill 3E **39**
Aislaby Ho. TS14: Guis 5E **109**
Aislaby Rd.
    TS16: Ais, News 5F **145**
Ajax Way TS6: S Ban 3A **80**
Alan St. TS6: S Ban 2A **80**
ALBANY 2C **74**
Albany Ct. TS26: H'pool 3A **14**
Albany Rd. TS7: Mart 3C **132**
    TS20: Nort. 1B **74**
Albany St. TS1: Midd 4E **77**
Alberta Ho. TS4: Midd 1A **102**
Albert M. TS1: Midd 3F **77**
Albert Rd. TS1: Midd 3F **77**
    TS6: Est 1D **105**
    TS16: Eag 4C **126**
    TS18: S Tee 5A **74**
    TS19: S Tee. 5B **72**
Albert St. TS2: Midd 2F **77**
    TS24: H'pool 4C **14**
Albert Ter. TS1: Midd 5E **77**
Albion St. TS12: Boo 3C **112**
    TS14: Guis 1A **98**
    (not continuous)
Albion Ter. TS12: Salt. 5C **68**
    TS14: Guis 1F **139**
    TS24: H'pool 2F **13**
Albourne Grn. TS4: Midd 4B **102**
Albury Way TS3: Midd 1F **103**
Alconbury Way TS3: Midd . . 1F **103**
Aldbrough Cl. TS19: S Tee . . . 5B **72**
Aldeburgh Cl. TS25: H'pool . . 1E **31**
Aldenham Rd. TS14: Guis . . . 4C **138**

Aldergrove Dr. TS4: Midd. . . . 5B **102**
Alderlea TS7: Mart 2E **133**
Alderney Gro. TS17: T Tee . . . 4D **99**
Alderney Wlk. TS14: Guis . . . 3D **139**
Alder Rd. TS19: S Tee. 3F **73**
Alderson St. TS26: H'pool . . . 4A **14**
Alderwood TS8: C New. 3B **132**
Alderwood Cl. TS7: Orm 4B **104**
    TS27: H'pool 2C **6**
Aldridge Rd. TS3: Midd 3D **103**
Aldwark Cl. TS5: Midd 3C **130**
Aldwych Cl. TS6: Norm 3C **104**
Alexander Av. TS3: Midd 5E **79**
Alexandra Ho. TS12: Salt. . . . 3D **69**
Alexandra Rd. TS6: Gran 3D **81**
Alexandria Dr.
    DL2: M Geo. 1B **144**
Alford Cl. TS25: H'pool. 4A **20**
Alford La. TS19: S Tee 3D **73**
Alford Rd. TS12: Brot 3B **90**
Alfred St. TS10: Redc. 3D **49**
    TS24: H'pool 5F **9**
Alfriston Cl. TS17: I Bar . . . 1B **150**
Alice Row TS18: S Tee 1F **97**
Alice St. TS20: Nort 5B **54**
Allen Ct. TS9: Stok. 1A **168**
Allendale Cen. TS7: Orm 4A **104**
Allendale Ho. TS7: Orm 3B **104**
Allendale Rd. TS7: Orm 3A **104**
    TS18: S Tee 4E **73**
    TS23: Bill. 2C **54**
Allendale St. TS25: S Car. . . . 4E **21**
Allendale Tee TS11: N Mar. . . 2F **85**
Allen Gro. TS9: Stok. 1A **168**
Allensway TS17: T Tee 1E **129**
Allerford Cl. TS17: I Bar 3A **150**
Allerston Way TS14: Guis . . . 5E **109**
Allerton Balk TS15: Yarm . . . 1A **160**
Allerton Cl. TS24: H'pool 1B **14**
Allerton Pk. TS7: Nun. 4A **134**
Alliance St. TS18: S Tee 2F **97**
    TS24: H'pool 5F **9**
Allington Dr. TS23: Bill. 4D **39**
Allington Wlk. TS23: Bill 4D **39**
Allinson St. TS3: N Orm 4C **78**
Allison Av. TS17: T Tee 1D **151**
Allison Ho. TS17: T Tee 1C **98**
Allison Pl. TS24: H'pool 5E **9**
Allison St. TS14: Guis 2D **139**
    TS18: S Tee 5A **74**
Alloa Gro. TS25: H'pool 3A **20**
Alloway Gro. TS8: Hem 4F **131**
Alma Cen. TS18: S Tee 4A **74**
Alma Pde. TS10: Redc 3C **48**
Alma St. TS18: S Tee 4A **74**
    TS26: H'pool *3B* **14**
    (off York Rd.)
    TS26: H'pool 3F **13**
    (Mulgrave Rd., not continuous)
Almond Cl. TS4: Midd. 3F **101**
Almond Gro. TS11: M Sea . . . 5C **66**
    TS19: S Tee 5C **72**
Alness Gro. TS25: H'pool . . . 3A **20**
Alnmouth Dr. TS10: Redc. . . . 3D **65**
Alnport Rd. TS18: S Tee 4C **74**
Alnwick Cl. TS10: Redc 1F **65**
    TS27: H'pool 3C **6**

Alnwick Ct. TS4: Midd 2A **102**
Alnwick Gro. TS20: Nort. 4A **54**
Alnwick Ho. TS4: Midd 2B **102**
Alonby Cl. TS21: L New 1A **124**
Alpha Gro. TS20: Nort 2B **74**
Alpine Way TS20: Nort 1F **73**
Alston Grn. TS3: Midd 5D **79**
Alston St. TS26: H'pool 5B **14**
Althorpe Cl. TS3: Midd 2F **103**
Althorp Rd. TS10: Redc 4C **48**
Alton Rd. TS5: Midd 1B **100**
Alum Way TS12: Skel 3E **89**
Alva Gro. TS25: H'pool 3A **20**
Alverstone Av.
  TS25: H'pool 1B **20**
Alverton Cl. TS3: Midd 1F **103**
Alverton Grn. TS3: Midd 1F **103**
Alvingham Ter. TS3: Midd . . . 2F **103**
Alvis Cl. TS23: Bill 1B **56**
Alvis Ct. TS23: Bill 1B **56**
Alwent Rd. TS1: Midd. 3E **77**
Alwin Cl. TS17: I Bar 2B **150**
Alwinton Cl. TS7: Orm 4A **104**
Amberley Cl. TS10: Redc 4E **65**
  TS18: S Tee 2C **96**
Amberley Grn. TS3: Midd 5D **79**
Amberley Way TS16: Eag . . . 5A **126**
Amber St. TS1: Midd 4E **77**
  TS12: Salt. 3D **69**
Amberton Rd. TS24: H'pool . . . 1B **14**
Amberwood Cl.
  TS27: H'pool 2C **6**
Amberwood Wlk.
  TS24: H'pool *2C 6*
  (off Amberwood Cl.)
Amble Cl. TS26: H'pool 3D **13**
Amble Ct. TS26: H'pool 5F **13**
Ambleside Av. TS10: Redc. . . . 1C **64**
Ambleside Gro.
  TS5: Midd 4C **100**
Ambleside Rd.
  TS6: Norm. 2C **104**
  TS23: Bill. 4E **55**
Amble Vw. TS20: Nort 1C **74**
Ambrose Rd. TS6: Est 2E **105**
Amersham Rd. TS3: Midd . . . 3D **103**
Amerston Rd. TS22: Wyn 4B **26**
Amesbury Cres. TS8: Hem . . . 4F **131**
Ammerston Rd. TS1: Midd. . . . 3D **77**
Ampleforth Av. TS6: Est 1D **105**
Ampleforth Cl. TS12: Skel . . . 4D **89**
Ampleforth Rd. TS3: Midd . . . 2C **102**
  TS23: Bill. 1E **55**
Amroth Grn. TS3: Midd 5D **79**
Anchorage M. TS17: T Tee . . . 1C **98**
Anchor Ct. TS24: H'pool 1F **15**
Anchor Ho. TS24: H'pool 3D **15**
Anchor Retail Pk.
  TS24: H'pool 2B **14**
Ancroft Dr. TS7: Orm 4A **104**
Ancroft Gdns. TS20: Nort 1B **74**
Anderson Rd. TS17: T Tee . . . 2D **99**
Anderson St. TS7: T Tee. 3D **99**
Andover Way TS8: Hem 4E **131**
Andrew Pl. TS24: H'pool 4C **14**
Andrew St. TS24: H'pool 4C **14**
Angel Ct. TS9: Stok 1B **168**
Angle Ct. TS4: Midd 5A **78**
Anglesey Av. TS3: Midd 3E **103**
Anglesey Gro. TS26: H'pool . . . 5E **7**
Anglesey Wlk. *TS14: Guis* . . . *3D 139*
  (off Hutton La.)
Angle St. TS4: Midd 4A **78**
Angling Grn. TS13: Skin. 2A **92**
Angrove Cl. TS9: G Ayt. 3C **166**
  TS15: Yarm 4E **149**
Angrove Dr. TS9: G Ayt. 3C **166**
Angus St. TS26: H'pool 3A **14**

Anlaby Cl. TS23: Bill. 2E **39**
Anna Ct. *TS26: H'pool* *5A 14*
  (off Flaxton St.)
Annandale Cres.
  TS24: H'pool 3F **7**
Annan Rd. TS23: Bill. 3E **39**
Ann Crooks Way
  TS24: H'pool 5F **9**
Anne St. TS1: Midd 4C **76**
Annfield Cl. TS23: Bill 4D **39**
Annigate Cl. TS22: Wyn 2E **37**
Annigate (Samsung) Rdbt.
  TS22: Wyn 1A **38**
Ann St. TS6: S Ban 2A **80**
Ansdale Rd. TS3: Midd 5A **80**
Anson Ho. TS17: T Tee. 1D **129**
Anstey Ho. TS20: Nort 5A **54**
Antrim Av. TS19: S Tee 4A **72**
Appleby Av. TS3: Midd 5D **79**
Appleby Cl. TS11: N Mar 2F **85**
Appleby Ct. TS24: H'pool 1B **14**
Appleby Ho. TS17: T Tee . . . 1D **129**
Appleby Rd. TS23: Bill 5E **39**
Applegarth TS8: C New 1B **154**
Applegarth, The
  TS14: Guis. 1F **139**
Apple Orchard Bank
  TS11: Skel, Uple 4E **87**
Applethwaite Gdns.
  TS12: Skel. 2C **88**
Appleton Cl. TS14: Guis 5E **109**
Appleton Rd. TS5: Midd 3B **100**
Appletree Gdns.
  TS7: Orm. 4B **104**
Applewood Cl. TS27: H'pool . . . 2B **6**
Appley Cl. TS16: P Tee 1D **127**
Apsley St. TS1: Midd 5F **77**
Apsley Way TS17: I Bar 4F **127**
Arabella Cl. TS24: H'pool. 5E **9**
Arabella St. TS24: H'pool 5E **9**
Arbroath Gro. TS25: H'pool . . . 3F **19**
Arcade, The TS9: G Ayt 2D **167**
Arch Ct. TS24: H'pool 5C **8**
Archer Cl. TS4: Midd 4A **102**
Archer Rd. DL2: M Row 4A **144**
Archer St. TS17: T Tee 2C **98**
  TS24: H'pool 3C **14**
Archibald St. TS5: Midd. 5C **76**
Arden Cl. TS14: Guis 4D **139**
Arden Gro. TS19: S Tee 1B **96**
Ardrossan Cl. TS25: H'pool . . 3A **20**
Ardrossan Rd.
  TS25: H'pool 3A **20**
Arening Ct. TS17: I Bar. 5F **127**
Argory, The TS17: I Bar 1B **150**
Argyle Rd. TS6: Gran 2D **81**
Argyll Ct. TS20: Nort 1A **74**
Argyll Rd. TS7: Mart. 3C **132**
  TS20: Nort 1F **73**
  TS25: H'pool 3A **20**
Arisaig Cl. TS16: Eag 1C **148**
Arkendale TS8: Hem 5D **131**
Arken Ter. TS20: Nort. 2B **74**
Arkgrove Ho. TS24: H'pool. . . 2D **15**
Arkgrove Ind. Est.
  TS18: S Tee 3D **75**
Arkley Cres. TS24: H'pool 4A **8**
Ark Royal Cl. TS25: S Car . . . 3D **21**
Arlington Cl. TS18: S Tee . . . 2F **97**
Arlington Rd. TS5: Midd 3E **101**
Arlington St. TS13: Loft 5C **92**
  TS18: S Tee 2F **97**
  (not continuous)
Armadale TS10: Redc. 3E **65**
Armadale Ct. TS19: S Tee . . . 4F **71**
Armadale Gro.
  TS25: H'pool 3F **19**
Armitage Rd. TS10: Redc. . . . 2E **63**

Arncliffe Av. TS18: S Tee 3F **97**
Arncliffe Gdns.
  TS26: H'pool 4A **14**
Arncliffe Rd. TS5: Midd 5B **76**
Arnold Gro. TS25: H'pool 2E **19**
Arnside Av. TS3: Midd 5D **79**
Arran Cl. TS17: T Tee 2C **128**
Arrandale TS8: Hem. 1D **153**
Arran Gro. TS25: H'pool 3A **20**
Arran Wlk. TS14: Guis 3D **139**
Arrathorne Rd. TS18: S Tee . . 3A **96**
Arthur St. TS9: G Ayt 1D **167**
  TS10: Redc 3B **48**
Arthur Ter. TS11: N Mar 1A **86**
Arundel Ct. TS17: I Bar 4F **127**
Arundel Grn. TS3: Midd. 2B **79**
Arundel Rd. TS6: Gran 4E **81**
  TS23: Bill 5D **39**
Arundel St. TS10: Redc 3B **48**
Ascot Av. TS5: Midd 2B **100**
Ascot Dr. TS18: S Tee 3F **75**
Ascot Rd. TS10: Redc 1D **65**
Ashberry Cl. TS12: Moor 3B **142**
Ashbourne Lodge
  TS23: Bill 4D **55**
Ashbourne Rd. TS19: S Tee . . 3A **74**
Ashbrooke Way
  TS5: Midd 1B **100**
Ashburn St. TS25: S Car 4E **21**
Ashburton Cl. TS8: Midd 2B **132**
Ashby Gro. TS25: H'pool 1E **31**
Ashby Rd. TS23: Bill. 5D **39**
Ashcombe Cl. TS22: Bill. 4A **38**
Ashdale TS8: Hem 5D **131**
Ashdale Cl. DL2: M Geo 2C **144**
Ashdown Cl. TS17: T Tee . . . 2C **128**
Ashdown Way TS23: Bill. 4A **40**
Ashes, The TS25: S Car 5E **21**
Ashfield Av. TS4: Midd 2F **101**
Ashfield Cl. TS25: Grea 3E **31**
Ashford Av. TS5: Midd 3A **100**
Ashford Cl. TS14: Guis. 4D **139**
Ashford Grange
  TS12: Boo 3B **112**
Ash Grn. TS8: C New 1B **154**
Ash Gro. TS6: S Ban 3B **80**
  TS13: Loft 5B **92**
  TS15: K'ton 4C **160**
Ashgrove Av. TS25: H'pool . . . 1B **20**
Ashgrove Pl. TS25: H'pool . . . 1B **20**
Ash Hill TS8: C New 5C **132**
Ashkirk Rd. TS6: Norm. 1C **104**
Ashley Gdns. TS24: H'pool. . . 1F **13**
Ashling Way TS5: Midd 1C **100**
Ashmead Vw. TS18: S Tee . . 4D **73**
Ashridge Cl. TS11: N Mar . . . 2F **85**
  TS17: I Bar 5C **128**
Ash Rd. TS14: Guis. 1E **139**
Ashton Rd. TS20: Nort 5E **53**
Ash Vale Holiday Pk.
  TS27: H'pool 2B **6**
Ashville Av. TS16: P Tee 3C **126**
  TS20: Nort. 4F **53**
Ashwood Cl. TS7: Orm 4B **104**
  TS27: H'pool 2C **6**
Ashwood Dr. TS9: Stok. 4C **164**
Askern Dr. TS5: Midd 5E **101**
Aske Rd. TS1: Midd 4E **77**
  TS10: Redc 4D **49**
Askewdale TS14: Guis 3A **138**
Askgrigg Wlk. TS3: Midd . . . 2C **102**
Askham Cl. TS4: Midd 2F **101**
Askrigg Rd. TS18: S Tee. 5D **73**
Askwith Rd. TS5: Midd. 2D **101**
Aspen Dr. TS5: Midd 2F **101**
Aspen Gdns. TS19: S Tee . . . 1B **72**
Aspen Rd. TS16: Eag 1B **148**

Astbury TS8: Mart 1E **155**
Aster Cl. TS7: Mart 2B **132**
Asterley Dr. TS5: Midd 4A **100**
Astley Cl. TS19: S Tee 5B **72**
Aston Av. TS3: Midd 4E **79**
Astonbury Grn. TS4: Midd . . 4B **102**
Aston Dr. TS14: Guis 2B **128**
Aston Rd. TS22: Bill 5B **38**
Atherstone Dr. TS14: Guis . . 3E **139**
Atherton Way TS15: Yarm . . 1A **160**
Atholl Gro. TS10: Redc 5A **48**
Atkin Av. 3A **20**
Athol St. TS1: Midd 5E **77**
Atkinson Ind. Est.
  TS25: H'pool 5C **14**
Atlas Wynd TS15: Yarm . . 3B **148**
Attingham Cl. TS8: Hem . . . 4F **131**
Attlee Rd. TS6: Gran 4E **81**
Attlow Wlk. TS3: Midd 1F **103**
Atwater Cl. TS15: Yarm 5D **149**
Atwick Cl. TS23: Bill 2E **39**
Aubrey Ct. TS20: Nort 1B **74**
Aubrey St. TS1: Midd 5F **77**
Auckland Av. TS7: Mart 3E **133**
Auckland Rd. TS23: Bill 3A **40**
Auckland St. TS14: Guis 1E **139**
Auckland Way TS18: S Tee . . 2B **96**
  TS26: H'pool 4C **12**
Audrey Gro. TS18: S Tee 2C **96**
Aurora Ct. TS2: Midd 1C **76**
Austen Cl. TS23: Bill 2D **39**
Austin Av. TS18: S Tee 2F **97**
Autumn Gro. TS19: S Tee . . . 1C **96**
Avalon Ct. TS8: Hem 4F **131**
Avebury Cl. TS17: I Bar 1C **150**
Avens Way TS17: I Bar 4B **128**
Avenue, The TS5: Midd 5D **101**
  (Cowley Rd.)
  TS5: Midd 2E **101**
  (Cumberland Rd.)
  TS6: Norm 5C **80**
  TS7: Nun 3F **133**
  TS9: Stok 1C **168**
  TS10: Redc 4D **49**
  TS12: Brot 2C **90**
  TS14: Guis 3B **138**
  TS16: P Tee 3C **126**
  TS17: T Tee 3D **99**
  TS19: S Tee 5B **72**
  (not continuous)
  TS22: Wyn 1B **36**
Avenue Pl. TS14: Guis 1F **139**
Avenue Rd. TS24: H'pool . . . 3B **14**
  (not continuous)
Aviemore Rd. TS8: Hem 4E **131**
Avill Gro. TS17: I Bar 3A **150**
Avoca Ct. TS10: Redc 3B **48**
Avon Cl. TS12: Salt 5C **68**
  TS12: Skel 3D **89**
  TS17: T Tee 5D **99**
Avon Ct. TS12: Ling 4E **113**
Avondale Cl. TS6: Est 4E **81**
Avondale Gdns.
  TS24: H'pool 1A **14**
Avon Dr. TS14: Guis 3C **138**
Avon Gro. TS22: Bill 4A **38**
Avon Rd. TS10: Redc 1A **64**
  TS20: Nort 1C **74**
Avon St. TS12: Salt 4C **68**
  TS18: S Tee 5E **97**
Avro Cl. TS11: M Sea 4B **66**
Axbridge Ct. TS23: Bill 4D **39**
Axminster Rd. TS8: Hem . . . 4F **131**
Axton Cl. TS17: T Tee 3B **128**
Aycliffe Cl. TS19: S Tee 5A **72**
Aycliffe Rd. TS7: Mart 3C **132**
Aylsham Cl. TS17: I Bar 1C **150**
Aylton Dr. TS5: Midd 3C **130**
Ayresome Ct. TS15: Yarm . . . 5D **149**

Ayresome Grange Rd.
  TS5: Midd 5C **76**
Ayresome Grn. La.
  TS5: Midd 5C 76
  (off West La.)
  TS5: Midd 5C **76**
  (Heywood St.)
Ayresome Pk. Rd.
  TS5: Midd 5D **77**
Ayresome Rd. TS5: Midd 4B **76**
Ayresome St. TS1: Midd 5C **76**
Ayr Gro. TS25: H'pool 3A **20**
Aysdale Ga. TS12: Char 4F **141**
Aysgarth TS19: S Tee 3E **97**
Aysgarth Rd. TS5: Midd 2C **100**
  TS18: S Tee 5D **73**
Ayton Bank TS9: G Ayt 4F **159**
Ayton Ct. TS14: Guis 1D **139**
Ayton Cres. TS6: Est 2E **105**
Ayton Dr. TS10: Redc 2B **64**
Ayton Pl. TS20: Nort 3B **74**
Ayton Rd. TS9: Stok 1D **169**
  TS17: T Tee 5C **98**
Azalia Gro. TS10: Redc 4E **65**
Azalia Rd. TS19: S Tee 3A **74**

B

Bk. Amber St. TS12: Salt 3D **69**
Bk. Garnet St. TS12: Salt 3C **68**
Back La. TS9: G Bro 5F **169**
  TS9: N Ros 2B **158**
  TS12: Skel 2F **111**
  TS13: Hind 5D **121**
  TS16: Egg 2C **148**
  TS21: L New 3A **94**
  (not continuous)
Back La. Cotts. TS12: Skel . . . 5A **88**
Bk. Throston St.
  TS24: H'pool 1F 15
  (off Throston St.)
Bk. Turner St. *TS10: Redc . . . 3C 48*
  (off Turner St.)
Bacon Wlk. TS25: H'pool 2D **19**
Baden St. TS26: H'pool 5A **14**
Bader Av. TS17: T Tee 2B **128**
Badger La. TS17: I Bar 4C **128**
Badminton Av. TS12: Skel . . . 4C **88**
Badsworth Cl. TS14: Guis . . . 4D **139**
Baffin Ct. TS17: T Tee 1D **129**
Bailey Gro. TS3: Midd 5C **78**
Bailey St. TS26: H'pool 4B **14**
Bainton Ct. TS23: Bill 2E **39**
Bakehouse Sq.
  TS14: Guis 2E **139**
Baker Cl. TS27: H'pool 3D **7**
Baker St. TS1: Midd 3E **77**
Bakery Dr. TS19: S Tee 3D **73**
Bakery Ho. *TS19: S Tee 3D 73*
  (off Daylight Rd.)
Bakery St. TS18: S Tee 5A **74**
Balaclava St. TS18: S Tee . . . 5A **74**
Bala Cl. TS17: I Bar 1E **149**
Balcary Ct. TS25: H'pool 4F **19**
Balcary Gro. TS25: H'pool . . . 4F **19**
Balder Rd. TS20: Nort 5A **54**
Baldoon Sands TS5: Midd . . 2B **130**
Balfour Ter. TS5: Midd 3B **100**
Baliol Cft. TS21: L New 5A **94**
Ballater Gro. TS25: H'pool . . . 4A **20**
Balliol Ct. TS9: Stok 1B **168**
Balmoral Av. TS17: T Tee . . . 3D **99**
  TS23: Bill 5E **39**
Balmoral Cl. TS25: H'pool . . . 4A **20**
Balmoral Dr. TS4: Midd 2A **102**
Balmoral Rd. TS3: Midd 3E **103**
  TS12: Ling 5F **113**
  TS25: H'pool 4F **19**

Balmoral Ter. *TS12: Salt 4D 69*
  (off Windsor Rd.)
  TS18: S Tee 2E **97**
Balmor Rd. TS6: Norm 2C **104**
Baltic Cl. TS18: S Tee 4B **74**
Baltic Rd. TS18: S Tee 4B **74**
Baltic St. TS25: H'pool 5C **14**
Bamburgh Cl. TS10: Redc . . . 1E **65**
Bamburgh Ct. TS17: I Bar . . . 4F **127**
  TS27: H'pool 3D **7**
Bamburgh Dr. TS7: Orm 4A **104**
Bamburgh Ho. TS4: Midd . . . 2B **102**
Bamburgh Rd. TS27: H'pool . . 3D **7**
Bamford Rd. TS17: T Tee 5C **98**
Bamletts Wharf Ind. Est.
  TS23: Bill 4C **56**
Bamletts Wharf Rd.
  TS23: Bill 5B **56**
Banbury Gro. TS5: Midd 5B **100**
Banff Gro. TS25: H'pool 4A **20**
Bangor Cl. TS6: Est 4E **81**
Bangor St. TS26: H'pool 5A **14**
Bankfields Ct. TS6: Est 3D **105**
Bankfields Rd. TS6: Est 3D **105**
Bank La. TS6: Est 2F **105**
Bank Rd. TS23: Bill 4D **55**
Bank Sands TS5: Midd 3B **130**
Bankside TS15: Yarm 3E **149**
Bankside Ct. TS6: Est 2F **105**
Bankston Cl. TS26: H'pool . . . 2C **12**
Bank St. TS10: Redc 3C **48**
  TS14: Guis 2F **139**
Bank Ter. TS21: T The 2E **51**
Bannockburn Way
  TS23: Bill 3F **39**
Baptist St. TS24: H'pool 1F **15**
Barbara Mann Ct.
  TS26: H'pool 3A **14**
  (not continuous)
Barberry Cl. TS17: I Bar 4C **128**
Barclays Ho. TS17: T Tee 5C **74**
Barden Rd. TS3: Midd 1C **102**
Bardsey Sq. TS17: T Tee 4D **99**
Bardsey Wlk. TS14: Guis . . . 4D **139**
Bardsley Cl. TS16: P Tee 1D **127**
Barford Cl. TS10: Redc 3B **64**
  TS20: Nort 4E **53**
  TS25: H'pool 2E **31**
Bargate TS3: N Orm 4B **78**
Barholm Cl. TS3: Midd 2F **103**
Barker Rd. TS5: Midd 2C **100**
  TS17: T Tee 3D **99**
Barkers Pl. TS24: H'pool 1F **15**
Barkery, The TS8: Newb 4B **154**
Barkston Av. TS17: T Tee . . . 3B **128**
Barkston Cl. TS22: Bill 4B **38**
Barlborough Av.
  TS18: S Tee 3D **73**
Barle Cl. TS17: I Bar 3B **150**
Barley Cl. TS26: H'pool 2E **13**
Barley Hill Cl. TS6: Est 3E **105**
Barlow Cl. TS14: Guis 3E **139**
Barlow Ct. TS23: Bill 3E **39**
Barmet Ind. Est.
  TS12: Ling 3F **113**
Barmoor Gro. TS20: Nort 3A **54**
Barmouth Rd. TS6: Est 5E **81**
Barmpton Rd. TS23: Bill 3E **39**
Barnaby Av. TS5: Midd 5C **76**
Barnaby Cl. TS11: M Sea 5E **67**
Barnaby Cres. TS6: Est 2E **105**
Barnaby Pl. TS14: Guis 2C **138**
Barnaby Rd. TS7: Nun 3B **134**
Barnack Av. TS7: Mart 2E **133**
Barnard Av. TS19: S Tee 1C **96**
Barnard Cl. TS17: T Tee 2C **98**
Barnard Ct. TS4: Midd 2A **102**
Barnard Gallery 5B **74**

Borrowdale Gro.
TS5: Midd 4C 100
TS16: Egg 2C 148
Borrowdale Rd. TS6: Gran . . . 4F 81
Borrowdale St.
TS25: H'pool 1B 20
Borrowdale Wlk.
TS6: Gran 4F 81
Borton Wlk. TS19: S Tee. 4F 73
Boscombe Gdns.
TS8: Hem. 5F 131
Boston Cl. TS25: H'pool 5F 19
Boston Dr. TS7: Mart 4D 133
Boston Wlk. TS20: Nort 1C 74
Boswell Gro.
TS25: H'pool 2E 19
Boswell St. TS1: Midd 3F 77
Bosworth Way TS23: Bill. 4F 39
Botanical Gdns. 2E 131
Botany Way TS7: Nun. 3A 134
Bothal Dr. TS19: S Tee 3A 72
Bothal Wlk. TS19: S Tee. 2A 72
(not continuous)
Bottomley Mall TS1: Midd 2E 77
BOULBY. 1D 119
Boulby Bank TS13: Boul 1C 118
Boulby Barns Cotts.
TS13: Boul 1D 119
(not continuous)
Boulby Dr. TS13: Loft 5C 92
Boulby Rd. TS6: Midd 1D 61
TS10: Redc 1F 63
TS13: C How 2F 91
Boulby Wlk. TS6: Est 5F 81
Boulevard, The TS1: Midd 3F 77
(off Russell St.)
Boundary Rd. TS1: Midd 2E 77
TS6: Norm. 3C 104
Bournemouth Av.
TS3: Midd 3F 103
Bournemouth Dr.
TS24: H'pool 2D 7
Bourton Ct. TS3: Midd 4D 103
Bousdale Cotts.
TS14: Guis 4A 138
BOWESFIELD 4A 98
Bowesfield Cvn. Pk.
TS18: S Tee. 3A 98
Bowesfield Cres.
TS18: S Tee 3A 98
Bowesfield Ind. Est.
TS18: S Tee 5A 98
Bowesfield La.
TS18: S Tee 5A 98
(not continuous)
Bowesfield Nth. Ind. Est.
TS18: S Tee. 3B 98
Bowesfield Riverside Ind. Est.
TS18: S Tee. 4A 98
Bowes Grn. TS24: H'pool 2D 7
Bowes Rd. TS2: Midd. 1D 77
TS23: Bill 4D 39
Bowes Rd. Ind. Est.
TS2: Midd 5D 57
Bowfell Cl. TS16: Eag. 4B 126
Bowfell Rd. TS3: Midd 1C 102
Bowhill Way TS23: Bill 3A 40
Bowland Cl. TS7: Nun. 4F 133
Bowland Rd. TS12: Skel. 2B 88
Bowley Cl. TS6: Norm 2B 104
Bowley Wlk. TS1: Midd. 3D 77
Bowline Ho. TS24: H'pool 2C 14
Bowness Cl. TS25: H'pool 2B 20
Bowness Gro. TS10: Redc 5C 48
Bowood Cl. TS17: I Bar. 4F 127
Bowron St. TS20: Nort 4B 74
Bowser St. TS24: H'pool 4C 14
Bow St. TS1: Midd 4D 77
TS14: Guis. 2F 139

Bow St. Bus. Cen.
TS14: Guis 2F 139
Box Dr. TS7: Nun 4B 134
Boxer Ct. TS6: S Ban 3A 80
Boyne Ct. TS21: Sed. 3C 22
Boynston Gro. TS21: Sed. 4D 23
Boynton Rd. TS4: Midd 1A 102
Brabazon Dr. TS11: M Sea . . . 3B 66
Brabourn Gdns. TS8: Hem . . . 5F 131
Brackenberry Cres.
TS10: Redc 2E 65
Brackenbury Wlk. TS6: Est . . . 5F 81
Bracken Cres. TS14: Guis 3B 138
Brackenfield Ct. TS6: Est 3E 105
Brackenhill Cl. TS7: Nun 5A 134
Bracken Rd. TS19: S Tee 1E 73
Brackenthwaite
TS5: Midd 2B 130
Bracknell Rd. TS17: T Tee 4E 99
Bradbury Rd. TS20: Nort 4B 54
Bradhope Rd. TS3: Midd 1B 102
Brading Ct. TS17: I Bar. 3E 127
Bradley Ct. TS23: Bill 5F 39
Bradley's Ter. TS9: G Ayt 1D 167
Bradshaw Ct. TS24: H'pool. . . . 3F 7
Braehead TS16: Eag. 5C 126
Braemar Gro. TS6: Norm 5B 80
Braemar Rd. TS5: Midd 3B 100
TS23: Bill. 4C 38
(not continuous)
Braeside TS15: K'ton 4D 161
Braeworth Cl. TS15: Yarm . . . 4F 149
Brafferton Dr. TS23: Bill 2F 39
Brafferton St. TS26: H'pool. . . . 3F 13
Brafferton Wlk.
TS5: Midd 1C 130
Braid Cres. TS23: Bill. 2D 55
Braidwood Rd.
TS6: Norm 2C 104
Braithwaite Cl. TS12: Skel 2B 88
Bramble Dykes TS10: Redc . . . 4E 65
Bramble Rd. TS19: S Tee 1E 73
BRAMBLES FARM 4F 79
Brambling Cl. TS20: Nort 4F 53
Bramcote Way
TS17: T Tee 3C 128
Bramfield Way
TS17: I Bar 3A 128
Bramham Down
TS14: Guis. 3E 139
Bramley Cl. TS25: H'pool. 4A 20
Bramley Gro. TS7: Mart 2E 133
Bramley Pde. TS18: S Tee 2A 98
Brampton Cl. TS8: Hem 3E 131
Bramwith Av. TS3: Midd. 3D 103
Brancepath Wlk.
TS24: H'pool 3F 7
Brancepeth Av. TS3: Midd . . . 3C 102
Brancepeth Cl.
TS11: N Mar 2A 86
Brancepeth Ct. TS23: Bill 4C 38
Brandlings Ct.
TS15: Yarm 3B 148
Brandon Cl. TS23: Bill 3D 39
TS25: H'pool 2D 31
Brandon Rd. TS3: Midd 1F 103
Brankin Ct. TS12: Skel 3F 89
Branklyn Gdns.
TS17: I Bar 1B 150
Branksome Av. TS5: Midd 4E 101
Branksome Gro.
TS18: S Tee. 3B 96
Bransdale TS14: Guis. 3A 138
Bransdale Av. TS10: Redc . . . 1F 63
Bransdale Cl. TS19: S Tee 4E 73
Bransdale Gro.
TS25: S Car. 4E 21
Bransdale Rd. TS3: Midd. 1C 102

Brantingham Dr.
TS17: I Bar 4E 127
Brantwood Cl. TS17: I Bar . . . 1C 150
Brass Castle La.
TS8: Mart, Nun 3D 155
Brass Wynd TS7: Nun. 5F 133
Braygate Mill La.
TS12: Brot. 5E 91
TS13: C How 5E 91
Breakwater Ho.
TS24: H'pool 3D 15
Brechin Dr. TS17: T Tee 3D 129
Brechin Gro. TS25: H'pool . . . 4A 20
Breckland Wlk.
TS3: Midd 2D 103
Breckon Hill Rd.
TS4: Midd 4A 78
Brecon Cres. TS17: I Bar 1F 149
Brecon Dr. TS10: Redc. 2A 64
Brecon Gdns. TS6: Est 4D 81
Brecongill Cl.
TS24: H'pool 1B 14
Brenda Rd. TS25: H'pool 1B 20
Brendon Cres. TS23: Bill 1E 55
Brendon Gro. TS17: I Bar. 3B 150
Brenkley Cl. TS20: Nort 4E 53
Brent Ct. TS23: Bill. 2C 54
Brentford Cl. TS12: Brot. 3C 90
Brentford Rd. TS20: Nort 2A 74
Brentnall St. TS1: Midd 3E 77
Brereton Rd. TS4: Midd 4A 102
Bretby Cl. TS4: Midd 3A 102
Brettenham Av.
TS4: Midd 5B 102
(not continuous)
Breward Wlk. TS24: H'pool . . . 2B 14
Brewery St. TS24: H'pool. 4B 14
Brewery Ter. TS9: Stok. 1B 168
Brewery Yd. TS9: Stok 1B 168
TS15: Yarm 3B 148
Brewsdale TS3: N Orm. 3C 78
Briardene Av. TS5: Midd. 4E 101
Briardene Ct. TS19: S Tee . . . 1A 72
Briardene M. TS25: H'pool. . . . 2B 20
Briardene Wlk.
TS19: S Tee. 1A 72
Briargate TS6: Est. 1F 105
Briar Gro. TS10: Redc 5C 48
Briarhill Gdns.
TS26: H'pool 2E 13
Briar Rd. TS17: T Tee 5C 98
Briarvale Av. TS5: Midd. 3D 101
Briar Wlk. TS18: S Tee 2D 97
TS26: H'pool 2A 14
Brickton Rd. TS5: Midd 1B 100
Bridge Ct. TS6: Norm. 2C 104
TS15: Yarm 2B 148
Bridgend Cl. TS6: Gran. 3E 81
Bridgepool Cl. TS24: H'pool. . . 4B 8
Bridge Rd. TS9: Stok 1B 168
TS10: Redc 3A 48
TS18: S Tee. 2B 98
Bridge St. TS9: G Ayt 2C 166
TS15: Yarm 2B 148
TS17: T Tee 2C 98
TS20: Nort. 3B 74
TS24: H'pool 4D 15
Bridge St. E. TS2: Midd 2F 77
Bridge St. W. TS2: Midd. 2E 77
Bridnor Rd. TS3: Midd 3C 102
Bridport Cl. TS18: S Tee. 4D 75
Bridport Gro. TS8: Hem 5F 131
Brierley Dr. TS21: T The. 4D 25
TS22: Wyn 4C 26
Brierley Grn. TS7: Mart 4E 133
(not continuous)
BRIERTON 3B 18
Brierton La. TS22: Bri 3B 18
TS25: H'pool 3B 18

Castle Grange TS12: Skel. 5B 88
Castle Howard Cl.
   TS27: H'pool 3D 7
Castlemartin TS17: I Bar 3F 149
Castlereagh TS22: Wyn 5C 26
Castlereagh Cl.
   TS21: L New 1A 124
Castlereagh Rd.
   TS19: S Tee 4F 73
Castle Rd. TS10: Redc 1E 65
Castleton Av. TS5: Midd 3B 100
Castleton Dr. TS22: Bill 5B 38
Castleton Rd. TS6: Est 5F 81
   TS18: S Tee 3F 97
   TS25: S Car 4E 21
Castleton Wlk.
   TS17: T Tee 2B 128
Castle Way TS4: Midd. 2F 101
   TS18: S Tee 1B 98
Castlewood TS3: Midd 2F 103
Castle Wynd TS7: Nun 5A 134
Catcote Rd. TS25: H'pool 5E 13
Caterton Cl. TS15: Yarm 5E 149
Cat Flatt La. TS11: M Sea 4A 66
   TS10: M Sea, Redc 3F 65
Cathedral Dr. TS19: S Tee 4A 72
Cathedral Gdns. TS2: Midd . . 2E 77
Catherine Gro.
   TS24: H'pool 4C 14
   (off Sheerness Gro.)
Catherine Rd. TS24: H'pool . . . 4C 14
Catherine St. TS12: Ling 4E 113
   TS24: H'pool 1F 15
Catterall Ho. TS3: Midd 5D 79
Cattersty Way TS12: Brot 1B 90
Cattistock Cl. TS14: Guis 3F 139
Caudwell Cl. TS19: S Tee. 1A 72
Causeway, The TS23: Bill. 1D 55
Cavendish Rd. TS4: Midd. . . . 3A 102
Caversham Rd.
   TS4: Midd 4B 102
Cawdor St. TS11: N Mar. 2F 85
Cawood Dr. TS5: Midd 4E 101
Cawthorn Cl. TS8: Hem 4C 130
Caxton Gro. TS25: H'pool 1E 19
Caxton St. TS5: Midd 5E 77
Cayton Cl. TS10: Redc 3B 64
Cayton Dr. TS5: Midd 4E 101
   TS17: T Tee 3B 128
   TS22: Bill 4B 38
Cecil Ho. TS25: H'pool 2B 20
Cecil St. TS1: Midd 3D 77
   TS18: S Tee 2A 98
Cedar Cl. TS6: Est 1D 105
Cedar Ct. TS17: T Tee. 4C 98
Cedar Cres. TS16: P Tee. 2C 126
Cedar Dr. TS8: Thor 1B 152
Cedar Gro. DL2: M Geo 3A 144
   TS10: Redc 4E 49
   TS12: Brot 2A 90
   TS13: Loft 5B 92
   TS17: T Tee 4C 98
Cedar Ho. TS19: S Tee 3C 72
Cedarhurst Dr.
   TS12: Ling 4E 113
Cedar Lodge DL2: M Geo. . . . 1D 145
Cedar Rd. TS7: Mart. 2F 133
   TS7: Orm. 5B 104
Cedar St. TS18: S Tee 5B 74
Cedar Ter. TS2: P Cla 5F 57
Cedar Wlk. TS24: H'pool 1A 14
Cedarwood Av. TS9: Stok. . . . 4C 164
Cedarwood Glade
   TS8: Stain 5C 130
Celandine Cl. TS7: Mart. 1C 132
Celandine Way
   TS19: S Tee 3C 72
Cemetery Rdbt.
   TS14: Guis 4F 109

Cennon Gro. TS17: I Bar 1F 149
Centenary Cres.
   TS20: Nort. 1A 74
Central Arc. TS15: Yarm. . . . 3B 148
Central Av. TS5: Midd. 1B 100
   TS23: Bill 3D 55
Central M. TS1: Midd 3F 77
Central Rd. TS24: H'pool 5D 9
Central St. TS15: Yarm. 3B 148
Central Ter. TS10: Redc 3C 48
Central Way TS9: G Ayt 1D 167
Central Way Bungs.
   TS9: G Ayt. 1D 167
Centre Ct. TS5: Midd 3C 130
Centre Mall TS1: Midd 3E 77
Centre Rd. TS8: Hem 4E 131
Ceylon Sq. TS16: Eag. 3A 126
Chadburn Grn. TS4: Midd . . . 4F 101
Chadburn Rd. TS20: Nort. 2A 74
Chadderton Cl. TS12: Boo . . . 2B 112
Chadderton Dr. TS17: T Tee . . 5E 99
Chadwell Av. TS3: Midd. 3D 103
Chaffinch Cl. TS26: H'pool . . . 5E 7
Chalcot Wlk. TS3: Midd 5E 79
Chaldron Way TS16: Eag 3A 126
Chalfield Cl. TS17: I Bar 1C 150
Chalford Oaks TS5: Midd . . . 4A 100
Chalk Cl. TS18: S Tee. 2A 98
Chalk Wlk. *TS18: S Tee 2A 98*
   (off Chalk Cl.)
Challacombe Cres.
   TS17: I Bar 3A 150
Challoner Rd.
   TS15: Yarm 5B 148
   TS24: H'pool 1F 13
Challoner Sq. TS24: H'pool . . 1F 13
Chaloner M. TS14: Guis 2E 139
Chaloner St. TS14: Guis 2E 139
Chamomile Dr.
   TS19: S Tee 2C 72
Chancel Way TS6: Est. 1E 105
Chancery Ri. TS17: T Tee 2B 128
Chandlers Cl. TS24: H'pool . . . 3D 15
Chandlers Ridge
   TS7: Nun 4A 134
Chandlers Wharf
   TS18: S Tee 2B 98
Chantry Cl. TS3: Midd 3C 102
   TS20: Nort. 5A 54
Chapelbeck Bungs.
   TS14: Guis 2D 139
Chapel Cl. TS3: Midd 3F 103
   TS11: M Sea 4C 66
Chapel Ct. TS23: Bill 4D 55
Chapel Gdns. TS21: Car. 5D 51
Chapelgarth TS8: Stain. 5C 130
Chapel Rd. TS23: Bill. 4D 55
Chapel Row TS13: Loft. 5C 92
Chapel St. TS6: Laze 4C 82
   TS11: M Sea 4C 66
   TS12: Brot. 2C 90
   TS13: Skin. 2A 92
   TS17: T Tee 2C 98
Chapel Yd. *TS13: Stait 1C 120*
   (off Beckside)
   TS15: Yarm 3B 148
Chapman Cl. TS3: Midd 1E 103
Chapman St. TS20: Nort 1B 74
Chards Cotts. TS12: Salt 1C 88
Chard Wlk. TS3: Midd 3C 102
Charlbury Rd. TS3: Midd 5D 79
Charles St. TS1: Midd 3A 78
   TS10: Redc 3D 49
   TS11: N Mar 2A 86
   TS17: T Tee 3C 98
   TS24: H'pool 4C 14
   TS25: S Car 4E 21
Charlock TS8: C New 2C 154

Charlotte Grange
   TS26: H'pool 4A 14
Charlotte St. TS2: Midd 2E 77
   TS10: Redc. 3D 49
   TS12: Skel. 4D 89
   TS26: H'pool 5A 14
Charlton Rd. TS10: Redc 5F 47
CHARLTONS 2F 141
Charltonsfield
   TS12: Moor. 4B 142
Charltons Gth. TS14: Guis . . . 1E 139
Charltons Pond (Nature Reserve)
   . . . . 2F 55
Charnley Grn. TS4: Midd . . . 5A 102
Charnwood Cl.
   TS11: M Sea 5C 66
Charnwood Dr. TS7: Orm. . . . 1B 134
Charrington Av.
   TS17: T Tee 3B 128
Charterhouse St.
   TS25: H'pool 1A 20
Chart Ho. TS24: H'pool 3D 15
Chartwell Cl. TS11: M Sea . . . 3B 66
   TS17: I Bar 1C 150
Charwood TS3: Midd. 1F 103
Chase, The TS10: Redc 5D 49
   TS19: S Tee. 5B 72
Chatham Gdns.
   TS24: H'pool 1A 14
Chatham Rd. TS16: Eag 4F 125
   TS24: H'pool 1F 13
Chatham Sq. TS24: H'pool . . . 1A 14
Chathill Wlk. TS7: Orm 4A 104
Chatsworth Ct.
   TS19: S Tee 3D 73
Chatsworth Gdns.
   TS22: Bill. 5C 38
Chatsworth Ho. TS3: Midd . . . 5D 79
Chatton Cl. TS3: Midd 3D 103
Chaucer Av. TS25: H'pool. . . . 1E 19
Chaucer Cl. TS23: Bill 3D 39
Chaytor Lee TS15: Yarm. 4C 148
Cheadle Wlk. TS3: Midd 2D 103
Cheam Av. TS3: Midd. 5D 79
Cheddar Cl. TS6: Gran 4E 81
Cheetham St. TS6: Gran 2D 81
Chelker Cl. TS26: H'pool 3C 12
Chelmsford Av.
   TS18: S Tee 1C 96
Chelmsford Rd.
   TS5: Midd 1E 101
Chelmsford St.
   TS17: T Tee 2C 98
Chelmsford Wlk.
   TS5: Midd 2E 101
Chelsea Gdns. TS20: Nort . . . 4E 53
Chelston Cl. TS26: H'pool . . . 2C 12
Cheltenham Av.
   TS7: Mart 4D 133
   TS17: T Tee 3C 98
Cheltenham Cl. TS5: Midd . . . 1F 101
Cheltenham Rd.
   TS18: S Tee. 3F 75
Chepstow Cl. TS23: Bill 5D 39
Chepstow Wlk. TS26: H'pool . . 5E 7
Cheriton Grn. TS3: Midd 5D 79
Cherry Cl. TS19: S Tee 3A 74
Cherry Gth. TS17: I Bar 4A 128
Cherry Tree Cl. TS7: Orm. . . . 4B 104
Cherry Tree Dr. TS21: Sed . . . 3D 23
Cherry Tree Gdns.
   TS20: Nort. 1C 74
Cherry Trees TS10: Redc 3B 48
Cherry Wlk. TS24: H'pool 1A 14
Cherrywood Av. TS9: Stok . . . 5C 164
Cherrywood Ct.
   TS5: Midd 2E 131
Chertsey Av. TS3: Midd 5D 79
Chervil Ct. TS8: C New. 1C 154

Cherwell Ter. TS3: Midd 4E **79**
Chesham Cl. TS20: Nort 5B **54**
Chesham Gro. TS20: Nort 5C **54**
Chesham Rd. TS20: Nort 5B **54**
Chesham St. TS5: Midd 1E **101**
Cheshire Rd. TS20: Nort 1C **74**
Chesneywood TS3: Midd 1F **103**
Chester Rd. TS10: Redc 1F **65**
   TS26: H'pool 2F **13**
Chester St. TS1: Midd 5D **77**
Chesterton Av.
   TS17: T Tee 2B **128**
Chesterton Ct. TS20: Nort . . . 1B **74**
Chesterton Rd.
   TS25: H'pool 2E **19**
Chesterwood TS3: Midd 1F **103**
Chestnut Av. TS10: Redc 5E **49**
Chestnut Cl. TS6: Laze 4C **82**
   TS12: Salt 5A **68**
Chestnut Dr. TS7: Mart 3E **133**
Chestnut Gro. TS12: Brot 2A **90**
   TS17: T Tee 4C **98**
Chestnut Lodge
   DL2: M Geo. 1D **145**
Chestnut Rd. TS16: P Tee . . . 2C **126**
   TS21: Sed 3D **23**
Chestnut Row TS25: Grea. . . . 3E **31**
Chestnut Sq. TS19: S Tee . . . 3F **73**
Chetwode Ter. *TS3: Midd . . . 3E 103*
   (off Carmarthen Rd.)
Chevin Wlk. TS3: Midd. 2C **102**
Cheviot Cres. TS23: Bill 2D **55**
Cheviot Dr. TS12: Skel 3C **88**
Chez Nous Av.
   TS25: H'pool 1B **20**
Chichester Cl. TS25: H'pool . . 1F **31**
Chilcroft Cl. TS22: Bill 5A **38**
Childeray St. TS18: S Tee. . . . 1F **97**
Child St. TS12: Brot 2B **90**
   TS14: Guis 2E **139**
Chillingham Ct. TS23: Bill . . . 3E **39**
Chiltern Av. TS10: Redc 2A **64**
Chilton Cl. TS5: Midd 5C **100**
   TS19: S Tee. 1A **72**
Chiltons Av. TS23: Bill 4E **55**
Chine, The TS12: Salt 4B **68**
Chingford Av. TS3: Midd. 2F **103**
Chingford Gro. TS19: S Tee . . 4C **72**
Chipchase Rd. TS5: Midd . . . 1D **101**
Chippenham Rd.
   TS4: Midd 5A **102**
Chivers Ct. TS18: S Tee 4D **73**
Chopwell Cl. TS19: S Tee. . . . 1B **72**
Christchurch Dr.
   TS18: S Tee 2B **96**
Christine Ho. TS17: T Tee . . . 2B **98**
Christopher St. TS20: Nort . . . 3B **74**
   TS26: H'pool 3A **14**
Church Cl. TS7: Orm 4A **104**
   TS8: Stain 5C **130**
   TS11: M Sea 4D **67**
   TS13: Loft 5C **92**
   TS16: Egg 2C **148**
   TS17: T Tee 3B **98**
   TS24: H'pool 1F **15**
Church Dr. TS9: G Ayt. 2C **166**
   TS12: Boo 3C **112**
Churchend Cl. TS23: Bill 4D **55**
Church Farm Flats
   TS21: Redm 1B **70**
Church Fld. Way
   TS17: I Bar 4A **128**
Church Howle Cres.
   TS11: M Sea 4E **67**
Churchill Cl. TS6: Est 5E **81**
   TS9: G Ayt. 1D **167**
   TS22: Wyn. 1E **37**
Churchill Dr. TS11: M Sea . . . 4B **66**
Churchill Ho. TS17: T Tee. . . . 1C **98**

Churchill Rd. TS6: Est 5E **81**
Church La. DL2: M Geo 4A **144**
   TS5: Midd 5C **100**
   TS6: Est 3D **81**
   TS6: Est, Gran. 3D **81**
   TS7: Nun 1B **156**
   TS7: Orm 4F **103**
   (not continuous)
   TS9: N Ros 2B **158**
   TS11: M Sea 3D **67**
   TS12: Skel 4A **88**
   TS14: Guis 1E **139**
   TS21: Redm 1B **70**
Church M. TS23: Bill 4D **55**
Church Mt. TS6: Est 1E **105**
Church Rd. TS16: Egg 2C **148**
   TS18: S Tee 5B **74**
   TS23: Bill 4D **55**
Church Row TS13: Loft 5C **92**
   TS22: Wolv 2C **38**
   TS24: H'pool 5B **14**
Church Sq. TS24: H'pool . . . 3C **14**
Church St. TS10: Redc 3A **48**
   TS11: M Sea 3C **66**
   TS13: Stait 1C **120**
   TS14: Guis 1F **139**
   TS24: H'pool 3C **14**
   TS25: S Car 4E **21**
Church St. M. *TS14: Guis . . . 1F 139*
   (off Church St.)
Church St. Sth.
   TS11: M Sea 4D **67**
Church Vw. TS18: S Tee 4A **74**
   TS21: L New 1A **124**
   TS21: Sed 4C **22**
Church Wlk. TS3: Midd 5F **79**
   TS14: Guis. 1F **139**
   TS24: H'pool 1F **15**
Churchyard Link Rd.
   TS18: S Tee 1A **98**
Cinderwood TS3: Midd 1F **103**
Cinnabar Rd. TS19: S Tee . . . 3B **72**
Clairville Ct. TS4: Midd 5A **78**
Clairville Rd. TS4: Midd. 5A **78**
Clairville Sports Stadium . . 5A **78**
Clapham Grn. TS3: Midd . . . 1B **102**
Clapham Rd. TS15: Yarm. . . 5B **148**
Claremont Ct. TS17: T Tee . . . 1C **98**
Claremont Dr. TS7: Mart. . . . 4E **133**
   TS26: H'pool 4F **13**
Claremont Gdns.
   TS19: S Tee 5B **72**
Claremont Grn. TS21: Sed . . . 5C **22**
Claremont Pk.
   TS26: H'pool 5F **13**
Clarence Rd. TS7: Nun 4B **134**
   TS16: Eag 4C **126**
   TS24: H'pool 2B **14**
Clarence Row TS18: S Tee . . 4B **74**
Clarence St. TS18: S Tee . . . 4B **74**
   TS23: Bill 3D **57**
   TS24: H'pool 5F **9**
Clarendon Rd. TS1: Midd . . . 4E **77**
   (not continuous)
   TS17: T Tee 5D **99**
   TS20: Nort. 2A **74**
Clarendon St. TS10: Redc . . . 3D **49**
Clarkson Ct. TS25: H'pool. . . . 3F **19**
Clarkson's Wood Nature Reserve
   . . . . 2F **115**
Clark St. TS24: H'pool 4C **14**
Claude Av. TS5: Midd. 3D **101**
CLAVERING 2C **6**
Clavering Rd. TS27: H'pool . . . 2C **6**
Claxton Cl. TS19: S Tee 1A **72**
Claydon Gro. TS17: I Bar . . 1B **150**
Claygate TS23: Bill. 3D **39**
Clay La. Commercial Pk.
   TS6: S Ban 1B **80**

Claymond Ct. TS20: Nort 5A **54**
Claymore Rd. TS25: H'pool . . 5F **19**
Clayton Ct. TS18: S Tee 4A **98**
Claywood TS3: Midd 1F **103**
Cleadon Av. TS23: Bill 3E **39**
Cleadon Wlk. TS19: S Tee . . . 2B **72**
Clearpool Cl. TS24: H'pool. . . . 5C **8**
Clearwater Bus. Pk.
   TS17: T Tee 5C **74**
Clearwater Ho.
   TS17: T Tee 5B **74**
Cleasby Way TS16: Eag 3A **126**
Cleatlam Cl. TS19: S Tee 2B **72**
Cleator Dr. TS14: Guis 4D **139**
Clee Ter. TS23: Bill 1E **55**
Clements Ri. TS20: Nort. 5F **53**
Clepstone Av. TS5: Midd . . . 3C **100**
Clevecoat Wlk. TS27: Hart . . . 4F **5**
Clevegate TS7: Nun 4F **133**
Cleveland Av. TS5: Midd . . . 3D **101**
   TS9: Stok 5C **164**
   TS20: Nort. 1B **74**
Cleveland Bus. Cen.
   TS1: Midd 3F **77**
Cleveland Cen. TS1: Midd . . . 3E **77**
Cleveland Cl. TS7: Orm . . . 5A **104**
Cleveland Ct. TS6: S Ban . . . 2B **80**
Cleveland Craft Cen. 3E **77**
Cleveland Gdns.
   TS16: Eag 5B **126**
Cleveland Ind. Est.
   TS18: S Tee. 4D **75**
Cleveland Retail Pk.
   TS6: S Ban 4A **80**
Cleveland Rd. TS24: H'pool . . 5C **8**
Cleveland Sq. *TS1: Midd . . . 3E 77*
   (off Cleveland Cen.)
Cleveland St. TS2: Midd 2F **77**
   TS6: Est 1F **105**
   TS6: Norm 2D **105**
   TS9: G Ayt. 1D **167**
   TS10: Redc 3C **48**
   TS12: Salt 4D **69**
   TS13: Live 1A **116**
   TS13: Loft 5C **92**
   TS14: Guis 1D **139**
   TS24: H'pool 5F **9**
Cleveland Vw. TS3: Midd . . . 1E **103**
   TS11: M Sea 4A **66**
   TS12: Skel 1A **112**
Cliff, The TS25: S Car 3E **21**
Cliff Cotts. TS5: Midd 2C **100**
   TS11: M Sea 3D **67**
Cliff Cres. TS13: Loft 5A **92**
Cliffden Ct. TS12: Salt 4D **69**
Cliffe Av. TS13: C How 3E **91**
Cliffe Ct. TS25: S Car 3E **21**
Cliffe St. TS12: Brot 2C **90**
Cliffe Ter. TS9: G Ayt 1D **167**
Cliff Ho. TS11: M Sea. 3D **67**
Clifford Cl. TS24: H'pool. 4F **7**
Clifford St. TS10: Redc. 3C **48**
Cliffport Ct. TS18: S Tee 4C **74**
Cliff Rd. TS13: Stait 2C **120**
Cliff St. TS11: N Mar 2A **86**
Cliff Ter. TS11: M Sea 3D **67**
   TS13: Live 5A **92**
   TS13: Skin. 2A **92**
   TS24: H'pool 1F **15**
Cliffwood Cl. TS6: Est. 2F **105**
Clifton Av. TS16: P Tee 3C **126**
   TS18: S Tee 3F **97**
   TS22: Bill. 5B **38**
   TS26: H'pool 4F **13**
Clifton Gdns. TS16: P Tee . . 3D **127**
Clifton Ho. TS17: T Tee. 2B **98**
   TS19: S Tee 3E **73**

Coronation Dr. TS25: S Car . . . 5D **15**
Coronation Grn.
   TS3: Midd 4F **103**
Coronation Rd. TS13: Loft . . . 5B **92**
Coronation St.
   TS3: N Orm 4C **78**
   TS13: Bill. 3F **91**
Coronation Ter. TS14: Guis. . . 1E **139**
Corporation Rd. TS1: Midd. . . 3E **77**
   TS10: Redc 4A **48**
   TS24: H'pool 5E **9**
Corporation St.
   TS18: S Tee 5A **74**
Corsham Wlk. TS3: Midd 3D **103**
Cortland Rd. TS7: Nun 3C **134**
Coryton Wlk. TS3: Midd 3D **103**
Costain Gro. TS20: Nort 4B **54**
Costa St. TS1: Midd 5D **77**
   TS6: S Ban. 2F **79**
Cotgarth Way TS19: S Tee . . . 2A **72**
Cotherstone Ct. TS16: Eag . . . 5F **125**
Cotherstone Dr.
   TS5: Midd 2C **130**
Cotherstone Rd.
   TS18: S Tee 3F **97**
Cotswold Av. TS3: Midd 5D **79**
Cotswold Cres. TS23: Bill. . . . 2D **55**
Cotswold Dr. TS10: Redc 1A **64**
   TS12: Skel 3C **88**
Cottage Farm TS18: S Tee . . . 1D **97**
Cottersloe Rd. TS20: Nort . . . 4B **54**
Cottingham Dr. TS3: Midd . . . 5D **79**
Cottonwood TS3: Midd 1F **103**
Coulby Farm Way
   TS8: C New 5B **132**
Coulby Mnr. Farm
   TS8: C New 3A **132**
   (not continuous)
Coulby Mnr. Way
   TS8: C New 3F **131**
COULBY NEWHAM 4B **132**
Coulson Cl. TS15: Yarm 1B **160**
Coulthard Ct. TS6: S Ban 2A **80**
Coulton Gro. TS22: Bill. 5A **38**
Council of Europe Blvd.
   TS17: T Tee 5B **74**
   TS18: S Tee, T Tee. 5B **74**
Coundon Grn. TS19: S Tee . . . 2B **72**
Countisbury Rd.
   TS20: Nort. 3E **53**
County Gymnastics Cen. . . . 4C **102**
Courageous Cl.
   TS25: S Car. 3D **21**
Courtney Wlk. TS3: Midd 5E **79**
Court Rd. TS4: Midd. 2A **102**
Covent Cl. TS6: Norm 4C **104**
Coverdale TS8: Hem 5D **131**
Coverdale Bldgs.
   TS12: Brot. 2C **90**
Coverdale Rd. TS19: S Tee. . . . 1C **96**
COWBAR 1C **120**
Cowbar Bank TS13: Stait 1C **120**
Cowbar Cotts. TS13: Stait . . . 1B **120**
Cowbar La. TS13: Boul. 1F **119**
Cowbridge La.
   TS23: C Bew 3B **40**
Cow Cl. La. TS12: Moor. 4C **142**
   (not continuous)
   . . . . 5D **143**
Cowdray Cl. TS14: Guis 4F **139**
Cowley Cl. TS16: P Tee 1D **127**
   TS25: S Car 2E **21**
Cowley Rd. TS5: Midd 5D **101**
COWPEN BEWLEY 4C **40**
Cowpen Bewley Rd.
   TS23: C Bew, Bill. 4C **40**
   . . . . 2C **40**

   Vis. Cen. 3C **40**
Cowpen Cres. TS19: S Tee . . . 2B **72**
Cowpen La.
   TS23: Bill, C Bew. 3E **55**
Cowpen La. Est.
   TS23: Bill. 2A **56**
Cowpen La. Ind. Est.
   TS23: Bill. 5A **40**
   . . . . 4F **41**
Cowper Gro. TS25: H'pool . . . 2D **19**
Cowper Rd. TS20: Nort 3C **74**
Cowscote Cres. TS13: Loft. . . 4A **92**
Cowshill Grn. TS19: S Tee . . . 2B **72**
Cowton Way TS16: Eag. 3B **126**
Coxgreen Cl. TS19: S Tee. . . . 2B **72**
Coxhoe Rd. TS23: Bill. 5F **39**
Coxmoor Way TS11: N Mar. . . 2F **85**
Coxwold Cl. TS5: Midd 5E **101**
Coxwold Rd. TS18: S Tee 1D **97**
Coxwold Way TS23: Bill 2B **56**
Crabtree Wlk. TS7: Nun 1D **135**
Cradley Dr. TS5: Midd 3C **130**
Cradoc Gro. TS17: I Bar 1F **149**
Cragdale Rd. TS3: Midd 1C **102**
Cragghall Rdbt. TS12: Brot . . 2D **91**
Craggs St. TS4: Midd 3A **78**
   TS19: S Tee 4F **73**
Cragside TS12: Brot 2C **90**
   TS21: Sed 5C **22**
Cragside Ct. TS17: I Bar. 1B **150**
Cragston Cl. TS26: H'pool . . . 2D **13**
Cragston Ct. TS10: Redc 4E **65**
Craigearn Rd. TS6: Norm. . . . 1C **104**
Craigweil Cres.
   TS19: S Tee 3F **73**
Craister Rd. TS20: Nort 4B **74**
Crall Wlk. TS25: H'pool 4F **19**
Cramlington Cl. TS8: Hem . . . 4E **131**
Cranage Cl. TS5: Midd 3B **100**
Cranberry TS8: C New 5D **133**
Cranbourne Dr. TS10: Redc . . 4E **65**
Cranbourne Ter.
   TS18: S Tee 2F **97**
Cranbrook TS8: Mart 5E **133**
Cranfield Av. TS3: Midd 4F **79**
   (not continuous)
Cranford Av. TS6: S Ban 4B **80**
Cranford Cl. TS6: S Ban 4B **80**
Cranford Gdns. TS5: Midd . . . 4B **100**
Cranleigh Rd. TS18: S Tee . . . 1E **97**
Cranmore Rd. TS3: Midd 5C **78**
Cranstock Cl. TS22: Bill 5A **38**
Cranswick Cl. TS23: Bill 2F **39**
Cranswick Dr. TS5: Midd 5E **101**
Cranwell Gro. TS17: T Tee . . . 3D **129**
Cranwell Rd. TS25: H'pool. . . 5D **19**
Cranworth Grn.
   TS17: T Tee 2D **99**
Cranworth St. TS17: T Tee . . . 2C **98**
Crathorne Cres.
   TS5: Midd 1B **100**
Crathorne Pk. TS6: Norm . . . 2C **104**
Crathorne Rd. TS20: Nort. . . . 5B **54**
Craven St. TS1: Midd 4D **77**
Craven Va. TS14: Guis 3E **139**
Crawcrook Wlk.
   TS19: S Tee 2B **72**
Crawford St. TS25: S Car 4E **21**
Crawley Rd. TS17: T Tee 4E **99**
Crayke Rd. TS18: S Tee 2D **97**
Creekwood TS3: Midd. 1F **103**
Cremorne Cl. TS7: Mart 2C **132**
Crescent, The
   DL2: M Geo 2C **144**
   TS5: Midd 2D **101**
   TS7: Nun 3B **134**
   TS7: Orm 4F **103**

Crescent, The
   TS11: M Sea 4D **67**
   TS12: Salt 5C **68**
   TS16: Eag 1B **148**
   TS17: T Tee 4C **98**
   TS21: Car 5C **50**
   TS26: H'pool 3E **13**
Crescent Av. TS23: Bill 4E **55**
Crescent Rd. TS1: Midd 5C **76**
Cresswell Cl. TS8: Hem 4E **131**
Cresswell Cl. TS26: H'pool . . . 3D **13**
Cresswell Dr. TS26: H'pool . . . 3D **13**
Cresswell Rd. TS6: Gran 2E **81**
   TS26: H'pool 3D **13**
Crest, The TS26: H'pool 2D **13**
Crestwood TS3: Midd 2F **103**
   TS10: Redc 4D **65**
Cribyn Cl. TS17: I Bar 1F **149**
Cricket La. TS6: Norm 3C **104**
Crieff Wlk. TS25: H'pool. 4F **19**
Crimdon Cl. TS8: Hem 5E **131**
Crimdon Wlk. TS19: S Tee . . . 1A **72**
Crinklewood TS3: Midd. 2F **103**
Crispin Cl. TS12: Brot 2C **90**
   TS21: Sed 4D **23**
Crisp St. TS20: Nort 2B **74**
Croft, The TS7: Mart. 3D **133**
Croft Av. TS5: Midd. 4B **100**
Croft Dr. TS7: Nun 4B **134**
Crofton Av. TS4: Midd. 2F **101**
Crofton Cl. TS18: S Tee 4D **75**
CROFT ON HEUGH 1F **15**
Crofton Rd. TS18: S Tee. 4D **75**
Croft Rd. TS16: Eag 1B **148**
Crofts, The TS21: Stil 2B **50**
Croft St. TS18: S Tee 4B **74**
Croft Ter. TS24: H'pool 1F **15**
   (not continuous)
Cromer Ct. TS16: Eag. 1C **148**
Cromer St. TS4: Midd 4A **78**
Cromer Wlk. TS25: H'pool . . . 5E **19**
Cromore Cl. TS17: T Tee 2C **128**
Cromwell Av. TS13: Loft 5D **93**
   TS18: S Tee. 4B **74**
Cromwell Grn. TS18: S Tee . . 5B **74**
Cromwell Rd. TS6: S Ban. . . . 3A **80**
Cromwell St. TS3: N Orm. . . . 4B **78**
   TS24: H'pool 5C **14**
Cromwell Ter. TS17: T Tee . . . 3C **98**
Crookers Hill TS7: Nun. 5A **134**
Crookhall Wlk. TS19: S Tee . . 2B **72**
CROOKSBARN 3B **54**
Crooks Barn La.
   TS20: Nort 3A **54**
Crook St. TS20: Nort 4A **54**
Cropton Cl. TS10: Redc 3B **64**
Cropton Way TS8: C New 4B **132**
Crosby Ct. TS16: Eag 5D **127**
Crosby Ho. TS3: Midd 5D **79**
Crosby St. TS20: Nort. 3B **74**
Crosby Ter. TS2: P Cla 5A **58**
Crosby Wlk. TS17: T Tee 3C **98**
Crossbeck Ter. TS6: Norm . . . 2D **105**
Crossbeck Way TS7: Orm. . . . 4B **104**
Crosscliff TS8: Hem 4E **131**
Cross Fell TS10: Redc 1B **64**
Crossfell Rd. TS3: Midd 2C **102**
Crossfields TS8: C New 1B **154**
Cross La. TS9: L Ayt 4E **167**
   TS13: Loft. 3B **92**
Cross Row TS12: Boo 3B **112**
Cross St. TS6: Est 1F **105**
   TS14: Guis. 2E **139**
   TS20: Nort. 5B **54**
   TS21: Sed 4D **23**
   TS23: Bill 3D **57**
Crosswell Pk. TS17: I Bar. . . . 2F **149**
Crosthwaite Av.
   TS4: Midd 2F **101**

Crowhurst Cl. TS14: Guis 4E **139**
Crowland Av. TS3: Midd 2A **104**
Crowland Rd. TS25: H'pool 1D **31**
Crow La. TS6: O Lac. 5A **82**
Crowood Av. TS9: Stok. 5C **164**
Croxdale Gro. TS19: S Tee 1B **96**
Croxdale Rd. TS23: Bill 4E **39**
Croxden Gro. TS3: Midd 3E **103**
Croxton Av. TS3: H'pool 1F **31**
Croxton Cl. TS19: S Tee 5F **71**
Croydon Rd. TS1: Midd 5A **78**
Crummackdale
   TS17: I Bar 3B **150**
Crummock Rd. TS10: Redc . . . 5C **48**
Culgarth Av. TS3: Midd 1C **102**
Cullen Rd. TS25: H'pool 4F **19**
Culloden Way TS23: Bill 4A **40**
Culross Gro. TS19: S Tee 5F **71**
Cumberland Cres.
   TS23: Bill 3D **55**
Cumberland Gro.
   TS20: Nort 4F **53**
Cumberland Ho.
   TS5: Midd 2E **101**
Cumberland Rd.
   TS5: Midd 1E **101**
Cumbernauld Rd.
   TS17: T Tee 4E **99**
Cumbria Wlk. TS25: H'pool . . 5B **14**
Cumnor Wlk. TS3: Midd 5D **79**
Cundall Rd. TS26: H'pool 3F **13**
Cunningham Cl. TS12: Brot . . . 1B **90**
Cunningham Cl. TS21: Sed . . . 2C **22**
Cunningham Dr.
   TS17: T Tee 3D **129**
Cunningham St. TS5: Midd . . 5C **76**
Curlew La. TS20: Nort 3A **54**
Curran Av. TS5: Midd 2B **100**
Curson St. TS6: Est. 2F **105**
Curthwaite TS5: Midd 2A **130**
Custom Ho. TS2: Midd 1F **77**
Cuthbert Cl. TS17: T Tee. 3C **98**
Cutler Cl. TS7: Mart 2E **133**
Cypress Ct. TS19: S Tee 3A **74**
Cypress Rd. TS7: Mart 2E **133**
   TS10: Redc 5F **49**

D

Dabholm Rd. TS6: Midd 5E **45**
Dacre Cl. TS17: T Tee. 5C **98**
Daimler Dr. TS23: Bill. 5B **40**
Daisy Ct. TS19: S Tee 3C **72**
Dalby Cl. TS10: Redc 3C **64**
   TS22: Bill. 5A **38**
Dalby Ct. TS8: C New 5B **132**
Dalby Vw. TS8: C New 5B **132**
Dalby Way TS8: C New 4B **132**
Dalcross Ct. TS8: Hem 5E **131**
   (not continuous)
Dale Cl. TS19: S Tee 2A **72**
Dale Gth. TS11: M Sea 5E **67**
Dale Gro. TS19: S Tee 1B **96**
DALEHOUSE 2B **120**
Dalehouse Bank
   TS13: Stait 3B **120**
Dales Pk. Rd. TS8: Hem . . . 5D **131**
Daleston Av. TS5: Midd 3D **101**
Daleston Cl. TS26: H'pool . . . 2C **12**
Dale St. TS1: Midd 3E **77**
   TS11: N Mar 1A **86**
Dale Ter. TS12: Ling. 4E **113**
Daleville Ct. TS4: Midd 3F **101**
Dalewood Wlk. TS9: Stok . . . 5C **164**
Dalkeith Cres. TS8: New 4B **132**
Dalkeith Rd. TS25: H'pool . . . 3E **19**
Dallas Ct. TS8: Hem 5E **131**
   (not continuous)

Dallas Rd. TS25: H'pool 3E **19**
Dalmuir Cl. TS16: Eag 5C **126**
Dalry Gro. TS25: H'pool 4E **19**
Dalston Ct. TS7: Orm 4B **104**
Dalton Bk. La. TS22: Clax . . . 2D **17**
   TS27: D Pie 2D **17**
Dalton Ct. TS10: Redc 4F **65**
Dalton Gro. TS20: Nort 2A **74**
   TS23: Bill 3E **39**
Dalton Hgts. TS27: D Pie 1E **17**
DALTON PIERCY 1E **17**
Dalton St. TS26: H'pool 4A **14**
Daltry Cl. TS15: Yarm 5E **149**
Dalwood Ct. TS8: Hem 5E **131**
Dam St. TS13: Loft. 5C **92**
Danby Cl. TS20: Nort 3B **74**
Danby Dale Av.
   TS10: Redc 1A **64**
Danby Gro. TS17: T Tee 4D **99**
   TS25: S Car 4E **21**
Danby Rd. TS6: Est 5F **81**
   TS20: Nort 3B **74**
Danby Wlk. TS23: Bill. 5C **38**
Danby Wynd TS15: Yarm 3B **148**
Danesbrook Ct.
   TS17: I Bar 3B **150**
Danesfort Av. TS14: Guis . . . 2D **139**
Daniel Ct. TS4: Midd 5A **78**
Dante Rd. TS7: Mart. 2B **132**
Daphne Rd. TS19: S Tee. 3A **74**
Darcy Cl. TS15: Yarm 1A **160**
Darenth Cres. TS3: Midd . . . 2D **103**
Darlington Bk. La.
   DL2: Sadb 1A **94**
   TS19: S Tee 4D **71**
   TS21: S Tee, W Hill 4D **71**
Darlington La. TS19: S Tee . . . 3B **72**
   (not continuous)
   TS20: Nort 1F **73**
Darlington Rd. TS18: S Tee . . . 3A **96**
   TS21: Elt 4E **95**
   TS21: L New 1F **123**
Darlington St. TS17: T Tee . . . 2C **98**
   TS24: H'pool 1F **15**
Darlington Ter.
   *TS13: Stait 1C **120***
   (off High St.)
Darnall Grn. TS4: Midd 5B **102**
Darnbrook Way TS7: Nun . . . 4F **133**
Darnton Dr. TS4: Midd 5B **102**
Darras Wlk. TS3: Midd. 5D **79**
Dartmouth Gro.
   TS10: Redc 2D **65**
Darvel Rd. TS25: H'pool. 3E **19**
Darwen Ct. TS8: Hem 5E **131**
Darwin Cl. TS19: S Tee 1B **72**
Darwin Gro. TS25: H'pool . . . 1D **19**
Dauntless Cl. TS25: S Car . . . 3E **21**
Davenport Rd.
   TS15: Yarm 1A **160**
Daventry Av. TS19: S Tee 2E **73**
David Lloyd Leisure
   Teeside. 5D **75**
David Rd. TS20: Nort 2C **74**
Davison Cl. TS22: Wyn. 2E **37**
Davison Dr. TS24: H'pool 3F **7**
Davison St. TS1: Midd 3E **77**
   TS12: Ling 4E **113**
Davy Rd. TS6: S Ban. 3F **79**
Dawdon Cl. TS19: S Tee. 1B **72**
Dawley Cl. TS17: T Tee. 4E **99**
Dawlish Cl. TS10: Redc 3A **64**
Dawlish Dr. TS25: H'pool 5A **20**
Dawlish Grn. TS4: Midd 5B **102**
Dawn Cl. TS20: Nort. 3A **54**
Dawson Ho. TS23: Bill 1D **55**
Dawson Sq. TS5: Midd 1B **100**
Dawsons Wharf Ind. Est.
   TS2: Midd 1E **77**

Daylight Rd. TS19: S Tee 3D **73**
Days Ter. TS12: Brot. 2B **90**
Day St. TS12: Brot 3B **90**
Deacon Gdns. TS25: S Car . . . 5E **21**
Deacon St. TS3: N Orm 4C **78**
Deal Cl. TS19: S Tee 2E **73**
Deal Ct. TS4: Midd 2A **102**
Deal Rd. TS10: Redc 2E **65**
   TS23: Bill 4D **39**
Deansgate TS6: Est 1A **106**
Dean St. TS18: S Tee 1A **98**
De Brus Ct. TS12: Salt 3C **68**
Debruse Av. TS15: Yarm. . . . 1A **160**
De Brus Pk. TS8: Mart 2E **155**
De Brus Way TS14: Guis. . . . 1E **139**
Deepdale TS13: Loft 3A **138**
Deepdale Av. TS4: Midd 2A **102**
   (Fairfield Rd.)
   TS4: Midd 3F **101**
   (Marton Burn Rd., not continuous)
   TS6: Gran 4F **81**
Deepdale La.
   TS13: Skin, Loft 3A **92**
Deepdale Rd. TS13: Loft 4A **92**
Deepdene Gro.
   TS10: Redc 3F **65**
Deepgrove Wlk. TS6: Est 5F **81**
Dee Rd. TS6: Est 5D **81**
Deerpool Cl. TS24: H'pool . . . 5C **8**
De Havilland Av.
   TS18: S Tee 5E **97**
De Havilland Dr.
   TS11: M Sea 3A **66**
Deighton Gro. TS23: Bill 4D **39**
Deighton Rd. TS4: Midd. . . . 1B **132**
De La Mare Dr. TS23: Bill . . . 2D **39**
Delamere TS22: Wyn 4B **26**
Delamere Dr. TS11: M Sea. . . 5B **66**
Delamere Rd. TS3: Midd 3D **103**
Delarden Rd. TS3: Midd 5D **79**
Delaval Rd. TS23: Bill. 5F **39**
Dell Cl. TS7: Mart. 3C **132**
Dellfield Cl. TS3: Midd. 3C **102**
Del Strother Av.
   TS18: S Tee 4E **73**
Denbigh Rd. TS23: Bill 4E **39**
Dene Cl. TS17: T Tee 4E **99**
Dene Gro. TS10: Redc 4D **49**
Dene Rd. TS4: Midd 2A **102**
Deneside Cl.
   TS15: Yarm. 4D **149**
Denevale TS15: Yarm. 4D **149**
Dene Wlk. TS11: M Sea 4B **66**
Denholme Av.
   TS18: S Tee 3E **97**
Denmark St. TS2: Midd 2D **77**
Dennison St. TS18: S Tee. . . . 3F **97**
Denshaw Cl. TS19: S Tee 5A **72**
Dentdale Cl. TS15: Yarm . . . 1B **160**
Denton Cl. TS5: Midd 2B **130**
   TS19: S Tee 1B **72**
Dent St. TS26: H'pool. 3B **14**
Denver Dr. DL2: M Geo 1B **144**
Depot Rd. TS2: Midd 1E **77**
Derby, The TS7: Mart 1B **132**
Derby Av. TS5: Midd 2A **100**
Derby Cl. TS17: T Tee. 3D **99**
Derby Rd. TS14: Guis. 3D **139**
Derby St. TS18: S Tee. 5A **74**
   TS25: H'pool 1B **20**
Derby Ter. TS17: T Tee 2D **99**
Derwent Av. TS14: Guis 3C **138**
Derwent Ho. TS23: Bill 3A **40**
Derwent Pk. TS13: Loft 5D **93**
Derwent Rd. TS10: Redc 5A **48**
   TS12: Skel 4B **88**
   TS17: T Tee. 5D **99**

Derwent St. TS1: Midd 4D **77**
  TS3: N Orm 4C **78**
  TS20: Nort. 2A **74**
  TS26: H'pool 3B **14**
Derwentwater Av.
  TS5: Midd 4C **100**
Derwentwater Rd.
  TS6: Gran 4F **81**
Desford Grn. TS3: Midd 1D **103**
Desmond Rd. DL2: M Geo . . 3A **144**
Deva Cl. TS4: Midd 2B **102**
Devon Cl. TS10: Redc 1B **64**
Devon Cres. TS12: Skel 4A **88**
  TS23: Bill 2F **55**
Devonport Rd. TS5: Midd . . . 2F **101**
  TS18: S Tee 4C **74**
Devon Rd. TS6: Gran 4E **81**
  TS14: Guis 3D **139**
Devonshire Rd.
  TS5: Midd 1D **101**
Devonshire St. TS18: S Tee . . 3F **97**
Devon St. TS25: H'pool 1B **20**
Dewberry Rd. TS8: C New . . . 1D **155**
Dewberry Cl. TS26: H'pool . . . 4D **7**
Dew La. TS7: Orm 5A **104**
Diamond Ct. TS3: S Tee 5F **97**
Diamond Hall Rdbt.
  TS21: Sed 5E **23**
Diamond Rd. TS17: T Tee . . . 4D **99**
Diamond St. TS1: Midd 4E **77**
  TS12: Salt 3C **68**
Dickens Ct. TS23: Bill. 3D **39**
Dickens Gro. TS25: H'pool . . . 1F **19**
Dickens St. TS24: H'pool 3F **7**
Didcot Cl. TS10: Redc 4E **65**
Dikes La. TS9: G Ayt 2F **167**
Diligence Way TS16: Eag. . . 4B **126**
Dillside TS19: S Tee 3C **72**
Dimmingdale Rd.
  TS12: Moor 5C **142**
Dinas Ct. TS17: I Bar 1F **149**
Dingleside TS19: S Tee 4C **72**
Dinsdale Av. TS5: Midd 5C **100**
Dinsdale Ct. TS23: Bill 4F **39**
Dinsdale Dr. TS16: Eag 5C **126**
Dinsdale Rd. TS19: S Tee. . . . 1B **72**
Diomed Ct. TS7: Mart. 1C **132**
Dionysia Rd. TS3: Midd 5C **78**
Dipton Grn. TS4: Midd 5B **102**
Dipton Rd. TS19: S Tee 1A **72**
Dishforth Cl. TS17: T Tee . . . 3D **129**
Dixon Gro. TS3: Midd 5C **78**

Dixons Bank
  TS7: Mart, Nun 3E **133**
Dixon St. TS12: Brot. 2B **90**
  TS12: Ling. 4E **113**
  TS12: Skel. 3C **88**
  TS13: C How 3F **91**
  TS3: S Tee. 5A **74**
Dobson Pl. TS24: H'pool 3E **7**
Dobson Ter. TS10: Redc. . . . 4D **49**
Dockside Rd. TS3: Midd. . . . 2C **78**
  TS6: Midd 1F **79**
Dock St. TS2: Midd 2F **77**
Dodford Rd. TS8: Hem 5E **131**
Dodsworth Wlk.
  TS27: H'pool 3D **7**
Doncaster Cres.
  TS19: S Tee 2F **73**
Donegal Ter. TS1: Midd 5C **76**
Donington Grn. TS3: Midd . . 2A **104**
Dorchester Cl. TS8: Midd. . . 2B **132**
  TS19: S Tee 2E **73**
Dorchester Dr. TS24: H'pool . . 2D **7**
Doric Ho. TS21: Sed. 4C **22**
Dorkings, The TS9: G Bro. . . 5F **169**
Dorlcote Pl. TS20: Nort 2B **74**
Dorman Mus. 5E 77
Dorman Rd. TS6: Est 1E **105**

Dorman's Cres.
  TS10: Redc 5F **47**
Dorman's Pond (Nature Reserve)
  . . . . 2C **58**
DORMANSTOWN. 1E 63
Dorman Way TS12: Skel. 5E **89**
Dorma Pk. Bungs.
  TS25: Grea 3E **31**
Dormor Way TS6: S Ban. . . . 3E **79**
Dornoch Sands TS5: Midd . . 3B **130**
Dorothy St. TS3: N Orm 4C **78**
Dorothy Ter. *TS17: T Tee . . . 3C 98*
  (off Langley Av.)
Dorrien Cres. TS3: Midd 5C **78**
Dorset Cl. TS5: Midd 1D **101**
  TS10: Redc 1B **64**
Dorset Cres. TS23: Bill. 1F **55**
Dorset Rd. TS12: Skel 4A **88**
  TS14: Guis 4C **138**
  TS20: Nort. 1C **74**
Dorset St. TS25: H'pool 1B **20**
Douglas Cl. TS18: S Tee 5F **97**
Douglas St. TS4: Midd 4A **78**
  (not continuous)
Douglas Ter. TS6: Norm. . . . 2D **105**
Douglas Wlk. *TS20: Nort 3B 74*
  (off Headlam Rd.)
Dovecote Cl. TS11: M Sea . . 4C **66**
Dovecot St. TS18: S Tee. . . . 1A **98**
  (not continuous)
Dovecot Theatre & Arts Cen.
  . . . . 1A **98**
Dovedale Av. TS6: Gran 4F **81**
Dovedale Cl. TS20: Nort 1C **74**
Dovedale Rd. TS20: Nort . . . 1C **74**
Dover Cl. TS10: Redc 2E **65**
  TS23: Bill. 5C **38**
Dover Rd. TS19: S Tee 2F **73**
  (not continuous)
Dover St. TS24: H'pool. 3C **14**
Dovey Ct. TS17: I Bar 1F **149**
Downe St. TS13: Live. 5A **92**
Downfield Way
  TS11: N Mar 2F **85**
Downham Av. TS3: Midd . . . 3C **102**
Downham Gro.
  TS25: H'pool 5E **19**
Downholme Gro.
  TS18: S Tee 3C **96**
Downside Rd. TS5: Midd . . . 3A **100**
Dowson Rd. TS24: H'pool 3F **7**
Doxford St. TS8: Hem 5E **131**
Doyle Wlk. TS25: H'pool 2D **19**
Doyle Way TS19: S Tee 4A **72**
Dragon Ct. TS20: Nort 5B **54**
Drake Cl. TS11: M Sea 4E **67**
Drake Ct. TS2: Midd 2C **76**
Drake Ho. TS24: H'pool 3D **15**
Drake Rd. TS20: Nort 1A **74**
Draycott Av. TS5: Midd 3D **131**
Draycott Cl. TS10: Redc 3B **64**
  TS20: Nort. 5E **53**
Drayton Rd. TS25: H'pool . . . 2D **19**
Driffield Way TS23: Bill. 2F **39**
Driftwell Dr. TS19: S Tee . . . 4A **72**
Drive, The TS8: Stain 5C **130**
  TS11: M Sea 4B **66**
  TS17: T Tee 2B **128**
  TS25: Grea 3E **31**
Droitwich Av. TS19: S Tee . . 2E **73**
Drovers La. TS21: Redm 1B **70**
Druridge Gro. TS10: Redc . . . 2F **65**
Dryburn Rd. TS19: S Tee . . . 1A **72**
Dryden Ct. TS23: Bill 2E **39**
Dryden Rd. TS25: H'pool . . . 2E **19**
Duchy Rd. TS26: H'pool 3C **12**
Duddon Sands TS5: Midd. . . 3B **130**
Duddon Wlk. TS19: S Tee . . . 5F **73**
Dudley Rd. TS23: Bill. 4D **39**

Dudley Wlk. *TS10: Redc. 2E 65*
  (off Carisbrooke Way)
Dufton Rd. TS5: Midd. 1C **100**
Dugdale St. TS18: S Tee. . . . 4C **74**
Dukeport Ct. *TS18: S Tee . . . 4C 74*
  (off Alnport Rd.)
Dukes Ct. TS17: T Tee 5D **129**
Duke St. TS26: H'pool 2F **13**
Dukesway TS17: T Tee 5D **129**
Dulas Cl. TS10: Redc 3E **65**
Dulverton Cl. TS17: I Bar . . . 3B **150**
Dulverton Way TS14: Guis . . 3F **139**
Dumbarton Av. TS19: S Tee . . 2F **73**
Dumfries Rd. TS25: H'pool. . . 4F **19**
Dunbar Av. TS4: Midd. 5B **102**
Dunbar Ct. TS13: Eas 2A **118**
Dunbar Dr. TS16: Eag. 1C **148**
Dunbar Rd. TS23: Bill. 5D **39**
  TS25: H'pool 3E **19**
Duncan Av. TS10: Redc 5A **48**
Duncan Pl. TS13: Loft 5C **92**
Duncan Rd. TS25: H'pool . . . 3E **19**
Duncombe Rd. TS4: Midd . . . 3A **78**
Dundas Arc. TS1: Midd. 2F **77**
Dundas St. TS1: Midd. 3E **77**
  (not continuous)
  TS10: Redc 3C **48**
  TS11: N Mar 1A **86**
  TS13: Loft 5B **92**
  TS19: S Tee 4F **73**
  TS24: H'pool 4C **14**
Dundas St. E. TS12: Salt . . . 4C **68**
Dundas St. W. TS12: Salt. . . 4C **68**
Dundas Ter. TS11: M Sea . . 5C **66**
  TS11: N Mar 1A **86**
Dundee Rd. TS25: H'pool . . . 4F **19**
Dundrennan TS18: S Tee . . . 2B **96**
Dunedin Ho. TS17: T Tee . . . 1B **98**
Dunelm Ct. TS21: Sed 4C **22**
Dunelm Rd. TS19: S Tee . . . 3C **72**
Duneside TS19: S Tee. 3C **72**
Dunford Cl. TS19: S Tee. . . . 1B **72**
Dunhallow Cl. TS14: Guis . . 4E **139**
Dunholm Av. TS3: Midd 3A **104**
Dunkeld Cl. TS19: S Tee. . . . 1B **72**
Dunkery Cl. TS17: I Bar 3A **150**
Dunlane Cl. TS5: Midd 5B **76**
Dunlin Cl. TS20: Nort 3B **54**
Dunlin Ho. TS24: H'pool 3D **15**
Dunlin Rd. TS26: H'pool. 5E **7**
Dunmail Rd. TS10: Redc 5B **48**
  TS19: S Tee 5F **73**
Dunmoor Gro. TS17: I Bar . . 2A **150**
Dunmow Av. TS3: Midd 3E **103**
Dunnet Cl. TS10: Redc 4C **64**
Dunning Rd. TS1: Midd 3F **77**
  (not continuous)
Dunning St. TS1: Midd 3F **77**
Dunoon Cl. TS19: S Tee 2F **73**
Dunoon Dr. TS25: H'pool. . . . 3E **19**
Dunottar Av. TS16: P Tee . . . 3C **126**
DUNSDALE 5C **84**
Dunsdale Cl. TS6: Est. 2E **105**
  TS11: M Sea 4E **67**
Dunsley Cl. TS3: Midd 1B **102**
Dunsley Ct. TS14: Guis. 1E **139**
Dunsley Dr. TS23: Bill. 4E **39**
Dunsop Av. TS4: Midd 5B **102**
Dunstable Cl. TS19: S Tee . . 2E **73**
Dunstable Rd. TS5: Midd. . . 5B **76**
Dunster Ho. TS3: Midd. 2D **103**
Dunster Rd. TS23: Bill 4E **39**
Dunston Cl. TS14: Guis 4E **139**
Dunston Rd. TS19: S Tee . . . 1B **72**
  TS26: H'pool. 3D **13**
Durham Ho. TS4: Midd. 2A **102**
Durham La. TS16: Eag 4A **96**
  TS21: Elt, P Tee, S Tee . . . 4A **96**

Durham La. Ind. Est.
TS16: Eag 3A **126**
Durham Rd. TS6: Est 5E **81**
TS10: Redc 1F **65**
TS12: Brot 2C **90**
TS19: S Tee 5C **52**
TS21: S Tee, T Lar, T The
. . . . 3C **34**
TS21: S Tee, T The 1D **51**
TS21: Sed 2C **22**
(Salter's La.)
TS21: Sed 4B **22**
(Sands Hall Rdbt.)
TS22: Wolv 2C **38**
Durham Rd. By-Pass
TS19: S Tee 3E **73**
Durham St. TS2: Midd 1F **77**
TS18: S Tee 5A **74**
TS24: H'pool 5E **9**
DURHAM TEES VALLEY AIRPORT
. . . . 2D **145**
Durness Gro.
TS25: H'pool 3E **19**
Durnford Rd. TS3: Midd . . . 2F **103**
DYKE HOUSE 1A **14**

E

Eaglebridge Ct. TS22: Wyn . . 2E **37**
Eagle Ct. TS18: S Tee 5F **97**
Eagle Pk. TS8: Mart 5F **133**
(not continuous)
EAGLESCLIFFE 5C **126**
Eaglescliffe Cl.
TS11: N Mar 2F **85**
Eaglescliffe Ind. Est.
TS16: Eag 3C **126**
Eaglesfield Rd.
TS25: H'pool 3D **19**
Eamont Gdns.
TS26: H'pool 4A **14**
Eamont Rd. TS20: Nort 5A **54**
Eamont Ter. TS26: H'pool 5A **14**
Earle Cl. TS15: Yarm 4E **149**
Earl's Ct. TS20: Nort 1B **74**
Earls Ct. Rd. TS8: Hem 5E **131**
Earlsdon Av. TS5: Midd 1B **130**
Earlsferry Rd.
TS25: H'pool 3D **19**
Earls Nook TS23: Bill 1A **56**
Earlston Wlk. TS25: H'pool . . 3D **19**
Earl St. TS24: H'pool 4D **9**
Earlsway TS17: T Tee 5E **129**
Earn Wlk. TS25: H'pool 3D **19**
Earsdon Cl. TS20: Nort 5E **53**
EASBY 5F **167**
Easby Av. TS5: Midd 3E **101**
Easby Cl. TS6: Est 5A **82**
TS10: Redc 2B **64**
TS14: Guis 2F **139**
Easby Ct. TS12: Skel 3E **89**
Easby Gro. TS6: Est 1D **105**
TS17: T Tee 4D **99**
Easby La. TS9: G Ayt 2C **166**
Easby Rd. TS23: Bill 1E **55**
Easdale Ct. TS17: T Tee 5E **99**
Easdale Wlk. TS5: Midd 3E **101**
EASINGTON 2A **118**
Easington Rd. TS19: S Tee . . 5B **52**
TS24: H'pool 1C **6**
Easson Rd. TS10: Redc 5C **48**
Easson St. TS4: Midd 1A **102**
East Av. TS23: Bill 4D **55**
Eastbank Rd. TS7: Orm 5B **104**
Eastbourne Av.
TS16: Egg 2C **148**
Eastbourne Gdns.
TS3: Midd 3F **103**

Eastbourne Rd.
TS5: Midd 2E **101**
TS19: S Tee 3A **74**
(not continuous)
Eastbury Cl. TS17: I Bar . . . 1C **150**
East Cres. TS5: Midd 2B **100**
TS13: Loft 5D **93**
Eastcroft TS3: Midd 1C **102**
Eastcroft Rd. TS6: Gran 2E **81**
East Dr. TS17: T Tee 1D **99**
East End TS9: Stok 1D **168**
TS21: Sed 4D **23**
Easter Pk. TS17: T Tee 5E **129**
EASTERSIDE 5B **102**
Easterside Rd. TS4: Midd . . 5B **102**
E. Farm Cl. TS6: Norm 3D **105**
Eastfield Rd. TS11: M Sea . . 4B **66**
Eastfields TS9: Stok 1C **168**
Eastgate Rd. TS5: Midd 3C **100**
Eastham Sands
TS5: Midd 3B **130**
EAST LOFTUS 5D **93**
Eastlowthian St. TS2: P Cla . . 5F **57**
East Mdws. TS11: M Sea . . . 4D **67**
E. Middlesbrough Ind. Est.
TS3: N Orm 3E **79**
(Telford Rd.)
TS3: N Orm 4D **79**
(Westerby Rd.)
Easton St. TS17: T Tee 3D **99**
East Pde. TS12: Skel 4B **88**
TS21: Sed 3D **23**
TS24: H'pool 5D **9**
Eastport Rd. TS18: S Tee . . . 4C **74**
East Pct. TS23: Bill 1D **55**
East Row TS5: Midd 2B **100**
TS6: Est 1F **105**
East Scar TS10: Redc 2E **65**
East Side TS7: Nun 2C **156**
East St. TS2: Midd 1F **77**
TS11: M Sea 4D **67**
TS13: Loft 5C **92**
East Ter. TS12: Skel 4B **88**
(off Marske La.)
TS12: Skel 4B **88**
(Rydal Rd.)
East Vw. DL2: M Row 4A **144**
East Vw. Ter. TS4: Midd . . . 1A **102**
TS25: S Car 3E **21**
E. Well Cl. TS21: Sed 4D **23**
Eastwood Rd. TS3: Midd . . 2A **104**
Ebchester Cl. TS19: S Tee . . 5B **52**
Eccleston Wlk. TS4: Midd . . 5A **102**
Eckert Av. TS5: Midd 2A **100**
Eckford Wlk. TS25: H'pool . . 3E **19**
Eco House 2F **131**
Eddison Way TS8: Hem 5E **131**
(not continuous)
Eddleston Wlk.
TS25: H'pool 3D **19**
Eden Dr. TS21: Sed 4D **23**
Edenhall Gro. TS10: Redc . . 2C **64**
Eden Rd. TS4: Midd 2F **101**
TS12: Skel 3C **88**
Eden St. TS12: Salt 4C **68**
TS24: H'pool 4B **14**
Eden Way TS22: Bill 4A **38**
Eder Rd. TS20: Nort 2B **74**
Edgar St. TS20: Nort 2B **74**
TS25: H'pool 1C **20**
Edgehill Way TS23: Bill 4A **40**
Edgeworth Ct. TS8: Hem . . . 5F **131**
Edgley Rd. TS19: S Tee 2B **96**

Edinburgh Av. TS5: Midd . . . 3D **101**
Edinburgh Cl. TS7: Nun . . . 3A **134**
Edinburgh Gro.
TS25: H'pool 4C **20**
Edith St. TS5: Midd 4B **76**
Edmondbyers Rd.
TS19: S Tee 5B **52**
Edmondsley Wlk.
TS19: S Tee 5C **52**
Edmundsbury Rd.
TS5: Midd 1F **101**
Ednam Gro. TS25: H'pool . . . 3E **19**
Edridge Grn. TS3: Midd 5E **79**
Edston Dr. TS14: Guis 5F **109**
Edwards St. TS6: Est 2F **105**
TS18: S Tee 2A **98**
(not continuous)
Edward St. TS3: N Orm 4C **78**
TS6: S Ban 3B **80**
Edzell Wlk. TS25: H'pool . . . 3D **19**
Egerton Cl. TS20: Nort 4E **53**
Egerton Rd. TS26: H'pool . . . 4C **12**
Egerton St. TS1: Midd 5F **77**
Egerton Ter. TS25: Grea 3E **31**
EGGLESCLIFFE 2C **148**
Egglescliffe Bank
TS16: Egg 2B **148**
Egglescliffe Cl.
TS19: S Tee 5C **52**
Egglescliffe Ct. TS16: Egg . . 2C **148**
Eggleston Cl. TS2: Midd 1C **76**
TS12: Skel 4D **89**
Eggleston Dr. TS16: Eag . . . 5A **126**
Eggleston Ter.
TS18: S Tee 1F **97**
Eggleston Rd. TS10: Redc . . 3C **64**
Eglinton Av. TS14: Guis 3E **139**
Eglinton Rd. TS6: Gran 2E **81**
Egmont Rd. TS4: Midd 5A **78**
Egton Av. TS7: Nun 4F **133**
Egton Cl. TS10: Redc 3C **64**
Egton Dr. TS25: S Car 5D **21**
Egton Rd. TS20: Nort 2B **74**
Eider Cl. TS17: I Bar 5B **128**
Elcho St. TS26: H'pool 3A **14**
Elcoat Rd. TS20: Nort 4B **54**
Elder Cl. TS26: H'pool 1D **13**
Elder Ct. TS1: Midd 3F **77**
Elder Gro. TS10: Redc 3F **65**
TS19: S Tee 2E **73**
Elderslie Wlk.
TS25: H'pool 3D **19**
Elderwood Ct. TS4: Midd . . . 3F **101**
Eldon Ct. TS23: Bill 3D **39**
Eldon Grove Community Sports Cen.
. . . . 4F **13**
Eldon St. TS17: T Tee 2C **98**
Eldon Wlk. TS17: T Tee 3D **99**
Eleanor Pl. TS18: S Tee 2A **98**
Elemere Ct. TS23: Bill 4E **39**
Elgin Av. TS3: Midd 3D **103**
TS6: Gran 2C **80**
Elgin Rd. TS17: T Tee 3D **129**
TS25: H'pool 3E **19**
Eliot Ct. TS23: Bill 3D **39**
Elishaw Grn. TS17: I Bar . . . 2A **150**
Elizabeth St. TS17: T Tee . . . 3C **98**
Elizabeth Ter. TS3: N Orm . . 4B **78**
Elizabeth Way TS25: S Car . . 4D **21**
Elkington Wlk. TS3: Midd . . 2A **104**
Elland Av. TS4: Midd 5B **102**
Ellary Wlk. TS25: H'pool . . . 3D **19**
Ellen Av. TS18: S Tee 2F **97**
Ellenport Ct. TS18: S Tee . . . 4C **74**
Ellerbeck Ct. TS9: Stok 3D **169**
Ellerbeck Way TS7: Orm . . . 4B **104**
TS9: Stok 3D **169**
Ellerburne St. TS17: T Tee . . 3D **99**

Ellerby Cl. TS10: Redc 2C **64**
Ellerby Grn. TS3: Midd 1C **102**
Ellerby Rd. TS6: Est 5F **81**
Ellers Bank TS11: Uple 2C **110**
Ellerton Cl. TS5: Midd 5E **101**
Ellerton Rd. TS18: S Tee 3A **96**
Ellesmere Wlk. TS3: Midd . . . 5E **79**
Ellett Ct. TS24: H'pool 4F **7**
Elliot St. TS1: Midd 3F **77**
 TS10: Redc 3B **48**
 TS12: Skel 5B **88**
Elliott St. TS26: H'pool 3A **14**
Elliotts Yd. *TS13: Stait 1C* **120**
 (off Beckside)
Elliott Wlk. TS18: S Tee 2A **98**
Ellis Gdns. TS8: Hem 5E **131**
Ellison St. TS26: H'pool 5A **14**
Elm Av. TS21: Sed 3D **23**
Elm Cl. TS6: Norm 5C **80**
 TS12: Salt 4A **68**
Elm Dr. TS7: Mart. 2D **133**
Elmfield Gdns.
 TS25: H'pool 3F **19**
Elm Gro. TS17: T Tee 4C **98**
 TS26: H'pool 3E **13**
Elm Ho. TS18: S Tee 5B **74**
Elmhurst Gdns.
 TS8: Hem 5E **131**
 (not continuous)
Elm Rd. TS10: Redc 4E **49**
 TS14: Guis 1E **139**
Elmstone Gdns. TS8: Hem . . 5E **131**
 (not continuous)
Elm St. TS1: Midd 3F **77**
 TS6: S Ban 2A **80**
ELM TREE 3C **72**
Elm Tree Av. TS19: S Tee 3B **72**
Elm Tree Cen. TS19: S Tee . . 4C **72**
Elm Tree Pk. TS25: S Car 3E **21**
Elm Wlk. TS13: Loft 5B **92**
Elmwood TS8: C New 3B **132**
Elmwood Av. *TS5: Midd 1B* **100**
 (off Northern Rd.)
Elmwood Cl. TS9: Stok 5C **164**
Elmwood Ct. TS19: S Tee . . . 3B **72**
Elmwood Gro. TS19: S Tee . . 4D **73**
Elmwood Pl. TS26: H'pool . . . 1E **13**
Elmwood Rd. TS16: P Tee . . . 2C **126**
 TS26: H'pool 2E **13**
Elphin Wlk. TS25: H'pool 3D **19**
Elsdon Gdns. TS17: I Bar . . . 2A **150**
Elsdon St. TS18: S Tee 1F **97**
Elstob Cl. TS19: S Tee 5B **52**
Elstone Rd. TS4: Midd 3A **78**
Elterwater Cl. TS10: Redc . . . 5B **48**
Eltham Cres. TS17: T Tee . . . 3E **129**
Eltisley Grn. TS3: Midd 5E **79**
ELTON 4E **95**
Elton Cl. TS19: S Tee 5C **52**
Elton Gro. TS19: S Tee 1A **96**
Elton Interchange
 TS21: S Tee 3F **95**
Elton La. TS16: Eag 1B **148**
ELTON PARK 5F **71**
Elton Rd. TS22: Bill 4B **38**
Elton St. TS10: Redc 4C **48**
Eltringham Rd.
 TS26: H'pool 4A **14**
Elvan Gro. TS25: H'pool 3E **19**
Elvington Cl. TS23: Bill 1F **39**
Elvington Grn. TS3: Midd . . . 1E **103**
ELWICK 4C **10**
Elwick Av. TS5: Midd 5C **100**
Elwick Cl. TS10: Redc 4F **65**
 TS19: S Tee 5B **52**
Elwick Ct. TS26: H'pool 5A **14**
Elwick Gdns. TS19: S Tee . . . 5B **52**
Elwick Rd. TS24: H'pool 5A **14**
 TS26: H'pool 2A **12**

Ely Cres. TS10: Redc 5F **49**
 TS12: Brot. 2C **90**
Ely St. TS4: Midd 4A **78**
Embleton Av. TS5: Midd 4C **100**
Embleton Cl. TS19: S Tee. . . . 5B **52**
Embleton Ct. TS10: Redc . . . 2D **65**
Embleton Gro. TS22: Wyn . . . 2E **37**
Embleton Rd. TS22: Bill 4B **38**
Embleton Wlk. TS19: S Tee . . 5B **52**
 (not continuous)
Embsay Cl. TS17: I Bar 2B **150**
Embsay Ct. TS4: Midd 3A **102**
Emerald St. TS1: Midd 4E **77**
 TS12: Salt 3C **68**
Emerson Av. TS5: Midd 3E **101**
Emerson Ct. TS4: H'pool. 3F **7**
Emily St. TS1: Midd 3F **77**
Emma Simpson Ct.
 TS18: S Tee 3C **96**
Emmerson St. TS5: Midd . . . 1E **101**
Emmetts Gdns.
 TS17: I Bar 1B **150**
Emsworth Dr. TS16: Eag. . . . 5A **126**
Endeavour, The TS7: Nun . . . 3A **134**
Endeavour Cl. TS25: S Car . . 3E **21**
Endeavour Dr. TS7: Orm. . . . 5B **104**
Endeavour Ho.
 TS17: T Tee 1B **98**
Enderby Gdns. TS8: Hem . . . 5E **131**
Endeston Rd. TS3: Midd 3E **103**
Endrick Rd. TS25: H'pool 3D **19**
Endsleigh Dr. TS5: Midd 3A **100**
Enfield Chase TS14: Guis . . . 3D **139**
Enfield Gro. TS6: Norm 4C **104**
Enfield Shop. Cen.
 TS14: Guis 3E **139**
Enfield St. TS1: Midd 4D **77**
Ennerdale Av. TS5: Midd . . . 4C **100**
Ennerdale Cres.
 TS12: Skel 3B **88**
Ennerdale Rd. TS18: S Tee . . 5D **73**
Ennis Rd. TS10: Redc 5E **47**
Ennis Sq. TS10: Redc 5E **47**
Enron Ho. TS17: T Tee 1C **98**
Ensign Ct. TS24: H'pool 3D **15**
Enterpen Cl. TS15: Yarm . . . 4F **149**
Enterprise Cen. TS2: Midd . . 1F **77**
Enterprise Cen. Annexe
 TS2: Midd 1E **77**
Enterprise Ho.
 TS25: H'pool 1C **20**
 (off Thomlinson Rd.)
Epping Av. TS3: Midd 3D **103**
Epping Cl. TS11: M Sea 4C **66**
 TS17: T Tee 2C **128**
Epsom Av. TS4: Midd 5B **102**
Epsom Rd. TS10: Redc 2D **65**
Epworth Grn. TS3: Midd 1E **103**
Erica Gro. TS7: Mart. 1C **132**
Eric Av. TS17: T Tee 3D **99**
Eridge Rd. TS14: Guis 3F **139**
Eriskay Wlk. TS25: H'pool . . . 3D **19**
Eris Rd. TS18: S Tee 5E **97**
Erith Gro. TS4: Midd. 1B **132**
Ernest St. TS26: H'pool 2A **14**
Ernest Wlk. TS26: H'pool . . . 2A **14**
Errington Gth. *TS11: M Sea . . 5E* **67**
 (off Hambleton Cres.)
Errington St. TS12: Brot. 3B **90**
Errol St. TS1: Midd 5F **77**
 TS24: H'pool 3B **14**
Erskine Rd. TS25: H'pool . . . 3D **19**
Escomb Cl. TS19: S Tee 5B **52**
Escombe Av. TS4: Midd 5B **102**
Escombe Rd. TS23: Bill 2E **39**
Escomb Ho. TS4: Midd. 2A **102**
Esha Ness Ct.
 TS25: H'pool 3D **19**
Esher Av. TS6: Norm 4C **104**

Esher St. TS1: Midd 4A **78**
Eshton TS22: Wyn 3B **26**
Eshwood Sq. TS1: Midd 3E **77**
Esk Cl. TS14: Guis 3D **139**
Esk Cl. TS14: Guis 3D **139**
Eskdale TS8: Hem 5D **131**
Eskdale Cl. TS15: Yarm 1B **160**
Eskdale Ct. TS25: H'pool 3D **19**
Eskdale Rd. TS10: Redc 1F **63**
 TS25: H'pool 4D **19**
Eskdale Ter. TS12: Ling 4E **113**
 TS14: Guis. 1E **139**
 (off Bolckow St.)
Esk Grn. TS16: Eag 1B **148**
Esk Gro. TS25: H'pool 3E **19**
Esk Rd. TS20: Nort 1A **74**
Esk St. TS3: N Orm. 4C **78**
Esk Ter. *TS13: Loft 5D* **93**
 (off Whitby Rd.)
Esplanade TS10: Redc 3C **48**
Essex Av. TS6: Gran 3D **81**
Essex Cl. TS10: Redc 1B **64**
Essex Cres. TS23: Bill. 2F **55**
Essex Gro. TS20: Nort 1C **74**
Essexport Rd. TS18: S Tee . . 4C **74**
Essex St. TS1: Midd 5D **77**
ESTON 1E **105**
Eston Leisure Cen. 4C **80**
Eston Leisure Complex 4C **80**
Eston Rd.
 TS6: Est, Laze, O Lac . . 1A **106**
 (not continuous)
 TS6: Gran 1C **80**
Eston Sports Academy 4C **80**
Eston Vw. TS3: Midd 2D **103**
Etherley Cl. TS19: S Tee 5B **52**
Etherley Wlk. TS19: S Tee . . . 5B **52**
 (not continuous)
Eton Rd. TS5: Midd 2C **100**
 TS18: S Tee 2F **97**
Eton St. TS25: H'pool 1A **20**
Ettersgill Cl. TS16: Eag 5A **126**
Ettersgill Av. TS3: Midd 4D **103**
Etton Rd. TS23: Bill. 1E **39**
Ettrick Wlk. TS25: H'pool . . . 3D **19**
Evans St. TS6: Gran 3D **81**
Evendale TS14: Guis 3A **138**
Evenwood Cl. TS19: S Tee . . 5B **52**
Evenwood Gdns.
 TS5: Midd 2D **131**
Everett St. TS26: H'pool 2F **13**
Evergreen Wlk. *TS4: Midd . . 3F* **101**
 (off Pinewood Av.)
Everingham Rd.
 TS15: Yarm 1A **160**
Eversham Rd. TS6: Gran . . . 2E **81**
Eversley Wlk. TS3: Midd 3D **103**
Evesham St. TS3: Midd. 3D **103**
Evesham Way TS23: Bill. 3A **40**
Ewbank Dr. TS18: S Tee 1F **97**
Ewbank Gdns. TS18: S Tee . . 1F **97**
Exchange Pl. TS1: Midd 2F **77**
Exchange Sq. TS1: Midd. . . . 2F **77**
Exchange Yd. TS18: S Tee . . 1A **98**
Exeter Rd. TS5: Midd 1F **101**
 TS6: Est. 1E **105**
Exeter St. TS12: Salt 4C **68**
 TS24: H'pool 4C **14**
Exford Cl. TS17: I Bar 3B **150**
Exmoor Gro. TS26: H'pool . . . 1D **13**
Exmouth Cl. TS10: Redc. . . . 3A **64**
Eyebright Cl. TS26: H'pool . . . 4D **7**
Ezard St. TS19: S Tee 4A **74**

F

Fabian Ct. Shop. Cen.
 TS6: Est. 5E **81**
Fabian Rd. TS6: Est 5C **80**

George St. TS10: Redc 4D **49**
  TS14: Guis 1D **139**
  TS17: T Tee 2C **98**
  TS24: H'pool 3C **14**
George Ter. TS12: Brot. 3B **90**
Georgiana Cl. TS17: T Tee . . . 2C **98**
GERRICK 5E **143**
Gerrie St. TS12: Boo 3C **112**
Gibb Sq. TS24: H'pool 5F **9**
Gibraltar Rd. TS16: Eag 4F **125**
Gibson Gro. TS24: H'pool . . . 2D **7**
Gibson St. TS3: N Orm. 4C **78**
Gifford St. TS5: Midd 1E **101**
Gilberti Pl. TS14: H'pool. 3F **7**
Gilkes St. TS1: Midd. 3E **77**
Gillercomb TS10: Redc 4C **64**
Gilling Rd. TS19: S Tee 5B **72**
Gilling Wlk. TS3: Midd 1C **102**
Gilling Way TS10: Redc 2E **65**
Gillpark Gro. TS25: S Car . . . 4D **21**
Gill St. TS12: Salt. 5C **68**
  TS14: Guis 1E **139**
  TS24: H'pool 4B **14**
Gilmonby Rd. TS3: Midd . . . 4D **103**
Gilmour St. TS17: T Tee 3C **98**
  (not continuous)
Gilpin Ho. TS20: Nort. 5A **54**
Gilpin Rd. TS17: T Tee 4C **98**
Gilpin Sq. TS19: S Tee 3F **73**
Gilside Rd. TS23: Bill 5F **39**
Gilsland Cl. TS5: Midd 2B **130**
Gilsland Gro. TS6: Norm . . . 2D **105**
Gilwern Ct. TS17: I Bar 2F **149**
Girrick Cl. TS8: Hem 5C **130**
Girton Av. TS3: Midd 4D **103**
Gisborne Gro. TS18: S Tee . . . 2C **96**
Gisburn Av. TS3: Midd 3D **103**
Gisburn Rd. TS23: Bill 5F **39**
Gladesfield Rd. TS20: Nort . . 2B **74**
Gladstone Ind. Est.
  TS17: T Tee 2C **98**
Gladstone St. TS6: Est 1F **105**
  TS12: Brot. 3A **90**
  TS13: C How 3F **91**
  TS13: Loft 5C **92**
  TS17: T Tee 2C **98**
  TS18: S Tee 2A **98**
  (not continuous)
  TS24: H'pool 1F **15**
Glaisdale Av. TS5: Midd 4E **101**
  TS10: Redc 1F **63**
  TS19: S Tee 3E **73**
Glaisdale Cl. TS6: Est 5A **82**
Glaisdale Gro. TS25: S Car . . 4E **21**
Glaisdale Rd. TS6: Est 5A **82**
  TS15: Yarm 4E **149**
Glamis Gro. TS4: Midd 3A **102**
Glamis Rd. TS23: Bill 4C **38**
Glamis Wlk. TS25: H'pool . . . 4E **19**
Glamorgan Gro.
  TS26: H'pool 1D **13**
Glasgow St. TS17: T Tee 2C **98**
Glastonbury Av. TS6: Est . . . 1E **105**
Glastonbury Ho.
  TS3: Midd 3E **103**
Glastonbury Rd.
  TS12: Skel. 4D **89**
Glastonbury Wlk.
  TS26: H'pool 1E **13**
Gleaston Cres. TS4: Midd . . . 4A **102**
Gleaston Wlk. TS4: Midd . . . 4A **102**
GLEBE 4E **53**
Glebe, The TS20: Nort 4E **53**
Glebe Gdns. TS8: Stain 5C **130**
  TS13: Eas 3A **118**
Glebe Rd. TS1: Midd 4D **77**
  TS9: Stok 2C **168**
Gledstone TS22: Wyn 3A **26**
Glen, The TS16: Egg 2C **148**

Glenarm Rd. TS22: Wyn 4F **27**
Glenbury Gro. TS10: Redc . . . 4F **65**
Glencairn Gro.
  TS25: H'pool 4D **19**
Glendale TS14: Guis 4A **138**
Glendale Av. TS26: H'pool . . 4F **13**
Glendale Rd. TS5: Midd 4E **101**
Glendue Cl. TS7: Nun 4A **134**
Gleneagles Cl. TS22: Bill . . . 5A **38**
Gleneagles Ct.
  TS4: Midd 4A **102**
Gleneagles Rd.
  TS4: Midd 4F **101**
  TS11: N Mar 1A **86**
  TS27: H'pool 2C **6**
Glenfall Cl. TS22: Bill. 5A **38**
Glenfield Cl. TS19: S Tee . . . 5A **72**
Glenfield Dr. TS5: Midd 4E **101**
Glenfield Rd. TS19: S Tee . . . 5A **72**
Glenfield Ter. TS13: Loft 5D **93**
Glenhow Gdns. TS12: Salt . . 4C **68**
Glenluce Cl. TS16: Eag 5C **126**
Glenmoor Gro.
  TS6: Norm 1C **104**
Glenn Cres. TS7: Mart 3D **133**
Glenside TS12: Salt 4D **69**
Glenston Cl. TS26: H'pool . . . 2C **12**
Glentower Gro.
  TS25: S Car. 4D **21**
Glentworth Av. TS3: Midd. . . 2A **104**
Glentworth Rd. TS3: Midd . . 2A **104**
Gloucester Cl. TS7: Nun. . . . 3A **134**
Gloucester Rd.
  TS14: Guis 4D **139**
Gloucester St.
  TS25: H'pool 1A **20**
Gloucester Ter. TS23: Bill . . . 1F **55**
Glyder Ct. TS17: I Bar. 1F **149**
Goathland Dr. TS25: S Car. . . 5D **21**
Goathland Gro.
  TS14: Guis 4D **139**
Goathland Rd. TS6: Est 5F **81**
Gofton Pl. TS6: Est. 4D **81**
Goldcrest TS14: Guis 2B **138**
Goldcrest Cl. TS17: I Bar . . . 5B **128**
Golden Boy Green Sports Cen.
  . . . . 2B **80**
Golden Lion M. TS9: Stok . . . 1C **168**
Goldfinch Rd. TS26: H'pool . . 5D **7**
Goldsmith Av. TS24: H'pool . . 2E **7**
Goldsmith Cl. TS23: Bill 3D **39**
Goodwin Cl. TS10: Redc 4B **64**
Goodwin Wlk.
  TS24: H'pool 4C **14**
Goodwood Rd. TS10: Redc . . 2D **65**
Goodwood Sq. TS17: T Tee. . 2F **99**
Goosepastures
  TS15: Yarm 4C **148**
Gooseport Rd. TS18: S Tee . . 4C **74**
Gordon Cres. TS6: Gran 3E **81**
Gordon Rd. TS10: Redc 4A **48**
Gordon St. TS26: H'pool 3F **13**
Gore Sands TS5: Midd 2A **130**
Gorman Rd. TS5: Midd 1D **101**
Gorsefields Ct. TS6: Est 3E **105**
Gorton Cl. TS23: Bill. 4C **38**
Gosford M. TS2: Midd 2E **77**
Gosford St. TS2: Midd 2F **77**
Gosforth Av. TS10: Redc . . . 4D **49**
  (not continuous)
Goshawk Rd. TS26: H'pool . . 5D **7**
Gough Cl. TS1: Midd 4D **77**
Goulton Cl. TS15: Yarm 4E **149**
Gower Cl. TS1: Midd 3D **77**
Gower Wlk. TS26: H'pool . . . 5E **7**
Grace Cl. TS25: S Car. 5E **21**
Graffenberg St.
  TS10: Redc 3D **49**
Grafton Cl. TS14: Guis 3E **139**

Graham St. TS13: Live 5A **92**
  TS24: H'pool 5E **9**
Graham Wlk. TS25: H'pool . . 4E **19**
Grainger Cl. TS16: Eag. 4B **126**
Grainger St. TS24: H'pool . . . 2B **14**
Grammar School La.
  TS15: Yarm 4B **148**
Grampian Rd. TS12: Skel. . . 3C **88**
  TS23: Bill 1D **55**
Granary, The TS22: Wyn . . . 5C **26**
Grange Av. TS18: S Tee 4D **73**
  TS23: Bill. 4E **55**
  TS26: H'pool 3F **13**
Grange Bungalow, The
  TS6: Gran 3E **81**
Grange Bus. Cen., The
  TS23: Bill 3F **55**
Grange Cl. TS6: Gran 3E **81**
  TS26: H'pool 3F **13**
Grange Cres. TS7: Mart 3D **133**
Grange Dr. TS9: Stok 1B **168**
Grange Est. TS6: Laze 3C **82**
Grange Farm TS8: C New. . . 3B **132**
Grange Farm Rd.
  TS6: Gran 3E **81**
GRANGEFIELD 5D **73**
Grangefield Rd.
  TS18: S Tee 5D **73**
Grangefields TS12: Brot. . . . 2A **90**
Grange La. TS13: Loft 3E **93**
Grange Rd. TS1: Midd 3E **77**
  (not continuous)
  TS17: T Tee 3C **98**
  TS20: Nort. 1B **74**
  TS26: H'pool 3F **13**
GRANGETOWN 3E **81**
Grangetown By-Pass
  TS6: Midd, Gran 2B **80**
Grange Vw. TS22: Wolv 3C **38**
Grangeville Av.
  TS19: S Tee 5A **72**
Grange Wood TS8: C New. . . 3F **131**
Grantham Av. TS26: H'pool. . . 4F **13**
Grantham Grn. TS4: Midd . . 5B **102**
Grantham Rd. TS20: Nort . . . 4F **53**
Grantley Av. TS3: Midd. 5A **80**
Grant St. TS10: Redc 3C **48**
Granville Av. TS26: H'pool . . . 3F **13**
Granville Gro. TS20: Nort . . . 1B **74**
Granville Pl. TS26: H'pool . . . 3F **13**
Granville Rd. TS1: Midd. 5E **77**
  TS6: Gran 3D **81**
Granville Ter. TS10: Redc . . . 3D **49**
Granwood Rd. TS6: Est. 2F **105**
Grasby Cl. TS3: Midd 2A **104**
Grasmere Av. TS5: Midd . . . 5C **100**
Grasmere Cres. TS12: Skel . . 4B **88**
Grasmere Dr. TS6: Norm . . . 1C **104**
Grasmere Rd. TS10: Redc . . 5C **48**
  TS18: S Tee 5E **73**
Grasmere St. TS26: H'pool . . 5A **14**
Grass Cft. TS21: L New 1A **124**
Grassholme Av.
  TS5: Midd 1B **100**
  (off Northern Rd.)
Grassholme Rd.
  TS26: H'pool 3C **12**
Grassholme Way
  TS16: Eag 4F **125**
Grassholm Rd. TS20: Nort. . . 1B **74**
Grassington Grn.
  TS17: I Bar 3B **150**
Grassington Rd.
  TS4: Midd 3A **102**
Graygarth Rd. TS3: Midd . . . 2C **102**
Gray's Rd. TS18: S Tee 5E **73**
Gray St. TS2: Midd 2F **77**
  TS24: H'pool 2A **14**
GRAYTHORP. 4C **32**

Graythorp Ind. Est.
TS25: H'pool 4D **33**
Graythorp Rd.
TS25: H'pool 4C **32**
Great Auk TS14: Guis 2B **138**
GREAT AYTON 2D **167**
Gt. Ayton Rd.
TS9: Nun, G Ayt 4C **156**
GREAT BROUGHTON 5F **169**
Great Gth. TS14: Guis 2D **139**
GREATHAM 3E **31**
Greatham Cl. TS5: Midd. 2C **130**
Greatham St.
TS25: H'pool 1C **20**
Green, The TS4: Midd 3A **102**
TS10: Redc 1E **63**
TS11: M Sea 4B **66**
TS12: Salt 1B **88**
TS15: K'ton 4D **161**
TS16: Egg 2C **148**
TS17: T Tee 1C **128**
TS20: Nort. 4A **54**
TS21: L New 1A **124**
TS22: Wolv 2C **38**
TS23: Bill 4D **55**
TS23: C Bew 4C **40**
TS25: Grea 3E **31**
TS25: S Car 3E **21**
TS27: Elw 4D **11**
Greenabella Marsh
(Nature Reserve) 1D **43**
Greenacre Cl. TS9: G Ayt . . . 3C **166**
TS11: M Sea 4C **66**
Greenacres TS8: Stain 5B **130**
Greenbank Av. TS5: Midd . . . 1B **100**
Green Bank Cl. TS12: Boo . . 2B **112**
Greenbank Ct.
TS26: H'pool 3E **13**
Greenbank Ter.
TS12: Boo 2B **112**
Green Cl. TS7: Nun 4A **134**
Greencroft TS10: Redc 3A **64**
Greencroft Wlk.
TS3: Midd 3E **103**
Green Dragon Mus. 5B **74**
Green Dragon Yd.
TS18: S Tee 5B **74**
Greenfield Dr. TS16: Eag . . 5B **126**
Greenfields Way
TS18: S Tee 1A **96**
Greenfinch Cl. TS26: H'pool. . . 5E **7**
Greenford Wlk. TS3: Midd . . 2A **104**
Greenham Cl. TS3: Midd . . . 2A **104**
Greenhead Cl. TS8: Hem . . . 3E **131**
Greenhow Gro.
TS25: S Car 4E **21**
Greenhow Rd. TS3: Midd . . . 1C **102**
Greenhow Wlk.
TS10: Redc 2B **64**
Greenland Av. TS5: Midd . . . 2A **100**
Greenland Rd. TS24: H'pool . . . 5C **8**
(not continuous)
Greenlands Rd.
TS10: Redc 5E **49**
Green La. TS5: Midd 4B **100**
TS8: Newb, Nun 5E **155**
TS9: L Ayt 5C **166**
TS10: M Sea, Redc 3A **66**
TS12: Skel 5B **88**
TS15: Yarm 2A **160**
TS17: T Tee 5B **98**
TS19: S Tee 2D **73**
(not continuous)
Green Lea TS27: Elw 4C **10**
Green Leas TS21: Car 5C **50**
Greenlee Cl. TS17: I Bar . . 2A **150**
Greenock Cl. TS11: N Mar . . . 2F **85**
Greenock Rd. TS25: H'pool . . . 4E **19**
Green Rd. TS12: Skel 4B **88**

Green's Beck Rd.
TS18: S Tee 2C **96**
Green Scar TS10: Redc 3E **65**
Greens Gro. TS18: S Tee 2C **96**
Greenshank Cl.
TS26: H'pool 5D **7**
Greenside TS6: Norm 4C **104**
TS17: I Bar 5B **128**
TS25: Grea 3E **31**
Green's La. TS18: S Tee 1C **96**
Greenstones Rd.
TS10: Redc 2E **65**
Green St. TS24: H'pool 5C **14**
Greens Valley Dr.
TS18: S Tee 2C **96**
Green Ter. TS25: S Car 4E **21**
Grn. Vale Gro. TS19: S Tee . . . 1A **96**
Green Way TS7: Nun 4A **134**
Greenway TS6: Est 1E **105**
TS17: I Bar 5B **128**
Greenway, The TS3: Midd . . . 5F **79**
Greenway Ct. TS3: Midd 5F **79**
Greenwood Av. TS5: Midd . . . 3D **101**
Greenwood Rd.
TS18: S Tee 2C **96**
TS23: Bill 1F **55**
TS24: H'pool 2B **14**
Greenwood Wlk.
TS10: Redc 2C **64**
Grenadier Cl. TS18: S Tee . . . 5D **73**
Grendale Ct. TS13: Loft 5C **92**
Grendon Wlk. TS3: Midd . . . 4D **103**
Grenville Cl. TS11: M Sea . . . 5E **67**
Grenville Rd. TS17: T Tee . . . 2D **129**
Gresham Rd. TS1: Midd. 4D **77**
Gresley Cl. TS12: Salt 4C **68**
Greta Av. TS25: H'pool 2A **20**
Greta Rd. TS10: Redc. 5A **48**
TS12: Skel 3C **88**
TS20: Nort. 5A **54**
Greta St. TS1: Midd 4D **77**
TS12: Salt 5C **68**
Gretton Av. TS4: Midd 5B **102**
Grewgrass La.
TS11: M Sea, N Mar . . . 4D **65**
Greylands Av. TS20: Nort . . . 1B **74**
Greymouth Cl. TS18: S Tee . . 2C **96**
Greys Cl. TS17: I Bar 1B **150**
Greystoke Ct. TS5: Midd . . . 4C **100**
Greystoke Gro. TS10: Redc . . 3C **64**
Greystoke Rd. TS10: Redc . . . 3C **64**
Greystoke Wlk. TS10: Redc . . 3C **64**
Greystone Rd. TS6: Gran . . . 2F **81**
Greystones Rdbt.
TS6: O Lac 5B **82**
Grey St. TS20: Nort 2B **74**
Grey Towers Dr. TS7: Nun . . 5A **134**
Grey Towers Farm Cotts.
TS7: Nun 5B **134**
Grey Towers Gdns.
TS7: Nun 2B **156**
Grey Towers Hall
TS7: Nun 2B **156**
Greywood Cl. TS27: H'pool . . . 2C **6**
Gribdale Rd. TS3: Midd 1D **103**
Griffin Rd. TS4: Midd 1A **102**
Griffiths Cl. TS15: Yarm 1B **160**
Griffiths Rd. TS6: Gran 4E **81**
Grimston Wlk. TS3: Midd . . 1B **102**
Grimwood Av. TS3: Midd . . . 4E **79**
GRINDON 3D **35**
Grinkle Av. TS3: Midd 3D **103**
Grinkle Ct. TS14: Guis 1E **139**
Grinkle La. TS13: Eas 5F **117**
Grinkle Rd. TS10: Redc 5F **47**
Grinton Rd. TS18: S Tee 3B **96**
Grisedale Cl. TS5: Midd. . . . 2C **130**
TS16: Egg 2C **148**
Grisedale Cres. TS6: Gran . . . 4F **81**

Gritten Sq. TS24: H'pool 4C **8**
Groom Ter. TS25: H'pool . . . 5A **20**
Grosmont Cl. TS10: Redc. . . . 3C **64**
Grosmont Dr. TS23: Bill 5C **38**
Grosmont Pl. TS6: Est 5F **81**
Grosmont Rd. TS6: Est 5E **81**
TS25: S Car 5E **21**
Grosvenor Ct.
TS17: I Bar 2B **150**
Grosvenor Gdns.
TS6: Norm 2D **105**
TS26: H'pool 3A **14**
(off Grosvenor St.)
Grosvenor Pl. TS14: Guis . . . 2D **139**
Grosvenor Rd. TS5: Midd. . . . 2D **100**
TS19: S Tee. 1C **96**
TS22: Bill 5B **38**
Grosvenor Sq. TS14: Guis . . 2D **139**
Grosvenor St. TS26: H'pool . . 3A **14**
(not continuous)
Grosvenor Ter.
TS13: C How 3F **91**
Grove, The TS5: Midd 3D **131**
TS7: Mart 5D **103**
TS14: Guis 4B **138**
TS15: Yarm 5C **148**
TS25: Grea 3E **31**
TS26: H'pool 3F **13**
Grove Bank TS15: K'ton 4C **160**
Grove Cl. TS26: H'pool 4F **13**
GROVE HILL 5A **78**
Grove Hill TS13: Skin 2A **92**
Grove Rd. TS3: N Orm 4A **78**
TS10: Redc 4D **49**
TS13: Skin. 2A **92**
Groves, The TS18: S Tee. . . . 2F **97**
Groves St. TS24: H'pool 1F **15**
Grove St. TS18: S Tee 2F **97**
(not continuous)
Grove Ter. TS20: Nort 2B **74**
Grundales Dr. TS11: M Sea . . 4C **66**
Guernsey Wlk.
TS14: Guis 3D **139**
Guildford Ct. TS6: Norm . . . 4D **105**
Guildford Rd. TS6: Norm . . . 4C **104**
TS23: Bill. 4C **38**
Guillemot Cl. TS26: H'pool . . . 5D **7**
GUISBOROUGH 2E **139**
Guisborough By-Pass
TS14: Guis 1C **138**
Guisborough Ct. TS6: Est . . . 1F **105**
Guisborough Forest &
Walkway Vis. Cen. 3F **137**
Guisborough Ho.
TS4: Midd 2B **102**
Guisborough La.
TS12: Skel 1F **111**
Guisborough Mus., The 1E **139**
Guisborough Pool 1D **139**
Guisborough Priory (remains)
. . . . 1F **139**
Guisborough Rd.
TS7: Nun 5A **134**
TS9: G Ayt 2C **166**
TS12: Moor 3A **142**
TS12: Salt 5B **68**
Guisborough Sports Cen. . . . 5F **109**
Guisborough St. TS6: Est . . . 2F **105**
Guiseley Way TS16: Eag . . . 3B **126**
Gulliver Rd. TS25: H'pool . . . 2D **19**
Gun Gutter TS13: Stait 1C **120**
Gunnergate Cl. TS12: Salt . . . 4A **68**
Gunnergate La.
TS7: Mart 4C **132**
TS8: C New 4C **132**
Gunnerside Rd.
TS19: S Tee 5A **72**
Gunners Va. TS22: Wyn 4A **26**
Gurney Ho. TS1: Midd 3F **77**

Gurney St. TS1: Midd 3F 77
　TS11: N Mar 1A 86
Guthrie Av. TS5: Midd 3A 100
Guthrie Wlk. TS25: H'pool 4D 19
Gwynn Cl. TS19: S Tee 4A 72
Gypsy La. TS7: Mart, Nun. . . . 3E 133

H

Hackforth Rd. TS18: S Tee 3B 96
Hackness Rd. TS5: Midd 4E 101
Hackworth Ct. TS18: S Tee 4A 74
Hadasia Gdns. TS19: S Tee . . . 5C 72
Haddon Rd. TS23: Bill 5C 38
Haddon St. TS1: Midd. 5F 77
Hadleigh Cl. TS21: Sed 5C 22
Hadleigh Cres. TS4: Midd . . . 2A 102
Hadleigh Wlk. TS17: I Bar . . 5A 128
Hadlow Wlk. TS3: Midd 1D 103
Hadnall Cl. TS5: Midd 5A 100
Hadrian Way TS17: I Bar 4E 127
Hadston Cl. TS10: Redc. 3D 65
Haffron Av. TS18: S Tee 4B 74
Hagg Farm Rdbt.
　TS12: Skel. 2E 89
Hailsham Av. TS17: T Tee . . . 5D 129
Haldane Gro. TS25: H'pool. . . 4E 19
Hale Rd. TS23: Bill 4E 39
Halidon Way TS23: Bill 4F 39
Halifax Cl. TS11: M Sea 4B 66
Halifax Rd. TS17: T Tee 2D 129
Hall Cl. TS11: M Sea 4C 66
　TS21: Car 5C 50
Hall Cl., The TS7: Orm. 4A 104
Hallcroft Cl. TS23: Bill 4D 55
Hall Dr. TS5: Midd 5C 100
Hall Farm Cl. TS22: Wolv. . . . 3B 38
Hallgarth TS9: G Bro. 5F 169
Hallgarth Cl. TS18: Midd . . . 2C 130
Hallgate Cl. TS18: S Tee 3A 96
Hall Grounds TS13: Loft. . . . 5C 92
Hallifield St. TS20: Nort. 2B 74
Hall Lea TS21: Sed 3C 22
Hall Moor Cl. TS15: K'ton . . . 4D 161
Halton Cl. TS23: Bill 2E 39
Halton Ct. TS3: Midd 5A 80
　TS23: Bill 2E 39
Halyard Way TS3: Midd 2B 78
Hambledon Cres.
　TS12: Skel. 3C 88
Hambledon Rd.
　TS5: Midd 2B 100
Hambleton Av. TS10: Redc. . . . 2A 64
Hambleton Cres.
　TS11: M Sea 5E 67
Hambleton Ga. TS9: Stok. . . . 2C 168
Hambletonian Yd.
　TS18: S Tee. 1A 98
　(off West Row)
Hambleton Rd. TS7: Nun . . . 3B 134
Hambleton Sq. TS23: Bill 1C 54
Hamilton Ct. TS21: T The 2E 51
Hamilton Gro. TS6: Norm . . . 5B 80
　TS10: Redc 4A 48
Hamilton Rd. TS19: S Tee. . . . 3F 73
　TS25: H'pool 4E 19
Hammond Cl. TS7: Mart. 3C 132
Hampden St. TS6: S Ban 3A 80
Hampden Way
　TS17: T Tee 2D 129
Hampshire Grn.
　TS20: Nort. 2C 74
Hampstead, The
　TS10: Redc 2E 65
Hampstead Gdns.
　TS26: H'pool 3E 13
Hampstead Gro.
　TS6: Norm. 4C 104

Hampstead Rd.
　TS6: Norm. 4C 104
Hampton Cl. TS7: Nun 3A 134
Hampton Gro. TS10: Redc . . . 5E 49
Hampton Rd. TS18: S Tee. . . 2E 97
Hamsterley Rd.
　TS19: S Tee 2C 72
Hamsterley Way
　TS12: Skel 3C 88
Hanbury Cl. TS17: I Bar 5B 128
Handale Cl. TS14: Guis 2A 140
Handale Ho. Rd.
　TS13: Eas 5F 117
Handley Cl. TS18: S Tee 1F 127
Hankin Rd. TS3: N Orm 4B 78
Hanover Ct. TS20: Nort. 5F 53
Hanover Gdns. TS5: Midd . . . 2C 100
Hanover Ho. TS12: Salt 3C 68
Hanover Pde. TS20: Nort 5F 53
Hanover Point TS20: Nort. . . . 5F 53
Hanson Ct. TS10: Redc 4C 48
Hanson Gro. TS3: Midd 5F 79
Hanson St. TS10: Redc 4C 48
Hanzard Dr. TS22: Wyn 4E 27
Harbottle Cl. TS17: I Bar . . . 2A 150
Harbourne Gdns.
　TS5: Midd 2D 131
Harbour Wlk. TS25: H'pool . . . 2C 14
Harcourt Rd. TS6: S Ban 3F 79
Harcourt St. TS26: H'pool . . . 3F 13
Hardale Gro. TS10: Redc 1A 64
Harding Row TS20: Nort 1B 74
Hardknott Gro. TS10: Redc . . 5B 48
HARDWICK. 1B 72
Hardwick Av. TS5: Midd. . . . 4C 100
Hardwick Cl. TS26: H'pool . . . 5C 12
Hardwick Hall Country Pk. . . 3A 22
Hardwick Rd. TS6: S Ban 2A 80
　TS19: S Tee 1C 72
　TS21: Sed 3C 22
　TS23: Bill 5F 39
Hardy Gro. TS23: Bill 3D 39
Harebell Cl. TS12: Skel 5B 89
　TS17: I Bar 4B 128
Hare Hills Rd. TS5: Midd . . . 2B 100
Haresfield Way
　TS17: I Bar 5B 128
Hareshaw Cl. TS17: I Bar. . . 2A 150
Harestones TS22: Wyn. 4B 26
Harewood Cres.
　TS19: S Tee 3B 72
Harewood Ho. TS4: Midd . . . 2B 102
Harewood Rd. TS17: T Tee. . . 2D 99
Harewood Way TS10: Redc . . . 2E 65
Harford St. TS1: Midd 5D 77
Harker Cl. TS15: Yarm 5B 148
Harland Pl. TS20: Nort. 5B 54
Harlech Cl. TS6: Est 5E 81
Harlech Ct. TS17: I Bar. 1F 149
Harlech Gro. TS11: N Mar . . . 2A 86
Harlech Wlk. TS26: H'pool . . . 1E 13
Harlow Cres. TS17: T Tee. . . . 5E 99
Harlsey Cres. TS18: S Tee . . . 3C 96
Harlsey Gro. TS18: S Tee . . . 3C 96
Harlsey Rd. TS18: S Tee 3C 96
Harpenden Wlk.
　TS3: Midd 1D 103
Harper Pde. TS18: S Tee 3D 97
Harper Ter. TS18: S Tee 3D 97
Harrier Cl. TS17: T Tee 1C 128
　TS26: H'pool 1D 13
Harriet Ho. TS17: T Tee 1B 98
　(off Sorbonne Cl.)
Harris Ct. TS17: T Tee 4D 99
Harris Gro. TS25: H'pool 4E 19
Harrison Pl. TS24: H'pool 4F 7
Harrison St. TS3: N Orm 4C 78
　(not continuous)

Harris St. TS1: Midd. 3E 77
Harris Wlk. TS14: Guis 3D 139
　(off Hutton La.)
Harrogate Cres.
　TS5: Midd 2E 101
Harrowgate La.
　TS19: S Tee 3A 72
Harrow Rd. TS5: Midd 3C 100
　TS18: S Tee 1E 97
Harrow St. TS25: H'pool 1A 20
Harsley Wlk. TS3: Midd 1D 103
HART. 4F 5
Hart Av. TS26: H'pool 2E 13
HARTBURN 2D 97
Hartburn Av. TS18: S Tee 1D 97
Hartburn Cl. TS5: Midd 1C 130
Hartburn La. TS18: S Tee . . . 2E 97
Hartburn Village
　TS18: S Tee. 3D 97
Hart Cl. TS19: S Tee. 2D 73
Harter Cl. TS7: Nun 4A 134
Hartforth Av. TS5: Midd 2C 130
Hartington Cl. TS17: T Tee . . . 3C 98
Hartington Rd. TS1: Midd. . . . 3E 77
　TS18: S Tee 1A 98
Hartington St. TS13: Loft 4A 92
Hartland Gro. TS3: Midd 3E 103
Hart La. TS26: H'pool. 4A 6
　TS27: Hart 4A 6
Hart La. Cotts.
　TS26: H'pool 2F 13
HARTLEPOOL 4B 14
Hartlepool Art Gallery 3B 14
Hartlepool Art Gallery and
　Info. Cen. 3C 10
　(off Hillcrest Gro.)
Hartlepool Cl. TS19: S Tee. . . 2C 72
Hartlepool Crematorium
　TS25: H'pool 3F 19
Hartlepool Historic Quay . . . 2C 14
Hartlepool Ind. Est.
　TS24: H'pool 5A 8
Hartlepool Power Station Vis. Cen.
　. . . . . 4F 33
Hartlepool Rd. TS21: Sed 1C 24
　TS22: Wyn 1C 24
Hartlepool St Hilda's Parish Church
　. . . . . 1F 15
　(off Church Wlk.)
Hartlepool United FC 3B 14
Hartley Cl. TS26: H'pool. 3A 14
Hartley St. TS26: H'pool. 3A 14
Harton Av. TS22: Bill. 5A 38
Hart Pastures TS27: Hart 4A 6
Hart Reservoirs (Nature Reserve)
　. . . . . 4D 7
Hart Rd. TS27: H'pool 3D 7
Hartsbourne Cres.
　TS11: N Mar 2F 85
Hartside Gdns.
　TS26: H'pool 2D 13
Hartside Gro. TS19: S Tee . . . 2E 73
HART STATION 1D 7
Hartville Rd. TS24: H'pool. . . . 1C 6
Hartwith Dr. TS19: S Tee 5B 52
Harvard Av. TS17: T Tee. 1C 98
Harvester Cl.
　TS25: S Car. 2D 21
Harvester Ct.
　TS7: Mart 1B 132
Harvey Ct. TS10: Redc 1F 63
Harvey Wlk. TS25: H'pool . . . 2D 19
Harwal Rd. TS10: Redc 4A 48
Harwell Cl. TS4: Midd 3A 102
Harwell Dr. TS19: S Tee 3A 72
Harwich Cl. TS10: Redc 2F 65
Harwich Gro. TS25: H'pool. . . 4B 20
Harwood Cl. TS2: Midd 1D 77
Harwood St. TS24: H'pool . . . 1A 14

Highfield Dr. TS16: Eag 5B **126**
Highfield Gdns.
 TS16: Eag 5B **126**
Highfield Rd. TS4: Midd. . . . 1A **102**
 (not continuous)
 TS6: Est. 1E **105**
 TS11: M Sea 4B **66**
 TS18: S Tee 2C **96**
High Force Rd. TS2: Midd . . . 1C **76**
Highgate TS6: Est. 1A **106**
High Gill Rd. TS7: Nun. 2A **134**
High Godfalter Hill
 TS7: Nun 2C **134**
HIGH GRANGE 3D **39**
High Grange Av.
 TS23: Bill 4D **39**
High Grange Ho.
 TS23: Bill 4D **39**
High Grn. TS9: G Ayt 2D **167**
Highland Rd. TS25: H'pool. . . 4E **19**
High La. TS8: Malt 2E **151**
HIGH LEVEN 4B **150**
Highlight, The
 TS24: H'pool 2C **14**
Highmead Wlk.
 TS3: Midd 4D **103**
High Newham Ct.
 TS19: S Tee 1B **72**
High Newham Rd.
 TS19: S Tee 1B **72**
High Peak TS14: Guis 4F **139**
Highpoint Pk. TS24: H'pool . . 2B **14**
High Rifts TS8: Stain 5B **130**
High Row TS13: Loft 4A **92**
High Stone Cl. TS10: Redc. . . 2E **65**
High St. TS2: P Cla 5F **57**
 TS6: Est. 5A **82**
 TS6: Est, Norm 2C **104**
 TS6: Laze 4C **82**
 TS7: Orm 4F **103**
 TS9: G Ayt 2C **166**
 TS9: G Bro. 5F **169**
 TS9: Stok 1B **168**
 TS11: M Sea 3C **66**
 TS12: Boo 2B **112**
 TS12: Brot 2B **90**
 TS12: Ling 3D **113**
 TS12: Moor 2B **142**
 TS12: Skel. 4B **88**
 TS13: Hind 5E **121**
 TS13: Loft 5C **92**
 TS13: Skin. 2A **92**
 TS13: Stait 1C **120**
 TS15: Yarm 2B **148**
 TS18: S Tee 5B **74**
 TS20: Nort. 5B **54**
 TS21: Sed 4D **23**
 TS22: Wolv 2C **38**
 TS24: H'pool 1F **15**
 TS25: Grea 2E **31**
High St. E. TS10: Redc. 3C **48**
High St. W. TS10: Redc 3A **48**
HIGH THROSTON. 1C **12**
High Tunstall Cotts.
 TS26: H'pool 4C **12**
Hilcott Cl. TS17: I Bar 4A **128**
Hilda Pl. TS12: Salt 4C **68**
Hilda Wlk. TS24: H'pool. 4D **15**
Hilden Pk. TS17: I Bar 4A **128**
Hilderthorpe TS7: Nun 3F **133**
Hilderthorpe Cl.
 TS17: I Bar 4A **128**
Hildewell TS13: Hind 5E **121**
Hildyard Cl. TS9: Stok 5B **164**
Hillbrook Cres.
 TS17: I Bar 4A **128**
Hill Cl. TS12: Skel 4B **88**
Hill Cres. TS10: Redc. 5E **47**
Hillcrest Av. TS18: S Tee 1C **96**

Hillcrest Dr. TS7: Nun 2B **134**
 TS13: Loft. 1B **116**
Hillcrest Gro. TS27: Elw. 3C **10**
Hillel Wlk. TS5: Midd. 2D **131**
Hill Ho. Farm TS20: Nort 2B **74**
Hillingdon Rd. TS3: Midd . . . 4D **103**
Hillington Gro.
 TS17: I Bar 4A **128**
Hillmorton Rd.
 TS17: I Bar 4A **128**
Hillocks La. TS12: Moor 3B **142**
Hill Ri. DL2: M Row 4A **144**
Hill Rd. TS23: Bill. 4D **55**
Hills, The TS12: Skel 4B **88**
Hillsford Cl. TS17: I Bar 4A **128**
Hillside Av. TS4: Midd 3F **101**
Hillside Cl. TS11: N Mar. 3F **85**
Hillside Rd. TS20: Nort 4B **54**
Hillston Cl. TS26: H'pool 2C **12**
Hill St. TS10: Redc. 3B **48**
Hill St. E. TS18: S Tee 4C **74**
Hill St. Shop. Cen.
 TS1: Midd 2E **77**
Hills Vw. Rd. TS6: Est 1F **105**
Hill Vw. TS17: I Bar 5A **128**
 TS25: Grea. 4F **31**
Hillview *TS3: Midd.* *3D 103*
 (off Delamere Rd.)
Hill Vw. Ter. TS11: N Mar. . . . 2A **86**
Hillway TS17: I Bar. 4A **128**
Hilston Cl. TS17: I Bar 5A **128**
Hind St. TS18: S Tee 2F **97**
 (not continuous)
Hinton Av. TS5: Midd 1B **100**
Hinton Ct. TS14: Guis 1F **139**
Hirdman Gro. TS24: H'pool . . 2E **7**
Hird Rd. TS15: Yarm 5A **148**
Hive Cl. TS19: S Tee 2F **73**
HM Bark Endeavour (Replica)
 Vis. & Heritage Cen. . . . 1B **98**
HMS Trincomalee 2C **14**
Hobdale Ter. TS12: Skel. 2B **112**
Hob Hill Cl. TS12: Salt 5B **68**
Hob Hill Cres. TS12: Salt 5B **68**
Hob Hill La.
 TS11: Salt, Uple. 3E **87**
Hobson Av. TS10: Redc 2E **63**
Hodges Ho. TS1: Midd 2F **77**
Hodgeson's Yd.
 TS18: S Tee *1B 98*
 (off Finkle St.)
Hodgson Ct. TS6: Est 2F **105**
Hogarth Cl. TS23: Bill. 3D **39**
Holbeck Av. TS5: Midd. 2D **131**
Holbeck Wlk. TS17: T Tee. . . . 3E **129**
Holburn Pk. TS19: S Tee 2D **73**
Holdenby Dr. TS3: Midd. 4D **103**
Holden Cl. TS6: Gran 2D **81**
Holdernesse TS22: Wyn 4A **26**
Holder St. TS10: Redc 4C **48**
Holdforth Cl. TS24: H'pool . . . 5F **7**
Holdforth Ct. TS24: H'pool . . . 5F **7**
Holdforth Rd. TS24: H'pool. . . 5F **7**
Holey Cl. TS8: Hem 4D **131**
Holgate, The TS5: Midd 5D **77**
Holland Rd. TS25: H'pool. . . . 1E **31**
Hollies, The TS10: Redc. 5E **49**
 TS23: Bill 4D **55**
Hollinside TS19: S Tee 2D **73**
Hollinside Rd. TS23: Bill 4F **39**
Hollins La. TS5: Midd 2C **100**

Hollis Ct. TS8: C New. 4B **132**
Hollowfield TS8: C New 3A **132**
 (not continuous)
Hollowfield Sq.
 TS8: C New 4A **132**
Hollybush Av. TS17: I Bar. . . . 4C **128**
Hollybush Est. TS12: Skel . . . 3D **89**
Hollygarth TS9: G Ayt. 2C **166**
Hollygarth Cl. TS9: G Ayt. . . . 2C **166**
Holly Hill Cl. TS7: Orm 5B **104**
Hollyhurst Av. TS4: Midd 3F **101**
Holly La. TS8: Stain 5C **130**
Hollymead Dr. TS14: Guis . . . 1E **139**
Hollymount TS23: Bill. 4D **55**
Hollystone Ct. TS23: Bill. 3E **39**
Holly St. TS1: Midd. 4F **77**
 TS20: Nort. 1B **74**
Holly Ter. TS2: P Cla. 4E **57**
Hollywalk Av. TS6: Norm 3C **104**
Hollywalk Cl. TS6: Norm 3C **104**
Hollywalk Dr. TS6: Norm 2D **105**
Hollywood Bowl
 Middlesbrough 1A **100**
Holmbeck Rd. TS12: Skel. . . . 4E **89**
Holme Ct. TS3: Midd 4F **103**
Holmefields Rd. TS6: Est 3E **105**
Holme Ho. Rd. TS18: S Tee . . 3E **75**
Holme Land TS17: I Bar 3A **128**
Holmes Cl. TS17: T Tee 5B **98**
Holmeside Gro. TS23: Bill . . . 3F **39**
Holmes Nature Reserve, The
 . . . . 1A **128**
Holmside Wlk. TS19: S Tee . . 2C **72**
Holms La. TS21: Car 3C **50**
Holmwood Av. TS4: Midd . . . 3F **101**
Holnest Av. TS3: Midd 2D **103**
Holnicote Cl. TS17: I Bar 3B **150**
Holt, The TS8: C New 3F **131**
Holtby Wlk. TS3: Midd. 1D **103**
 (Fransham Rd.)
 TS3: Midd 4D **103**
 (Hillingdon Rd.)
Holt St. TS24: H'pool 5B **14**
Holwick Rd. TS2: Midd. 2C **76**
Holyhead Cl. TS6: Est 4D **81**
Holyhead Dr. TS10: Redc. . . . 3E **65**
Holyrood Cl. TS17: T Tee 3D **99**
Holy Rood Ct. TS4: Midd 1A **102**
Holyrood Cres. TS27: Hart . . . 4F **5**
Holyrood La. TS4: Midd 1A **102**
Holyrood Wlk. TS25: H'pool . . 4E **19**
Holystone Dr. TS17: I Bar. . . . 2A **150**
Holywell Grn. TS16: Egg 5C **126**
Homebryth Ho. TS21: Sed . . . 3D **23**
Homerell Cl. TS10: Redc 2E **65**
Homer Gro. TS25: H'pool 2E **19**
Homerton Rd. TS3: Midd 1D **103**
Homestall TS21: Sed 1C **22**
Homestead Gth.
 TS17: I Bar 3A **128**
Honddu Ct. TS17: I Bar. 2F **149**
Honey Bee Cl. TS19: S Tee. . . 2F **73**
Honeycombe Av.
 TS19: S Tee 2F **73**
Honey Pot Gro.
 TS19: S Tee 2F **73**
Honeysuckle Cl.
 TS26: H'pool 4D **7**
Honeysuckle Ct.
 TS20: Nort. 1A **74**
Honey Way TS19: S Tee 2F **73**
Hong Kong Rd. TS16: Eag . . . 4F **125**
Honister Cl. TS19: S Tee. 4F **73**
Honister Gro. TS5: Midd 5B **100**
Honister Rd. TS10: Redc. 5B **48**
Honister Wlk. TS16: Eag 1C **148**
Honiton Way TS25: H'pool . . . 5F **19**
Hood Cl. TS24: H'pool 2E **7**

King Edward Ter.
TS11: M Sea 4D **67**
Kingfisher Dr. TS14: Guis . . . 2A **138**
Kingfisher Ho.
TS24: H'pool 3D **15**
Kingfisher Way
TS18: S Tee 5A **98**
TS26: H'pool 5D **7**
King Georges Ter.
TS6: S Ban 1F **79**
King Oswy Dr. TS24: H'pool . . 2D **7**
Kings Ct. TS20: Nort 5B **54**
Kingsdale Cl. TS15: Yarm . . 1B **160**
Kingsdown Way
TS11: N Mar 2A **86**
Kings Ho. TS1: Midd 3F **77**
Kingsley Av. TS25: H'pool. . . 2F **19**
Kingsley Cl. TS6: Gran 4E **81**
Kingsley Rd. TS6: Gran 4E **81**
TS18: S Tee 1C **96**
King's M. E. TS3: N Orm 4B **78**
King's M. W. TS3: N Orm . . . 4B **78**
Kingsport Cl. TS18: S Tee . . . 4D **75**
Kings Rd. TS3: N Orm 4B **78**
TS5: Midd 1C **100**
TS22: Bill 5C **38**
Kingston Av. TS5: Midd . . . 3D **101**
Kingston Rd. TS20: Nort 3B **74**
Kingston St. TS1: Midd 4E **77**
King St. TS6: S Ban 2A **80**
TS10: Redc 3D **49**
TS17: T Tee 3C **98**
TS18: S Tee 5B **74**
TS25: H'pool 1C **20**
Kingsway TS23: Bill 1D **55**
Kingsway Av. TS6: S Ban . . . 4B **80**
Kininvie Cl. TS10: Redc 4C **64**
Kininvie Wlk. TS19: S Tee . . . 1D **73**
Kinkerdale Rd. TS6: Midd . . . 2E **61**
Kinloch Rd. TS6: Norm 1C **104**
Kinloss Cl. TS17: T Tee 1E **129**
Kinloss Wlk. TS17: T Tee . . . 1E **129**
Kinmel Cl. TS10: Redc 3E **65**
Kinross Av. TS3: Midd 3E **103**
Kinross Gro. TS25: H'pool . . . 4D **19**
Kinterbury Cl. TS25: S Car . . 2D **21**
Kintra Rd. TS25: H'pool 4D **19**
Kintyre Dr. TS17: T Tee. . . . 2C **128**
Kintyre Wlk. TS14: Guis. . . . 4C **138**
(off Hutton La.)
Kinver Cl. TS3: Midd 2C **102**
Kipling Gro. TS19: S Tee . . . 1B **96**
Kipling Rd. TS25: H'pool . . . 1E **19**
Kirby Av. TS5: Midd 2B **100**
Kirby Cl. TS6: Est 5A **82**
TS23: Bill. 5F **39**
Kirby Wlk. TS10: Redc 2C **64**
Kirkbright Cl. TS12: Ling . . . 4E **113**
Kirkby La. TS9: G Bro 5F **169**
TS9: Kirk 5D **169**
Kirkdale TS14: Guis 3A **138**
TS17: T Tee 1C **98**
Kirkdale Cl. TS19: S Tee. . . . 4E **73**
Kirkdale Way TS5: Midd 5E **101**
Kirkfell Cl. TS16: Eag 4B **126**
Kirkgate Rd. TS5: Midd 3C **100**
Kirkham Rd. TS7: Nun 3B **134**
Kirkham Row TS4: Midd. . . . 4B **102**
Kirk Hill TS21: Car, Redm. . . 1B **70**
Kirklands, The
TS11: M Sea 3D **67**
Kirkland Way TS3: Midd. . . . 3D **103**
KIRKLEATHAM 5A **64**
Kirkleatham Av.
TS11: M Sea 3D **67**
Kirkleatham Bus. Pk.
TS10: K'ham 4A **64**
Kirkleatham By-Pass
TS10: K'ham, Redc 1A **84**

Kirkleatham La.
TS10: K'ham, Redc 4A **48**
Kirkleatham St.
TS10: Redc 4A **48**
Kirkleavington Hall Dr.
TS15: K'ton 2D **161**
KIRKLEVINGTON 4D **161**
Kirklevington Wlk.
TS17: I Bar 2A **150**
Kirknewton Cl. TS19: S Tee . . . 1D **73**
Kirknewton Gro.
TS17: I Bar 2A **150**
Kirknewton Rd.
TS6: Norm. 2C **104**
Kirk Rd. TS15: Yarm 5E **149**
Kirkstall Av. TS3: Midd 3E **103**
Kirkstall Ct. TS12: Skel 4D **89**
Kirkstone Gro. TS10: Redc. . . 1C **64**
TS24: H'pool 5F **7**
Kirkstone Rd. TS3: Midd . . . 2C **102**
Kirk St. TS21: Stil 2A **50**
Kirkwall Cl. TS19: S Tee 4F **71**
Kirkwood Dr. TS10: Redc . . . 4E **65**
Kirriemuir Rd.
TS25: H'pool 4D **19**
Kitchen Gdn., The
TS26: H'pool 3E **13**
Kittiwake Cl. TS26: H'pool . . . 1D **13**
Knaith Cl. TS15: Yarm 1A **160**
Knapton Av. TS22: Bill 5A **38**
Knaresborough Av.
TS7: Mart 4D **133**
Knaresborough Cl.
TS27: H'pool 3D **7**
Knayton Gro. TS19: S Tee. . . . 1A **96**
Knighton Ct. TS17: T Tee 5E **99**
Knightsbridge Gdns.
TS26: H'pool 3E **13**
Knightsport Rd.
TS18: S Tee 4C **74**
Knitsley Wlk. TS19: S Tee . . . 1C **72**
Knole Rd. TS23: Bill 5E **39**
Knowles Cl. TS15: K'ton. . . . 4C **160**
Knowles St. TS18: S Tee 5B **74**
Kreuger All. TS3: N Orm 4B **78**
Kyle Av. TS25: H'pool 1A **20**

L

Laburnum Av. TS17: T Tee . . . 5C **98**
Laburnum Ct. TS18: S Tee . . . 1F **97**
Laburnum Gro. TS2: P Cla . . . 5F **57**
Laburnum Rd. TS6: Norm . . . 5C **80**
TS7: Orm. 5B **104**
TS10: Redc 4E **49**
TS12: Brot. 2A **90**
TS16: P Tee 2C **126**
Laburnum St. TS26: H'pool . . . 3A **14**
Lacey Gro. TS26: H'pool. . . . 2F **13**
Lackenby La. TS6: Gran 4F **81**
(not continuous)
Lackenby Rd. TS6: Laze 4C **82**
Ladgate Grange
TS3: Midd 2D **103**
Ladgate La. TS3: Midd. 5C **102**
TS4: Midd 5C **102**
TS8: Midd 2E **131**
TS8: Midd 2E **131**
Ladle, The TS4: Midd. 5D **103**
Ladyfern Way TS20: Nort . . . 1F **73**
Lady Hullocks Ct.
TS9: Stok 2B **168**
Lady Mantle Cl.
TS26: H'pool 4C **6**
Ladyport Grn. TS18: S Tee . . . 4C **74**
Ladysmith St. TS25: H'pool . . . 1C **20**
Lagonda Ct. TS23: Bill 5C **40**

Lagonda Rd. TS23: Bill. 5B **40**
Laindon Av. TS6: Midd 1B **132**
Laing Cvn. Site TS10: Redc . . . 4F **47**
Laing Cl. TS6: Gran 2D **81**
Laing St. TS18: S Tee 5A **74**
Laird Rd. TS25: H'pool. 4D **19**
Lakes Av. TS10: Redc. 5C **48**
Lakeston Cl. TS26: H'pool . . . 2D **13**
Lambert Rd. TS24: H'pool . . . 3F **7**
Lambert Ter. TS13: Eas 2A **118**
Lambeth Rd. TS5: Midd 2D **101**
Lambfield Way
TS17: I Bar 3A **128**
Lamb La. TS17: I Bar 1A **150**
Lambourne Dr. TS7: Mart. . . . 2E **133**
Lambton Cres. TS21: Sed 4C **22**
(not continuous)
Lambton Lodge TS21: Sed. . . . 4C **22**
Lambton Rd. TS4: Midd 1A **102**
(not continuous)
TS19: S Tee 4F **73**
TS23: Bill 5F **39**
Lambton St. TS6: Norm . . . 2D **105**
TS24: H'pool 4C **14**
Lammermuir Rd. TS23: Bill . . . 1C **54**
Lamonby Cl. TS7: Nun 4F **133**
Lamont Gro. TS25: H'pool . . . 4C **18**
Lamport Cl. TS18: S Tee 4D **75**
Lamport St. TS1: Midd 4C **76**
Lanark Cl. TS19: S Tee 4B **72**
Lanark Rd. TS25: H'pool 4C **18**
Lanberry Grn. TS4: Midd . . . 1B **102**
Lancaster Cl. TS24: H'pool . . 1B **14**
Lancaster Dr. TS11: M Sea. . . . 3B **66**
Lancaster Ho. TS6: Est. 4E **81**
Lancaster Rd. TS5: Midd . . . 2E **101**
TS16: Eag 4E **125**
TS24: H'pool 1B **14**
Lancaster Rd. Nth.
TS24: H'pool 5B **8**
Lancaster Way
TS17: T Tee 3D **129**
Lancefield Rd. TS20: Nort . . . 4B **54**
Lancelot St. TS26: H'pool . . . 2F **13**
Lanchester Av. TS23: Bill . . . 4C **38**
Lanchester Rd. TS6: Gran . . . 2D **81**
Landseer Dr. TS23: Bill 3D **39**
Lane, The TS21: Sed 3D **23**
Lane End Cotts.
TS15: K'ton 1D **161**
Lanehouse Rd.
TS17: T Tee 4C **98**
Lane Pl. TS6: Gran. 3D **81**
Laneside Rd. TS18: S Tee . . . 2C **96**
LANGBAURGH 5F **157**
Langbaurgh Cl.
TS9: G Ayt. 1D **167**
Langbaurgh Cl. TS12: Salt. . . . 3C **68**
Langdale TS14: Guis 3A **138**
Langdale Cl. TS16: Egg 1B **148**
Langdale Cres. TS6: Gran . . . 5F **81**
Langdale Gro. TS5: Midd . . . 4D **101**
Langdale Rd. TS23: Bill 4E **55**
Langdon Sq. TS8: C New . . . 3B **132**
Langdon Way TS16: Eag. . . . 5A **126**
Langfield Wlk. TS19: S Tee . . 5A **72**
Langleeford Way
TS17: I Bar 2A **150**
Langley Av. TS17: T Tee. . . . 3D **99**
Langley Cl. TS10: Redc 3D **64**
Langley Ct. TS3: Midd 3D **103**
Langmire Rd. TS3: Midd . . . 2C **102**
Langsett Av. TS3: Midd . . . 2C **102**
Langthorne Gro.
TS18: S Tee 2A **96**
Langthorpe TS7: Nun 3F **133**
Langthwaite Wlk.
TS10: Redc 3C **64**

Lowfields Grn.
TS17: I Bar 5B **128**
Lowfields Wlk.
TS17: I Bar 4B **128**
Low Fold TS10: Redc 1B **64**
LOW GRANGE 4E **39**
Low Grange Av. TS23: Bill 2E **39**
Low Grn. TS9: G Ayt 2B **166**
Lowick Cl. TS19: S Tee 4B **72**
Low La. TS5: Midd 3C **130**
TS8: Midd 3C **130**
TS15: T Tee 1E **151**
TS17: H Lev, T Tee 4B **150**
Lowmead Wlk.
TS3: Midd 4D **103**
Lowood Av. TS7: Mart 3C **132**
Lowson St. TS21: Stil 1B **50**
Low Stanghow Rd.
TS12: Ling 5E **113**
Lowther Cl. TS22: Bill 4A **38**
Lowthian Rd. TS26: H'pool . . 3A **14**
LOW THROSTON 1E **13**
Loxley Rd. TS3: Midd 1A **104**
Loyalty Cl. TS25: H'pool 2B **20**
Loyalty Ct. TS25: H'pool 2B **20**
Loyalty M. TS25: H'pool 2B **20**
Loyalty Rd. TS25: H'pool 3B **20**
Loy La. TS13: Loft 5E **93**
(not continuous)
Lucan St. TS24: H'pool 3B **14**
Luccombe Cl. TS17: I Bar . . . 3B **150**
Lucerne Ct. TS7: Mart 2C **132**
Lucerne Dr. TS14: Guis 3B **138**
Lucerne Rd. TS10: Redc 5C **48**
Luce Sands TS5: Midd 3B **130**
Lucia La. TS14: Guis 3C **138**
Ludford Av. TS3: Midd 3D **103**
Ludham Gro. TS19: S Tee 3C **72**
Ludlow Cres. TS10: Redc 1E **65**
Ludlow Rd. TS23: Bill 5D **39**
Luff Way TS10: Redc 2E **65**
Lufton Cl. TS17: I Bar 4E **127**
Lullingstone Cres.
TS17: I Bar 3F **127**
Lulsgate TS17: T Tee 1E **129**
Lulworth Cl. TS10: Redc 3E **65**
Lulworth Gro. TS24: H'pool . . . 2D **7**
Lumley Rd. TS10: Redc 4D **49**
TS23: Bill 5E **39**
Lumley Sq. TS24: H'pool 1F **15**
Lumley St. TS13: Loft 4A **92**
Lumley Ter. TS14: Guis 1F **139**
Lumpsey Cl. TS12: Brot 2B **90**
Lundy Ct. TS17: I Bar 1B **150**
Lundy Wlk. TS14: Guis 3D **139**
(off Hutton La.)
Lunebeck Wlk.
TS17: T Tee 3E **129**
Lunedale Av. TS5: Midd 4D **101**
Lunedale Rd. TS23: Bill 2D **55**
Lune Rd. TS16: Eag 2B **148**
TS20: Nort 1A **74**
Lune St. TS12: Salt 4C **68**
Lustrum Av. TS18: S Tee 3F **75**
Lustrum Bus. Pk.
TS18: S Tee 3E **75**
Lustrum Retail Pk.
TS18: S Tee 3F **75**
Lutton Cres. TS22: Bill 5A **38**
Luttrell Ho. TS3: Midd 2C **102**
Lycium Cl. TS7: Mart 1C **132**
Lydbrook Rd. TS5: Midd 1B **100**
Lydd Gdns. TS17: T Tee 1E **129**
Lynas Pl. TS10: Redc 3C **48**
Lyn Cl. TS17: I Bar 3B **150**
Lyndale TS14: Guis 4A **138**
Lyndon Way TS18: S Tee 5A **72**
Lynmouth Cl. TS8: Hem 4C **130**
Lynmouth Rd. TS20: Nort 4E **53**

Lynmouth Wlk.
TS26: H'pool 1E **13**
Lynnfield Rd. TS26: H'pool . . . 3B **14**
Lynn St. TS24: H'pool 3C **14**
Lynn St. Sth. TS24: H'pool 4C **14**
Lynton Ct. TS26: H'pool 1E **13**
Lynwood Av. TS6: Midd 4E **101**
Lysander Cl. TS11: M Sea 4B **66**
Lytham Wlk. TS16: Eag 5C **126**
Lythe Pl. TS4: Midd 4A **102**
Lythe Wlk. TS6: Est. 5F **81**
Lyttleton Dr. TS18: S Tee 2C **96**
Lytton St. TS4: Midd 4A **78**

M

Macaulay Rd.
TS25: H'pool 2D **19**
McAuley Ct. TS3: Midd 1C **102**
Mac Bean St. TS3: N Orm 4C **78**
McClean Av. TS10: Redc 5F **47**
McCreaton St. TS3: N Orm . . . 5C **78**
McDonald Pl. TS24: H'pool . . . 1F **15**
(off Cliff Ter.)
Mackie Dr. TS14: Guis 1F **139**
Macklin Av.
TS23: Bill, C Bew. 1A **56**
McLean Rd. TS12: Brot 2C **90**
MacNay St. TS12: Salt 4C **68**
Macrae Rd. TS25: H'pool 5C **18**
Madison Sq. TS19: S Tee 4B **72**
Magdalene Dr. TS27: Hart 3F **5**
Magdalen St. TS3: N Orm 4B **78**
Magister Rd. TS17: T Tee . . . 1C **128**
Magnolia Ct. TS10: Redc 4E **65**
TS18: S Tee 1F **97**
Maidstone Dr. TS7: Mart 2E **133**
Mainsforth Dr. TS5: Midd . . . 1D **131**
TS23: Bill 2F **39**
Mainsforth Flats
TS24: H'pool 4D **15**
Mainsforth Ter.
TS24: H'pool 3C **14**
TS25: H'pool 1D **21**
Mainside TS21: Redm 1B **70**
Major Cooper Ct.
TS25: S Car 4E **21**
Major St. TS18: S Tee 4B **74**
Majuba Rd. TS10: Redc 3A **48**
Malcolm Dr. TS19: S Tee 3A **72**
Malcolm Gro. TS10: Redc . . . 5E **49**
TS17: T Tee 5D **99**
Malcolm Rd. TS25: H'pool . . . 5D **19**
Malden Rd. TS20: Nort 5B **54**
Maldon Rd. TS5: Midd 1B **100**
Malham Gill TS10: Redc 1B **64**
Malham Gro. TS17: I Bar 5C **128**
Malin Gro. TS10: Redc 4C **64**
Mallaig Vw. TS19: S Tee 4B **72**
Mallard Cl. TS14: Guis 3A **138**
Mallard Ct. TS10: Redc 1F **63**
Mallard La. TS20: Nort 4A **54**
Mallards, The TS8: Hem 1A **154**
Malleable Way
TS18: S Tee 5D **75**
Malling Rd. TS20: Nort 2B **74**
Malling Wlk. TS3: Midd 1D **103**
Mallory Cl. TS1: Midd 3D **77**
Mallory Rd. TS20: Nort 5A **54**
Mallowdale
TS7: Mart, Nun 4F **133**
Malltraeth Sands
TS5: Midd 2A **130**
Malmo Cl. TS10: K'ham 4F **63**
Malta Rd. TS16: Eag. 4F **125**
MALTBY 1F **151**
Maltby Ct. TS14: Guis 1D **139**
Maltby Ho. TS4: Midd 2A **102**

Maltby Pl. TS17: T Tee 4C **98**
Maltby Rd. TS8: Thor 1A **152**
Maltby St. TS3: N Orm 4C **78**
Maltings, The TS17: H'pool . . 5B **14**
Malton Dr. TS19: S Tee 3A **72**
Malton Ter. TS21: Sed 4D **23**
Malvern Av. TS10: Redc 2A **64**
TS12: Skel 3C **88**
Malvern Cl. TS9: Stok 2B **168**
Malvern Dr. TS5: Midd 2C **130**
TS9: Stok 2B **168**
Malvern Rd. TS18: S Tee 1E **97**
TS23: Bill. 1C **54**
Mandale Ho. TS17: T Tee . . . 3D **99**
TS24: H'pool 2C **14**
Mandale Ind. Est.
TS17: T Tee 2C **98**
Mandale Retail Pk.
TS18: S Tee 4D **75**
Mandale Rd. TS5: Midd . . . 4A **100**
TS17: T Tee 2B **98**
Mandale Rdbt. TS5: Midd . . 4A **100**
Manfield Av. TS5: Midd . . . 2A **100**
Manfield Cl. TS18: S Tee 1F **97**
Manitoba Gdns. TS4: Midd . . . 5A **78**
Manless Ter. TS12: Skel 5B **88**
Manners St. TS24: H'pool . . . 1F **15**
Manning Cl. TS17: T Tee . . . 1D **129**
Manning Way
TS17: T Tee 1D **129**
Mannion Cl. TS6: S Ban 2B **80**
Mannion Pk. Sports & Social Cen.
. . . . 2F **81**
Manor Cl. TS9: Stok 1C **168**
TS22: Wolv 3C **38**
TS27: Elw 4D **11**
Manor Ct. TS12: Moor 3B **142**
TS22: Wolv 3C **38**
Manor Dr. TS15: Hilt. 1E **163**
TS21: Stil 2B **50**
Mnr. Farm Way
TS8: C New 3A **132**
Manor Fld. TS27: D Pie 1E **17**
Manor Flds. TS22: Wyn 3A **26**
Manor Gth. TS15: K'ton . . . 4D **161**
Manor Gth. Dr.
TS26: H'pool 3E **13**
Manor Ga. TS21: L New . . . 1A **124**
Manor Grn. TS6: Norm 1C **104**
Manor Gro. TS9: G Bro 5F **169**
Manor Ho. M.
TS15: Yarm 3B **148**
Manor Pl. TS19: S Tee 4B **72**
Manor Rd. TS26: H'pool 3D **13**
Manorside TS9: Stok 1C **168**
Manor St. TS1: Midd 4D **77**
Manor Wlk. TS21: Stil 2B **50**
Manor Way TS23: Bill 2B **56**
Manor Wood TS8: C New . . . 3F **131**
Mansepool Cl. TS24: H'pool . . 4B **8**
Mansfield Av. TS17: T Tee . . 2D **99**
(not continuous)
Mansfield Rd. TS6: Est. 2E **105**
Manston Ct. DL2: M Geo . . . 1A **144**
Man's Yd. TS13: Stait. 1C **120**
Mapel Ct. TS19: S Tee 3C **72**
Maple Av. TS4: Midd. 3F **101**
TS17: T Tee 5C **98**
Maple Gro. TS12: Brot 2A **90**
TS21: Sed 3D **23**
Maple Lodge
DL2: M Geo. 1D **145**
Maple Rd. TS19: S Tee 3F **73**
Maple Sq. TS10: Redc 4D **49**
Maple St. TS1: Midd. 4F **77**
Mapleton Cl. TS10: Redc 4C **64**
Mapleton Cres.
TS10: Redc 4B **64**

Meadow Vw. Rd.
TS5: Midd 1B **100**
Meadow Wlk. TS21: Car. 5C **50**
Meadway TS10: Redc. 3B **64**
Measham Cl. TS20: Nort 5F **53**
Meath St. TS1: Midd 5C **76**
Meath Way TS14: Guis 3D **139**
Medbourne Gdns.
TS5: Midd 2D **131**
Medina Cl. TS19: S Tee 4B **72**
Medina Gdns. TS5: Midd . . . 2E **131**
Medway Cl. TS12: Skel 2C **88**
Medway Ho. TS23: Bill 4D **55**
Medwin Cl. TS12: Brot 1A **90**
Megarth Rd. TS5: Midd 1D **101**
Meggitts Av. TS10: Redc 2E **63**
Meggitts La. TS10: K'ham . . . 2E **63**
Melbourne Cl. TS7: Mart 3E **133**
Melbourne St. TS1: Midd 4C **76**
TS18: S Tee 5A **74**
Melbreak Gro. TS5: Midd . . . 5B **100**
Meldreth Ho. TS12: Salt. 5C **68**
Meldrum Sq. TS19: S Tee . . . 4B **72**
Meldyke La. TS8: Stain 5C **130**
Meldyke Pl. TS8: Stain 5C **130**
Melford Gro. TS17: I Bar 1B **150**
Melgrove Way TS21: Sed 5C **22**
Melksham Sq.
TS19: S Tee 4B **72**
Mellanby La. TS25: Grea 3E **31**
Mellor St. TS19: S Tee 4F **73**
Melrose Av. TS5: Midd 3C **100**
TS23: Bill. 5E **39**
Melrose Cres. TS14: Guis . . . 2A **140**
Melrose Dr. TS18: S Tee 3E **97**
Melrose Ho. TS1: Midd 3F **77**
Melrose St. TS1: Midd 3F **77**
TS25: H'pool 1A **20**
Melsonby Av. TS3: Midd 3E **103**
Melsonby Ct. TS23: Bill 3A **40**
Melsonby Gro. TS18: S Tee . . 2A **96**
Melton Rd. TS19: S Tee 4B **72**
Melton Wlk. TS8: Hem 4D **131**
Melville Wlk. TS20: Nort 3C **74**
Memorial Dr. TS7: Mart 2D **133**
Mendip Av. TS12: Skel 3C **88**
Mendip Dr. TS10: Redc 2A **64**
Mendip Rd. TS23: Bill 1D **55**
Merchant Ho. *TS24: H'pool* . . *3D* **15**
(off Quayside)
Meredith Av. TS6: Norm 3C **104**
Mereston Cl. TS26: H'pool . . . 2C **12**
Merganser Rd.
TS26: H'pool 5D **7**
Meridian Way TS18: S Tee . . . 5D **73**
Merion Dr. TS11: N Mar 2F **85**
Merioneth Cl. TS17: I Bar . . . 1F **149**
Merlay Cl. TS15: Yarm 1A **160**
Merlin Cl. TS14: Guis 2A **138**
Merlin Rd. TS3: N Orm 4D **79**
TS19: S Tee 4B **72**
Merlin Way TS26: H'pool 4C **6**
(not continuous)
Merriman Grn. TS24: H'pool . . 3D **7**
Merring Cl. TS18: S Tee 1A **96**
Merrington Av. TS5: Midd . . . 2B **130**
Merryweather Ct.
TS15: Yarm 3C **148**
Merry Weather's Yd.
TS14: Guis 2E **139**
Mersehead Sands
TS5: Midd 2B **130**
Mersey Rd. TS10: Redc 4B **48**
Merville Av. TS19: S Tee 1C **96**
Meryl Gdns. TS25: H'pool . . . 5A **20**
Messines La. TS21: Stil 2A **50**
Metcalfe Cl. TS15: Yarm 1B **160**
Metcalfe Rd. TS6: S Ban 3F **79**

Metz Bri. Cvn. Site
TS2: Midd 2C **76**
Metz Bri. Rd. TS2: Midd 2D **77**
Mews, The TS7: Orm 5A **104**
TS11: M Sea 4D **67**
TS16: Eag 3C **126**
Mexborough Cl.
TS19: S Tee 3D **73**
Meynell Av. TS14: Guis 3B **138**
Meynell Ho. TS17: T Tee 1D **129**
Meynell's Cotts.
TS15: Yarm 3B **148**
Meynell Wlk. TS15: Yarm . . . 5B **148**
Miall Ct. TS7: Nun 4F **133**
MICKLE DALES 4E **65**
Mickledales Dr.
TS11: M Sea 4C **66**
Micklemire La.
TS25: Grea 4F **31**
Mickleton Cl. TS16: Eag 5A **126**
Mickleton Rd. TS2: Midd 5C **56**
Micklow Cl. TS10: Redc 3C **64**
Micklow La. TS13: Loft 5C **92**
Micklow Ter. TS13: Loft 5D **93**
Midbourne Rd.
TS19: S Tee 3A **74**
Middle Av. TS23: Bill 4D **55**
Middlebank TS21: T The 2D **51**
Middle Bank Rd.
TS7: Orm 5B **104**
Middlefield Rd.
TS11: M Sea 4B **66**
TS19: S Tee 2C **72**
Middlegate TS24: H'pool . . . 1F **15**
Middleham Rd.
TS19: S Tee 1C **96**
Middleham Way
TS10: Redc 1F **65**
Middle Rd. TS17: I Bar 5B **128**
MIDDLESBROUGH 2E **77**
Middlesbrough Art Gallery . . 5E **77**
Middlesbrough By-Pass
TS1: Midd 2E **77**
TS3: Midd 3A **78**
TS4: Midd 3A **78**
Middlesbrough Cathedral . . 5C **132**
Middlesbrough FC 2B **78**
Middlesbrough Football Academy
. . . . 4C **80**
*Middlesbrough Football
Community Cen.* 4C **80**
MIMA 3F **77**
Middlesbrough Leisure Pk. . . 3A **78**
Middlesbrough Rd.
TS6: S Ban 3F **79**
TS7: Nun, Guis 2D **135**
TS14: Guis 2E **137**
TS17: T Tee 2D **99**
Middlesbrough Rd. E.
TS6: S Ban 2A **80**
(not continuous)
*Middlesbrough Tennis &
Badminton Club* 1A **102**
Middlesbrough Wharf Trad. Est.
TS2: Midd 5E **57**
(not continuous)
Middle St. TS18: S Tee 5A **74**
MIDDLETON 1C **14**
Middleton Av. TS5: Midd . . . 3B **100**
TS17: T Tee 3C **128**
TS22: Bill. 5B **38**
Middleton Cl. TS16: Eag. . . . 5F **125**
Middleton Ct. TS15: Yarm . . . 5C **148**
Middleton Dr. TS14: Guis . . . 3F **139**
Middleton Grange La.
TS24: H'pool 3B **14**
(not continuous)
Middleton Grange Shop. Cen.
TS24: H'pool 4B **14**

Middleton La.
DL2: M Geo 3A **144**
MIDDLETON ONE ROW 4A **144**
MIDDLETON-ON-LEVEN 4F **163**
Middleton Rd.
TS24: H'pool 2B **14**
Middleton Wlk.
TS18: S Tee 1F **97**
Middleway TS17: T Tee 2C **98**
Middlewood Cl.
TS27: H'pool 2C **6**
Middridge Gro. TS23: Bill . . . 3F **39**
Midfield, The TS5: Midd 5D **77**
Midfield Vw. TS19: S Tee . . . 4B **72**
Midhurst Rd. TS3: Midd 1A **104**
Midlothian Rd.
TS25: H'pool 4C **18**
Midville Wlk. TS3: Midd 2A **104**
Miers Av. TS24: H'pool 4F **7**
Milbank Rd. TS24: H'pool . . . 1B **14**
Milbank St. TS6: S Ban 2A **80**
TS18: S Tee 5A **74**
Milbank Ter. TS10: Redc 3C **48**
Milbourne Ct. TS21: Sed . . . 2C **22**
Milburn Cres. TS20: Nort . . . 2A **74**
Mildenhall Cl.
TS25: H'pool 2E **31**
Mildred St. TS26: H'pool . . . 2A **14**
MILE HOUSE 2E **73**
Miles St. TS6: S Ban 2B **80**
Milfoil Cl. TS7: Mart. 2B **132**
Milford Ho. TS3: Midd 4D **79**
Milholme Av. TS12: Skel 3D **89**
Mill, The TS9: G Ayt. 2D **167**
Millais Gro. TS23: Bill 2D **39**
Millbank TS13: Skin 4F **91**
Millbank Cl. TS27: Hart 3A **6**
Millbank Ct. TS18: S Tee . . . 5A **74**
Millbank La. TS17: T Tee . . . 1C **128**
Millbank Ter. TS21: Whit 3A **50**
Millbeck Ho. TS20: Nort 5B **54**
Millbeck Way TS7: Orm 4B **104**
Millbrook Av. TS3: Midd 4F **79**
(not continuous)
Millclose Wlk. TS21: Sed . . . 1D **23**
Mill Cotts. TS21: T The 2D **51**
Mill Ct. TS23: Bill 5E **55**
TS25: Grea 3E **31**
Millennium Ct. TS9: Stok . . . 2E **169**
Miller Cl. TS15: Yarm 5D **149**
Miller Cres. TS24: H'pool . . . 3D **7**
Millers La. TS12: Ling 2A **142**
Millfield Cl. TS16: Eag 1B **148**
TS17: T Tee 3E **99**
Millfield Rd. TS3: N Orm 5C **78**
Millford Rd. TS20: Nort 1F **73**
Millgin Ct. TS17: I Bar 4B **128**
Millholme Cl. TS12: Brot 3A **90**
Millholme Dr. TS12: Brot 3A **90**
Millholme Rdbt. TS12: Brot . . 4F **89**
Millholme Ter. TS12: Brot . . . 3A **90**
Mill House Leisure Cen. . . . 3B **14**
Millington Cl. TS23: Bill 1F **39**
Mill La.
DL2: L New, M Geo 1A **144**
(not continuous)
TS20: Nort. 4B **54**
TS21: Bis, Stil, Whit 4A **50**
TS21: L New 1A **144**
TS23: Bill. 4E **55**
Mill Mdw. Ct. TS20: Nort . . . 5B **54**
Millpool Ct. TS24: H'pool . . . 5C **8**
Mill Riggs TS9: Stok 1C **168**
Mills St. TS1: Midd 4C **76**
Millston Ct. TS26: H'pool . . . 2C **12**
Millstone Cl. TS10: Redc . . . 3E **65**
Mill St. TS14: Guis 2E **139**
TS20: Nort. 5A **54**
Mill St. E. TS18: S Tee 5B **74**

Mill St. W. TS18: S Tee 5A **74**
(not continuous)
Mill Ter. TS9: G Ayt 2C **166**
TS21: T The 2D **51**
TS25: Grea 3E **31**
Mill Vw. TS13: Loft 5B **92**
Mill Wynd TS15: Yarm 3B **148**
Milner Gro. TS24: H'pool 2B **14**
Milner Rd. TS20: Nort 4A **54**
Milne Wlk. TS25: H'pool 4C **18**
Milton Cl. TS12: Brot 1A **90**
Milton Ct. TS1: Midd 3D **77**
Milton Rd. *TS26: H'pool 3B 14*
(off Barbara Mann Ct.)
TS26: H'pool 3A **14**
(Thornville Rd.)
Milton St. TS12: Salt 4C **68**
Minch Rd. TS25: H'pool 5D **19**
Minerva M. TS15: Yarm 3C **148**
Miniott Wlk. TS8: Hem 4D **131**
Minskip Cl. TS14: Guis 5E **109**
Minsterley Dr. TS5: Midd 3A **100**
Missenden Gro.
TS3: Midd 3F **103**
Mitchell Av. TS17: T Tee 1D **129**
Mitchell St. TS26: H'pool 4A **14**
Mitford Cl. TS7: Orm 4B **104**
Mitford Ct. TS21: Sed 2C **22**
Mitford Cres. TS19: S Tee . . . 2A **72**
Moat, The TS23: Bill 1A **56**
Moat St. TS18: S Tee 1B **98**
Moffat Rd. TS25: H'pool 5C **18**
Monach Rd. TS25: H'pool 5D **19**
Monarch Gro. TS7: Mart 2E **133**
Mond Cres. TS23: Bill 5D **55**
Mond Ho. TS3: Midd 2D **103**
Monkland Cl. TS1: Midd 3E **77**
Monkseaton Dr. TS22: Bill . . . 5C **38**
Monkton Ri. TS14: Guis 5F **109**
Monkton Rd. TS25: H'pool . . . 5E **18**
Monmouth Dr. TS16: Eag 5C **126**
Monmouth Gro.
TS26: H'pool 5E **7**
Monmouth Rd. TS6: Est 4D **81**
Monreith Av. TS16: Eag 5C **126**
Montague St. TS1: Midd 3A **78**
TS24: H'pool 5F **9**
Montagu's Harrier
TS14: Guis 2B **138**
Montgomery Gro.
TS26: H'pool 1E **13**
Montreal Pl. TS4: Midd 1A **102**
Montrose Cl. TS7: Mart 3C **132**
Montrose St. TS1: Midd 3F **77**
TS12: Salt 5C **68**
Moorbeck Way TS7: Orm . . . 4B **104**
Moorberries TS15: Hilt 1F **163**
Moor Cl. TS12: Moor 3B **142**
TS15: K'ton 4D **161**
Moorcock Cl. TS6: Est 2F **105**
Moorcock Row
TS12: Ling 3D **113**
Moore St. TS10: Redc 3D **49**
TS24: H'pool 1A **14**
Moorgate TS6: Est 1A **106**
Moor Grn. TS7: Nun 5A **134**
Moorhen Rd. TS26: H'pool . . . 1D **13**
Moorholm La. TS13: Live 5E **115**
Moorhouse Est.
TS18: P Tee 5D **97**
Moor Pde. TS24: H'pool 5F **9**
Moor Pk. TS7: Nun 4A **134**
TS16: Eag 1C **148**
Moor Rd. TS3: N Orm 3B **78**
MOORSHOLM 3B **142**
Moorsholm Way
TS10: Redc 2C **64**
Moorside Cl. TS10: Redc 4F **65**
Moorston Cl. TS26: H'pool . . . 2C **12**

Moor Ter. TS24: H'pool 1F **15**
Moortown Rd. TS4: Midd 4A **102**
TS11: N Mar 2F **85**
Moor Vw. TS6: Norm 3D **105**
TS13: Hind 5E **121**
Moray Cl. TS4: Midd 2A **102**
Moray Rd. TS25: H'pool 1F **73**
Mordales Dr. TS11: M Sea . . . 5E **67**
Moreland Av. TS23: Bill 1D **55**
Moreland Cl. TS22: Wolv 2C **38**
Moreland St. TS24: H'pool . . . 5C **14**
Moresby Cl. TS4: Midd 3B **102**
Morison Gdns.
TS24: H'pool 5F **9**
Morlais Ct. TS17: I Bar 2F **149**
Morland Fell TS10: Redc 1C **64**
Morpeth Av. TS4: Midd 1B **132**
Morrison Rd. TS14: Guis 1F **139**
Morrison St. TS21: Stil 1B **50**
Morris Rd. TS6: Est 2E **105**
Mortain Cl. TS15: Yarm 5E **149**
Mortimer Dr. TS20: Nort 5F **53**
Morton Carr La. TS7: Nun . . . 3C **134**
Morton Cl. TS14: Guis 3C **138**
Morton St. TS26: H'pool 3A **14**
Morven Vw. *TS19: S Tee 4B 72*
(off Mosston Rd.)
Morville Ct. TS17: I Bar 1B **150**
Mosbrough Cl. TS19: S Tee . . . 3D **73**
Mosedale Rd. TS6: Gran 5E **81**
Moses St. TS3: N Orm 4B **78**
Mosman Ter. TS3: N Orm 4C **78**
Mossdale Gro.
TS14: Guis 3A **138**
Moss Gdns. TS8: Hem 4D **131**
Mosston Rd. TS19: S Tee 4B **72**
Moss Way TS18: S Tee 5E **97**
Mosswood Cres.
TS5: Midd 1B **130**
Motherwell Rd.
TS25: H'pool 5D **19**
Moulton Gro. TS19: S Tee . . . 5A **72**
Mount, The TS6: Norm 3C **104**
Mountbatten Cl.
TS24: H'pool 5C **8**
Mount Gro. TS20: Nort 4B **54**
MOUNT LEVEN 4E **149**
Mt. Leven Rd.
TS15: Yarm 4E **149**
MOUNT PLEASANT 2C **74**
Mt. Pleasant TS11: M Sea . . . 4D **67**
TS13: C How 3F **91**
TS14: Guis 4D **109**
TS21: Stil 2A **50**
Mt. Pleasant Av.
TS11: M Sea 4D **67**
Mt. Pleasant Bungs.
TS19: S Tee 5C **52**
Mt. Pleasant Cl.
TS21: Stil 2A **50**
Mt. Pleasant Grange
TS18: S Tee 3A **98**
Mt. Pleasant Gro.
TS21: Stil 2B **50**
Mt. Pleasant Rd.
TS20: Nort 2B **74**
Mt. Pleasant Wlk.
TS21: Stil 2A **50**
Mt. Pleasant Way
TS8: C New 1C **154**
Mountstewart TS22: Wyn 1E **39**
Mountston Cl.
TS26: H'pool 2D **13**
Mowbray Dr. TS8: Hem 4D **131**
Mowbray Gro. TS19: S Tee . . . 2A **72**
Mowbray Ho. TS4: Midd 3F **101**
Mowbray Rd. TS20: Nort 2A **74**
TS25: H'pool 1D **31**

Mowden Cl. TS19: S Tee 3D **73**
Moyne Gdns. TS25: H'pool . . . 5B **14**
Mr Twister's
Hartlepool 4B **20**
Mucky La. TS14: Guis 5B **110**
Muirfield TS7: Nun 4A **134**
Muirfield Cl. TS11: N Mar . . . 2A **86**
TS27: H'pool 2C **6**
Muirfield Rd. TS16: Eag 5C **126**
Muirfield Wlk. TS27: H'pool . . . 2C **6**
Muirfield Way TS4: Midd 4A **102**
Muir Gro. TS25: H'pool 5D **19**
Muker Gro. TS19: S Tee 1A **96**
Mulberry Cl. TS4: Midd 3F **101**
Mulberry Ct. TS14: Guis 5E **109**
Mulgrave Rd. TS5: Midd 2E **101**
TS26: H'pool 3F **13**
Mulgrave Wlk. *TS6: Est 5F 81*
(off Birchington Av.)
TS10: Redc 2B **64**
Mullroy Rd. TS25: H'pool 4C **18**
Munro Gro. TS25: H'pool 5D **19**
Murdock Rd. TS3: N Orm 4F **79**
Muriel St. TS1: Midd 5F **77**
TS10: Redc 4D **49**
TS13: C How 3F **91**
Murray St. TS26: H'pool 3A **14**
Murton Cl. TS17: T Tee 2B **128**
Murton Gro. TS22: Bill 5B **38**
Murton Scalp Rd.
TS12: Boo 3C **112**
Mus. of Hartlepool 2C **14**
Museum Rd. TS24: H'pool . . . 3B **14**
Musgrave St. TS24: H'pool . . . 4D **15**
Musgrave Ter. TS22: Wolv . . . 2C **38**
Musgrave Wlk.
TS24: H'pool 4C **14**
Muston Cl. TS5: Midd 5E **101**
Myrddin-Baker Rd.
TS6: Est 5E **81**
Myrtle Ct. TS17: T Tee 4C **98**
Myrtle Gro. TS17: T Tee 4C **98**
Myrtle Rd. TS16: P Tee 2C **126**
TS19: S Tee 3F **73**
Myrtle St. TS1: Midd 4F **77**
Myton Rd. TS17: I Bar 1A **150**
Myton Wlk. TS8: Hem 4D **131**
Myton Way TS17: I Bar 4F **127**

N

Nab Cl. TS6: Est 2E **105**
Nairnhead Cl. TS8: Hem 4D **131**
Naisberry Est.
TS26: H'pool 2C **12**
Nantwich Cl. TS8: Hem 4D **131**
Napier St. TS5: Midd 5E **77**
TS6: S Ban 2A **80**
TS20: Nort 2B **74**
Naseby Ct. TS12: Brot 3C **90**
TS23: Bill 3A **40**
Nash Gro. TS25: H'pool 2E **19**
Nature's World 2E **131**
Navenby Gro. TS25: H'pool . . . 1D **31**
Navigation Point Shop. & Hotel Cen.
TS24: H'pool 2D **15**
Navigation Way
TS17: T Tee 1E **99**
Navigator Ct. TS18: S Tee . . . 4A **98**
Naylor Rd. TS21: Sed 4D **23**
Neasham Av. TS7: Mart 4D **133**
TS23: Bill 3F **39**
Neasham Ct. TS18: S Tee . . . 5B **74**
Neasham Cl. TS9: Stok 5B **164**
Neasham La. TS9: Stok 5B **164**
Neath Ct. TS17: I Bar 2F **149**
Nederdale Cl.
TS15: Yarm 1B **160**

Needles Cl. TS10: Redc 4B 64
Nelson Av. TS23: Bill 2C 56
Nelson Cl. TS12: Brot. 1C 90
Nelson Ct. TS6: S Ban 2A 80
Nelson Sq. TS20: Nort 5A 54
Nelson St. TS6: S Ban 2F 79
Nelson St. Ind. Est.
   TS6: S Ban 2A 80
Nelson Ter. TS10: Redc 3B 48
   TS18: S Tee 5A 74
Neptune Cen. Swimming Baths
   . . . . 1D 103
Neptune Cl. TS25: S Car 2D 21
Neptune Ho. TS24: H'pool . . . 2D 15
Nesbit Rd. TS24: H'pool 3F 7
Nesham Av. TS5: Midd 2B 100
Nesham Rd. TS1: Midd 4C 76
   TS24: H'pool 5F 9
Netherby Cl. TS15: Yarm . . . 4E 149
Netherby Ga. TS26: H'pool . . . 2E 13
Netherby Grn. TS3: Midd . . . 3E 103
Netherfield Ho.
   TS3: Midd 2A 104
NETHERFIELDS 2A 104
Netherfields Cres.
   TS3: Midd 2A 104
Netley Gro. TS3: Midd 3F 103
Nevern Cres. TS17: I Bar . . . 2E 149
Neville Dr. TS21: Sed 2C 22
Neville Gro. TS14: Guis 3C 138
Neville Rd. TS18: S Tee 3A 76
Neville's Ct. TS5: Midd 3D 101
Newark Rd. TS25: H'pool 1D 31
Newark Wlk. TS20: Nort. 1C 74
Newbank Cl. TS7: Orm 5B 104
Newbiggin Cl. TS16: Eag 5F 125
Newbiggin Rd. TS23: Bill 2E 39
Newbridge Cl. TS5: Midd . . . 4E 101
Newbrook TS12: Skel 5B 88
NEW BROTTON 1A 90
Newburgh Ct. TS23: Bill 1A 56
Newburn Bri. Ind. Est.
   TS25: H'pool 5D 15
Newbury Av. TS5: Midd 2B 100
Newbury Rd. TS12: Brot. 3B 90
Newbury Way TS23: Bill 4F 39
NEWBY 4B 154
Newby Cl. TS5: Midd 4E 101
   TS20: Nort. 5A 54
Newby Gro. TS17: T Tee 4D 99
Newby Ho. TS4: Midd. 2A 102
Newby La. TS8: Newb 4E 153
Newcomen Ct. TS10: Redc. . . 3B 48
Newcomen Grn.
   TS4: Midd 1A 102
Newcomen Gro.
   TS10: Redc 3C 48
Newcomen Rd. TS6: S Ban . . 3F 79
Newcomen Ter.
   TS10: Redc 3B 48
   TS13: Loft 5B 92
New Company Row
   TS13: Skin. 2A 92
Newfield Cres. TS5: Midd . . 1B 130
Newgale Cl. TS17: I Bar 2E 149
Newgate TS6: Est 1F 105
New Grove Ter. TS13: Skin. . . 2A 92
Newham Av. TS5: Midd 4D 101
Newham Cres. TS7: Mart. . . . 3D 133
NEWHAM GRANGE 4E 73
Newham Grange Av.
   TS19: S Tee 4E 73
Newham Grange Leisure Farm
   . . . . 3A 132
Newham Way TS8: C New . . 4F 131
Newhaven Cl. TS8: Hem 4D 131
Newhaven Ct. TS24: H'pool . . 4C 14
Newholm Ct. TS25: H'pool . . 4A 20
Newholme Ct. TS14: Guis . . . 1D 139

Newholm Way TS10: Redc. . . 2B 64
Newick Av. TS3: Midd 1D 103
Newington Rd. TS4: Midd . . . 3A 102
Newlands Av. TS20: Nort 1B 74
   TS26: H'pool 4F 13
Newlands Gro. TS10: Redc . . 5B 48
   (not continuous)
Newlands Rd. TS1: Midd 4A 78
   TS12: Skel. 1A 112
   TS16: Eag 1B 148
Newley Ct. TS3: Midd. 2A 104
Newlyn Grn. TS3: Midd 3E 103
Newlyn Way TS10: Redc 3F 65
Newmarket Av. TS17: T Tee . . 2F 99
Newmarket Rd.
   TS10: Redc 1D 65
NEW MARSKE 1A 86
NEWPORT 4C 76
Newport Cl. TS17: I Bar 2E 149
Newport Cres. TS1: Midd . . . 3E 77
Newport Ho. TS17: T Tee . . . 2B 98
Newport Ind. Est.
   TS1: Midd 4D 77
Newport Rd. TS1: Midd 4C 76
   TS5: Midd 4B 76
Newport Way TS1: Midd. 3C 76
Newquay Cl. TS8: Hem 4D 131
   TS26: H'pool 2E 13
Newquay Dr. TS10: Redc . . . 3B 64
New Rd. TS14: Guis 2E 139
   TS23: Bill 5D 55
New Row TS14: Dun 1D 109
Newsam Cres. TS16: Eag. . . 1B 148
Newsam Rd. TS16: Eag 1B 148
NEW SKELTON 4D 89
NEWSTEAD 3D 139
Newstead Av. TS19: S Tee . . 3D 73
Newstead Farm La.
   TS14: Guis 2C 138
Newstead Rd. TS4: Midd . . . 5A 78
New St. TS17: T Tee 2C 98
NEWTON 4F 73
NEWTON BEWLEY 5F 29
Newton Cl. TS6: Est 2F 105
Newtondale TS14: Guis 3A 138
Newton Dr. TS17: T Tee . . . 2B 128
Newton Gro. TS22: Bill 5B 38
Newton Hanzard Long Dr.
   TS22: Wyn 2B 26
Newton Hanzard Short Dr.
   TS22: Wyn 3C 26
Newton Mall TS1: Midd 3E 77
   (off Cleveland Cen.)
Newton Rd. TS9: G Ayt. . . . 1D 167
   TS10: Redc 2B 64
NEWTON UNDER ROSEBERRY
   . . . . 2C 158
Newton Wlk. TS20: Nort. 3B 74
Newtown Av. TS19: S Tee . . . 4F 73
Nicholson Way TS24: H'pool . . 3E 7
Nicklaus Dr. TS16: Eag. . . . 5C 126
Nidderdale TS12: Skel 2B 88
Nightingale Cl. TS26: H'pool . . 5C 6
Nightingale Dr.
   TS19: S Tee 2C 72
Nightingale Rd. TS6: Est 5E 81
Nightingale Wlk.
   TS20: Nort. 4A 54
Nile St. TS2: Midd 2E 77
Nimbus Cl. TS7: Mart. 2C 132
Nine Acres TS27: Hart 4E 5
Nolan Ho. TS18: S Tee 4A 74
Nolan Pl. TS18: S Tee 4A 74
Nolton Ct. TS17: I Bar 2F 149
Nookston Cl. TS26: H'pool. . . 1D 13
Norcliffe St. TS3: N Orm . . . 4C 78
Norfolk Cl. TS10: Redc 1B 64
   TS25: H'pool 1B 20
Norfolk Cres. TS3: Midd . . . 3F 103

Norfolk Pl. TS3: Midd 1C 102
Norfolk Rd. TS12: Skel 4A 88
Norfolk St. TS18: S Tee 1F 97
Norfolk Ter. TS23: Bill 2F 55
Norham Wlk. TS7: Orm 4A 104
NORMANBY 2D 105
Normanby Ct. TS7: Mart. . . . 3C 132
Normanby Hall Pk.
   TS6: Norm. 3C 104
Normanby Rd.
   TS6: Est, S Ban 1A 80
   TS7: Orm. 3A 104
Norman Ter. TS6: S Ban 2F 79
Nth. Albert Rd. TS20: Nort . . . 3F 53
Northallerton Rd.
   TS17: T Tee 4D 99
Northall St. TS18: S Tee 3E 97
Northampton Ho. TS6: Est . . . 4E 81
Northampton Wlk.
   TS25: H'pool 5B 14
North Av. TS12: Salt 4B 68
Nth. Bank Cres. TS7: Orm . . 5B 104
Northbourne Rd.
   TS19: S Tee 3F 73
Northbrook Ct.
   TS26: H'pool 4E 13
North Cl. TS21: T The 1E 51
   TS27: Elw 3C 10
Northcote St. TS18: S Tee. . . 2F 97
Northdale Ct. TS3: Midd. . . . 1E 103
North Dr. TS7: Orm. 4A 104
   TS26: H'pool 3E 13
North End TS21: Sed 4C 22
Northern Av. TS5: Midd 1B 100
Northern Route TS1: Midd . . 1B 100
   TS5: Midd 1B 100
North Fen TS10: Redc 1B 64
Northfield Cl. TS9: Stok 1B 168
Northfield Dr. TS9: Stok . . . 1B 168
Northfield Rd.
   TS11: M Sea 4B 66
   TS22: Bill. 5C 38
Northfleet Av. TS3: Midd . . . 5E 79
Northgate TS14: Guis 1E 139
   TS24: H'pool 5E 9
Northgate Rd. TS5: Midd . . . 3D 101
North Grn. TS18: S Tee 2A 98
Northiam Cl. TS8: Hem 4D 131
Northland Av. TS26: H'pool. . . 4F 13
North La. TS27: Elw 3C 10
Northleach Dr. TS8: Hem . . . 4D 131
Nth. Liverton Ind. Est.
   TS13: Live 1A 116
Nth. Lodge Rdbt.
   TS14: Guis. 5F 109
Nth. Mt. Pleasant St.
   TS20: Nort. 2B 74
NORTH ORMESBY 4C 78
Nth. Ormesby By-Pass
   TS3: N Orm 3B 78
Nth. Ormesby Rd.
   TS4: Midd 3A 78
Northpark TS23: Bill 2E 39
North Pk. Rd. TS21: Sed . . . 3C 22
Northport Rd.
   TS18: S Tee 4C 74
North Ridge TS12: Skel 3B 88
North Rd. TS1: Midd 2D 77
   TS2: Midd 2D 77
   TS9: Stok 1B 168
   TS13: Loft 5C 92
   TS25: S Car 3E 21
North Row TS6: Laze 4C 82
Nth. Shore Link
   TS18: S Tee 5C 74
Nth. Shore Rd.
   TS18: S Tee 5B 74
North Side TS13: Stait 1C 120
NORTH SKELTON 5E 89

Powell St. TS26: H'pool 5A **14**
Powlett Rd. TS24: H'pool 5A **8**
Pragnell Ct. TS10: Redc 3F **65**
Preen Dr. TS5: Midd 4B **100**
Premier Pde. TS19: S Tee 1A **96**
Premier Rd. TS3: Midd 2D **103**
  TS7: Orm 5A **104**
  TS19: S Tee 5C **72**
Prescot Rd. TS3: Midd 3F **103**
Preseli Gro. TS17: I Bar 2F **149**
Preston Farm Bus. Pk.
  TS18: S Tee 5F **97**
Preston Farm Ind. Est.
  TS18: S Tee 1E **127**
                    (Concorde Way)
  TS18: S Tee 5E **97**
                          (Yarm Rd.)
Preston Hall Mus. 2D **127**
Preston La. TS18: P Tee 1D **127**
                    (not continuous)
PRESTON-ON-TEES 2D **127**
Preston Rd. TS18: S Tee. 1C **96**
Preston St. TS26: H'pool 2A **14**
Preston Way TS9: Stok. 5B **164**
Prestwick Cl. TS4: Midd 4A **102**
Prestwick Ct. DL2: M Geo . . . 1A **144**
  TS16: Eag 1C **148**
Preswick Cl. TS11: N Mar. 2F **85**
Price Av. TS5: Midd 3B **100**
Price Rd. TS10: Redc 1E **63**
Priestcrofts TS11: M Sea 4E **67**
Priestfield Av. TS3: Midd 4E **103**
Primrose Cl. TS14: Guis. 3B **138**
PRIMROSE HILL 3A **74**
Primrose Hill TS13: Skin 2A **92**
Primrose Hill Ind. Est.
  TS19: S Tee 4A **74**
Primrose Rd. TS26: H'pool . . . 4D **7**
Primrose St. TS19: S Tee 4F **73**
Primrose Ter. TS12: Salt 4C **68**
Princeport Rd. TS18: S Tee . . . 4C **74**
Prince Regent St.
  TS18: S Tee 1A **98**
Princes Rd. TS1: Midd 4D **77**
  TS12: Salt 5C **68**
Princess Av. TS18: S Tee 4B **74**
Princes Sq. TS17: T Tee 3D **129**
Princess St. TS2: Midd 2E **77**
  TS17: T Tee 2C **98**
  TS25: H'pool 1F **15**
Prince's Wharf TS17: T Tee . . . 1C **98**
Princeton Dr. TS17: T Tee. 1C **98**
Prior Ct. TS23: Bill 3A **40**
Priorwood Gdns.
  TS17: I Bar 2B **150**
Priory Cl. TS14: Guis 1E **139**
Priory Ct. TS14: Guis 1F **139**
  TS20: Nort. 5A **54**
  TS24: H'pool 5C **8**
                     (Cleveland Rd.)
  TS24: H'pool 1F **15**
                          (Union St.)
Priory Dr. TS8: Stain. 5C **130**
Priory Gdns. TS20: Nort 5A **54**
Priory Gro. TS10: Redc 4A **48**
Priory Pl. TS1: Midd 3E **77**
Priory Rd. TS5: Midd 3A **100**
Priory St. TS1: Midd 3E **77**
Prissick Farm Cotts.
  TS4: Midd 5C **102**
Prissick St. TS24: H'pool 1F **15**
Pritchett Rd. TS3: Midd 3F **103**
Proctor's Ct. TS25: S Car 4F **21**
Progress Ho. TS17: T Tee. 5C **74**
Promenade TS24: H'pool 4D **15**
                     (Mainsforth Flats)
  TS24: H'pool 1F **15**
                         (South Cres.)
Prospect, The TS5: Midd 3E **101**

Prospect Pl. TS12: Ling 4E **113**
  TS12: Skel. 5A **88**
  TS14: Guis 2E **139**
  TS20: Nort. 2B **74**
Prospect Ter. TS6: Est. 1F **105**
  TS11: M Sea 4D **67**
  TS12: Ling. 4E **113**
Prospect Way
  TS25: H'pool 4B **20**
Protear Gro. TS20: Nort 4C **54**
PS Wingfield Castle. 2C **14**
Puddlers Rd. TS6: S Ban 1A **80**
Pulford Rd. TS20: Nort. 5F **53**
Pump La. TS15: K'ton. 4E **161**
Punch St. TS1: Midd. 3C **76**
Purfleet Av. TS3: Midd 4E **79**
Pursglove Ter.
  TS14: Guis. 1F **139**
Purves St. TS19: S Tee. 4A **8**
Pybus Pl. TS10: Redc. 3C **48**
Pym St. TS6: S Ban 3A **80**
Pytchley Rd. TS14: Guis. 3E **139**

Q

Quarry Bank Rd.
  TS11: Uple 4C **86**
Quarry Dr. TS8: Stain 5C **130**
Quarry La.
  TS11: M Sea, Uple 1D **87**
                    (not continuous)
Quarry La. Rdbt.
  TS11: M Sea 1D **87**
Quarry Rd. TS16: P Tee 3D **127**
Quayside TS18: S Tee. 1B **98**
  TS24: H'pool 3D **15**
Quebec Gro. TS4: Midd 1A **102**
  TS23: Bill 3E **39**
Quebec Rd. TS18: S Tee. 3D **97**
Queen Anne Ter.
  TS18: S Tee 2D **97**
Queen Elizabeth Way
  TS17: I Bar 3F **127**
  TS18: S Tee 2A **128**
Queens Av. TS17: T Tee 3C **98**
Queensberry Av.
  TS26: H'pool 4F **13**
Queensbury Cl.
  TS10: Redc 3A **64**
Queens Ct. TS24: H'pool. 4F **7**
                     (off Warren Rd.)
Queens Dr. TS9: Stok. 5C **164**
  TS21: Sed 5B **22**
  TS22: Bill. 5C **38**
Queensland Av.
  TS10: Redc 5D **49**
Queensland Gro.
  TS18: S Tee 2D **97**
Queensland Rd.
  TS25: H'pool 4A **20**
Queens Mdw. Bus. Pk.
  TS25: H'pool 1F **31**
Queen's Pde. TS24: H'pool . . . 4B **14**
Queensport Cl.
  TS18: S Tee 4D **75**
Queens Rd. TS5: Midd 2D **101**
  TS13: Loft 4B **92**
Queens Sq. TS2: Midd 2F **77**
Queens Ter. TS2: Midd 2F **77**
  TS2: P Cla 5F **57**
Queen St. TS6: Laze 4C **82**
  TS6: S Ban 2A **80**
  TS10: Redc 3B **48**
  TS12: Boo 3B **112**
  TS13: C How 3F **91**
  TS18: S Tee 5B **74**
  TS24: H'pool 1F **15**
                          (Princess St.)

Queen St. TS24: H'pool 2D **15**
                          (Slake Ter.)
  TS25: S Car 3E **21**
Queen's Wlk. TS18: S Tee 5B **74**
Queensway TS3: N Orm 3E **79**
  TS12: Salt 4A **68**
  TS23: Bill 1D **55**
                    (not continuous)
  TS25: Grea 3E **31**
Queensway Ct. TS3: N Orm . . 3E **79**
Queensway Ho.
  TS3: N Orm. 4E **79**
Queen Ter. TS25: S Car 4E **21**
Quenby Rd. TS23: Bill. 5E **39**
Quorn Cl. TS14: Guis 4E **139**

R

Raby Cl. TS27: Hart 4A **6**
Raby Gdns. TS24: H'pool 1F **13**
Raby Rd. TS10: Redc 5E **49**
  TS18: S Tee 1D **97**
  TS24: H'pool 1A **14**
Raby Sq. TS24: H'pool 1A **14**
Raby St. TS24: H'pool. 1F **15**
Racecourse, The
  TS22: Wyn 5F **25**
Race Ter. TS9: G Ayt 2C **166**
Radcliffe Av. TS19: S Tee 1E **73**
Radcliffe Cres. TS17: T Tee . . . 1C **98**
Radcliffe Ter. TS24: H'pool. . . . 1F **15**
Radford Cl. TS19: S Tee. 4D **53**
Radlett Av. TS19: S Tee 1D **73**
Radnor Cl. TS19: S Tee. 1D **73**
Radnor Grn. TS3: Midd. 4E **103**
Radnor Gro. TS26: H'pool . . . 1D **13**
Radstock Av. TS19: S Tee 5E **53**
Radyr Cl. TS19: S Tee. 4C **52**
Raeburn St. TS26: H'pool 3F **13**
Rafton Dr. TS27: H'pool 2D **7**
Raglan Cl. TS19: S Tee. 4C **52**
Raglan Ter. TS23: Bill. 5E **39**
Ragpath La. TS19: S Tee 4D **53**
RAGWORTH 1F **73**
Ragworth Pl. TS20: Nort 4A **54**
Ragworth Rd. TS20: Nort. 5A **54**
Railway Cotts. TS7: Nun 3B **134**
  TS11: M Sea 5B **66**
  TS12: Skel 2C **88**
  TS13: C How 3E **91**
  TS13: Loft 5D **93**
  TS13: Skin. 3A **92**
  TS16: Eag 2B **148**
Railway Ho's. TS2: P Cla 1A **78**
Railway Pl. TS6: Gran 3D **81**
Railway St. TS18: S Tee 3B **74**
Railway Ter. TS12: Brot 3B **90**
  TS12: Skel 4F **89**
  TS13: Loft. 1D **117**
                          (Jackson St.)
  TS13: Loft. 5B **92**
                          (Station Rd.)
  TS16: Eag 3C **126**
  TS17: T Tee 2C **98**
Rainbow Leisure Cen. 4B **132**
Raincliffe Ct. TS8: C New. . . . 4B **132**
Rainford Av. TS19: S Tee 1E **73**
Rainham Cl. TS3: Midd 5A **80**
  TS17: I Bar 2B **150**
Rainsford Cres. TS3: Midd . . . 5F **79**
Rainton Av. TS5: Midd 1C **130**
Rainton Dr. TS17: T Tee 2B **128**
Rainton Gro. TS18: S Tee. . . . 2A **96**
Raisbeck Cl. TS11: M Sea . . . 4C **66**
Raisby Cl. TS5: Midd 3B **130**
Raisdale Cl. TS17: T Tee 1D **129**
Raisegill Cl. TS3: Midd 1B **102**
Raithwaite Cl. TS14: Guis . . . 1D **139**

Raithwaite Ho.
TS14: Guis. 1E **139**
Rake Av. TS19: S Tee. 5D **53**
Raleigh Cl. TS11: M Sea 5F **67**
Raleigh Ct. TS2: Midd 2C **76**
(not continuous)
Raleigh Rd. TS20: Nort 1A **74**
Raleigh Wlk. TS20: Nort 1A **74**
Ralfland Way TS7: Nun 4A **134**
Ralph Sq. TS19: S Tee. 3D **73**
Rampside Av. TS19: S Tee. . . . 4D **53**
Ramsbury Av.
TS19: S Tee. 5D **53**
Ramsey Cres.
TS15: Yarm 5B **148**
Ramsey Gdns.
TS17: I Bar 2E **149**
Ramsey Rd. TS10: Redc. 1F **63**
Ramsey Vw. TS20: Nort 1C **74**
Ramsey Wlk.
TS14: Guis 3D 139
(off Hutton La.)
Ramsgate TS14: Guis 1A **98**
Randolph St. TS12: Salt. 5C **68**
Raskelf Av. TS19: S Tee 1D **73**
Rathnew Av. TS19: S Tee 5C **52**
Raunds Av. TS19: S Tee 1D **73**
Raven Cl. TS14: Guis 3A **138**
Ravendale Rd. TS3: Midd. . . . 2F **103**
Raven La. TS20: Nort. 4A **54**
Ravenscar Cres.
TS19: S Tee 1F **73**
Ravenscroft Av.
TS5: Midd 3E **101**
Ravensdale Rd. TS5: Midd . . . 2B **130**
Ravensworth Av.
TS6: Norm. 1C **104**
Ravensworth Cres.
TS24: H'pool 1D **7**
Ravensworth Gro.
TS18: S Tee 2A **96**
Ravensworth Rd. TS23: Bill . . . 5E **39**
Ravenwood Cl. TS27: H'pool . . . 2B **6**
Rawcliffe Av. TS5: Midd 3C **130**
Rawley Dr. TS10: Redc. 3A **64**
Rawlings Ct. TS24: H'pool 4A **8**
Rawlinson Av. TS23: Bill. 4E **55**
Rawlinson St. TS13: C How . . . 2F **91**
Ray Ct. TS19: S Tee 1C **72**
Raydale TS8: Hem 5D **131**
Raydale Beck TS17: I Bar. . . . 3B **150**
Raylton Av. TS7: Mart 4D **133**
Reading Rd. TS20: Nort. 2A **74**
Rear High St. TS12: Skel 4B **88**
Rear Norton Rd.
TS18: S Tee. 5A 74
(off Norton Rd.)
Recreation Vw.
TS12: Moor 3B **142**
Rectory Av. TS14: Guis 2D **139**
Rectory Cl. TS14: Guis 2D **139**
Rectory La. TS14: Guis 3D **139**
TS21: L New 1A **124**
Rectory La. Ind. Est.
TS14: Guis. 3E **139**
Rectory Row TS21: Sed 4D **23**
Rectory Way TS25: S Car 5E **21**
Redbrook Av. TS19: S Tee 5D **53**
REDCAR. 3C **48**
Redcar Av. TS11: M Sea. 4B **66**
TS19: S Tee. 1E **73**
Redcar Cl. TS25: H'pool. 5A **14**
Redcar La. TS10: Redc 4D **49**
Redcar Leisure Cen. 3B **48**
Redcar Racecourse 5C **48**
Redcar Rd. TS6: Ban. 2A **80**
TS10: Redc, M Sea 3E **65**
TS11: M Sea 3A **66**
TS14: Dun, Guis 5D **85**

Redcar Rd. TS14: Guis 1E **139**
TS17: T Tee 5C **98**
(not continuous)
Redcar Rd. E. TS6: S Ban 2B **80**
Redcar St. TS2: Midd 2F **77**
Redditch Av. TS19: S Tee 5E **53**
Rede Ho. TS1: Midd 3F **77**
Redesdale Ct. TS2: Midd. 5D **57**
Redesdale Gro.
TS17: I Bar 2A **150**
Red Hall La. TS15: Cast. 3A **162**
Redhill Rd. TS19: S Tee 1D **73**
Red Ho. TS19: S Tee 5D **53**
Redland St. TS18: S Tee. 1A **96**
Red Lion St. TS10: Redc 3C **48**
REDMARSHALL. 1B **70**
Redmarshall Rd. TS21: Bis . . . 1A **70**
TS21: S Tee 3E **71**
TS21: Whit 3A **50**
Redmarshall St. TS21: Stil. . . . 2A **50**
Redmayne Cl. TS23: Bill. 4E **39**
Redmire Rd. TS18: S Tee. 1D **97**
Redruth Av. TS19: S Tee 1E **73**
Redshank Cl. TS26: H'pool . . . 5D **7**
Redstart Cl. TS26: H'pool. . . . 5E **7**
Redwing La. TS20: Nort 3B **54**
Redwing Rising TS14: Guis. . . 2B **138**
Redwood Cl. TS27: H'pool 1C **6**
Redwood Ct. TS7: Mart 2E **133**
Redwood Dr. TS12: Salt 5A **68**
Redworth Rd. TS23: Bill 5F **39**
Redworth St. TS24: H'pool 4C **14**
Redworth Wlk.
TS24: H'pool 4C **14**
Reed Cl. TS20: Nort 1C **74**
Reedsdale Cl. TS10: Redc 4F **65**
Reedston Rd. TS26: H'pool . . . 2C **12**
Reed St. TS17: T Tee 2C **98**
Reef Ho. TS24: H'pool 2C **14**
Reepham Cl. TS19: S Tee. 5C **52**
Reeth Rd. TS18: S Tee 3C **96**
Regal Ct. TS25: S Car 5F **21**
Regency Av. TS6: Norm 3D **105**
Regency Dr. TS25: H'pool 3B **20**
Regency Pk. TS17: I Bar 2C **150**
Regency W. Mall
TS18: S Tee 1A 98
(off West Row)
Regent Cinema
Redcar 3C **48**
Regent Ct. TS6: Gran 4E **81**
Regent M. *TS18: S Tee. 1A 98*
(off Prince Regent St.)
Regent Rd. TS4: Midd 2A **102**
Regent Sq. TS24: H'pool 1F **15**
Regent St. TS18: S Tee. 5A **74**
TS24: H'pool 1F **15**
Regent Wlk. TS10: Redc 3C **48**
Reid Ter. TS14: Guis. 1E **139**
Reigate Av. TS5: Midd 3E **101**
Reigate Cl. TS19: S Tee 5D **53**
Relton Way TS26: H'pool 3E **13**
Renfrew Rd. TS20: Nort 5B **54**
Rennie Rd. TS6: S Ban 4F **79**
Renown Wlk. TS6: S Ban 3B **80**
Renvyle Av. TS19: S Tee. 5C **52**
Repton Av. TS19: S Tee 1D **73**
Repton Rd. TS3: Midd 5A **80**
Resolution, The TS7: Nun . . . 3A **134**
Resource Cl. TS6: S Ban 3B **80**
Retford Cl. TS19: S Tee 5D **53**
Retford Gro. TS25: H'pool . . . 5E **19**
Rettendon Cl. TS19: S Tee . . . 5E **53**
Revesby Rd. TS3: Midd 3F **103**
Reynolds Ct. TS23: Bill 3D **39**
Reynoldston Av.
TS19: S Tee. 4D **53**
Rhinog Gro. TS17: I Bar 5F **127**

Rhobell Vw. TS17: I Bar 5E **127**
Rhodes Ct. TS17: T Tee 2D **129**
Rhondda Av. TS19: S Tee 1E **73**
Rhoosegate TS17: T Tee. 5E **99**
Rhyl Cl. TS19: S Tee. 5E **53**
Ribble Cl. TS22: Bill. 4A **38**
Ribbleton Cl. TS7: Mart 3F **133**
Ribchester Cl. TS19: S Tee . . . 5D **53**
Riccarton Cl. TS19: S Tee. . . . 5C **52**
Richard Ct. TS26: H'pool 4A **14**
Richard Hind Wlk.
TS18: S Tee 3F **97**
Richard Ho. TS17: T Tee. 1B **98**
Richardson Rd.
TS17: S Tee 5B **98**
TS18: S Tee 2F **97**
Richardson St.
TS26: H'pool 2A **14**
Richards Ter. TS12: Skel 4F **89**
Richard St. TS26: H'pool 4A **14**
Richmond Cl. TS6: Est 1D **105**
Richmond Dr. TS6: Gran 4E **81**
Richmond Cres. TS23: Bill . . . 5E **39**
Richmond Pl. TS17: T Tee . . . 5E **99**
Richmond Rd. TS10: Redc . . . 5E **49**
TS18: S Tee 2E **97**
Richmond St. TS2: Midd 1E **77**
TS18: S Tee 4A **74**
TS25: H'pool 1B **20**
Ricknall Cl. TS5: Midd 2B **130**
Ridge, The TS8: C New 2B **154**
TS12: Salt 1C **88**
Ridge La. TS13: Stait 5C **118**
Ridgeway TS8: C New 5A **132**
Ridley Av. TS5: Midd 4C **100**
Ridley Cl. TS20: Nort 4A **54**
TS26: H'pool 2A **14**
Ridley Dr. TS20: Nort 5F **53**
Ridley M. TS20: Nort 5B **54**
Ridley St. TS10: Redc 3C **48**
Ridley Ter. TS13: Skin 2A **92**
Ridlington Way
TS24: H'pool 2E **7**
Ridsdale Av. TS19: S Tee 1D **73**
Rievaulx Av. TS23: Bill 5C **38**
Rievaulx Cl. TS19: S Tee 5D **53**
Rievaulx Dr. TS5: Midd 4E **101**
Rievaulx Rd. TS12: Skel 3D **89**
Rievaulx Wlk. TS6: Est 1D **105**
Rievaulx Way TS14: Guis 2F **139**
RIFT HOUSE 2E **19**
Rifts Av. TS12: Salt. 4B **68**
Riftswood Dr. TS11: M Sea . . . 4B **66**
Rigby Ho. TS15: Yarm 4B **148**
Rigg, The TS15: Yarm 5C **148**
Riggston Pl. TS26: H'pool 2D **13**
Riley St. TS18: S Tee 1F **97**
Rillinton Cl. TS19: S Tee 5C **52**
Rillston Cl. TS26: H'pool 2D **13**
Rillstone Way TS10: Redc 4E **65**
Rimdale Dr. TS19: S Tee 4A **72**
Rimswell Pde. TS19: S Tee . . . 4A **72**
Rimswell Rd. TS19: S Tee 3A **72**
Ring Rd., The TS19: S Tee . . . 2E **73**
TS20: Nort. 2E **73**
Rings, The TS17: I Bar 4F **127**
Ringway TS17: T Tee 1E **129**
Ringway Gro.
DL2: M Geo 1A **144**
Ringwood Cres.
TS19: S Tee 1E **73**
Ringwood Rd. TS3: Midd . . . 1A **104**
Ripley Cl. TS3: Midd 5A **80**
Ripley Rd. TS20: Nort. 4F **53**
Ripon Cl. TS19: S Tee 1D **73**
Ripon Rd. TS7: Nun 3B **134**
TS10: Redc 1F **65**
TS12: Brot. 2C **90**
Ripon Way TS6: Est 5F **81**

Rowlands Gro. TS23: Bill 2A **40**
Roworth Rd. TS3: Midd 1A **104**
Roxburgh Cl. TS6: Norm . . . 5B **80**
ROXBY 5E **119**
Roxby Av. TS3: Midd. 4E **103**
  TS14: Guis 4D **139**
Roxby Cl. TS10: Redc. 2C **64**
  TS19: S Tee 1F **73**
  TS25: S Car. 5D **21**
Roxby La. TS13: Stait 5E **119**
Royal George Dr.
  TS16: Eag 4A **126**
Royce Av. TS23: Bill 5B **40**
Royce Cl. TS23: Bill 4B **40**
Royd, The TS15: Yarm 5B **148**
Royston Av. TS3: Midd 4E **103**
Royston Cl. TS19: S Tee 1F **73**
Royston Gro. TS25: H'pool . . . 1D **31**
Ruberry Av. TS19: S Tee. 5C **52**
Ruby Rd. TS17: T Tee. 4D **99**
Ruby St. TS1: Midd. 4E **77**
  TS12: Salt 3C **68**
Rudby Cl. TS15: Yarm 4E **149**
Rudd Cl. TS22: Wyn 1F **37**
Rudds Pl. TS5: Midd. 1E **101**
Rudland Way TS6: Est 5F **81**
Rudston Av. TS22: Bill 4A **38**
Rudston Cl. TS17: T Tee 2B **128**
Rudyard Av. TS19: S Tee 5C **52**
Rufford Cl. TS7: Mart 3F **133**
  TS14: Guis. 4E **139**
  TS17: I Bar 5C **128**
Ruff Tail TS14: Guis 2B **138**
Rugby Rd. TS18: S Tee 1F **97**
Rugby St. TS25: H'pool 1A **20**
Rugby Ter. TS2: P Cla 4E **57**
Rugeley Cl. TS19: S Tee. 1D **73**
Ruislip Cl. TS19: S Tee 1D **73**
Runciman Rd. TS24: H'pool . . . 4F **7**
Runcorn Av. TS19: S Tee 1D **73**
Runfold Cl. TS19: S Tee 4C **52**
Runnymead Grn.
  TS3: Midd 4E **103**
Runnymede TS7: Nun 4A **134**
Runnymede Cl.
  TS19: S Tee. 5D **53**
Runswick Av. TS5: Midd. . . . 2C **130**
  TS10: Redc. 5A **48**
  TS19: S Tee. 1D **73**
Runswick La. TS13: Hind 5F **121**
Runswick Rd. TS6: Est 5F **81**
Rupert St. TS18: S Tee 4C **74**
Rushleigh Av. TS5: Midd . . . 5B **100**
Rushmere TS8: Mart. 5E **133**
Rushmere Heath
  TS16: Eag 1C **148**
Rushpool Cl. TS10: Redc 2B **64**
Rushwarp Gro. TS25: S Car . . 5E **21**
Rushyford Av. TS19: S Tee . . . 1D **73**
Ruskin Av. TS5: Midd 4B **100**
  TS12: Salt 4B **68**
Ruskin Gro. TS25: H'pool . . . 1F **19**
Russell St. TS1: Midd. 3F **77**
  (not continuous)
  TS18: S Tee 5A **74**
  (not continuous)
  TS24: H'pool 5E **9**
Russell Wlk. TS17: T Tee. . . . 3C **98**
  TS25: H'pool 5B **14**
  (not continuous)
Rustington Cl. TS19: S Tee . . 5D **53**
Ruswarp Av. TS19: S Tee 1D **73**
Ruswarp Cl. TS6: Est 1F **105**
Ruswarp Rd. TS6: Est. 1F **105**
Ruth Av. TS3: Midd. 1E **103**
Rutherglen Wlk.
  TS16: Eag 1C **148**
Ruthin Cl. TS19: S Tee 5E **53**
Rutland Av. TS7: Mart 3C **132**

Rutland Cl. TS19: S Tee 5E **53**
Rutland Ct. TS1: Midd 3F **77**
Ryan Av. TS18: S Tee. 4B **74**
Ryans Row TS11: M Sea 4B **66**
Ryan Wlk. TS18: S Tee. 4B **74**
Rydal Av. TS5: Midd. 4C **100**
  TS6: Gran 4F **81**
  TS10: Redc 5B **48**
  TS23: Bill. 5E **55**
Rydal Rd. TS12: Skel 3B **88**
  TS18: S Tee 5E **73**
Rydal St. TS26: H'pool 5A **14**
Rydal Way TS21: Redm 1B **70**
Ryder Cl. TS11: N Mar 2F **85**
Ryde Rd. TS19: S Tee. 5D **53**
Rye Cl. TS16: Eag. 2B **148**
Ryedale TS14: Guis 4B **138**
Ryedale Cl. TS15: Yarm 1B **160**
Ryedale St. TS3: N Orm. 4C **78**
Ryefields Ho. TS6: Est 3E **105**
Ryehill Cl. TS7: Nun. 5A **134**
Ryehill Gdns.
  TS26: H'pool 2E **13**
Ryehills Dr. TS11: M Sea 3E **67**
Rye Hill Way TS8: C New . . . 2C **154**
Ryelands Pk. TS13: Eas 3A **118**
Ryhill Wlk. TS7: Orm 4A **104**
Ryhope Av. TS19: S Tee 5D **53**
Rylstone Ct. TS4: Midd 3A **102**
Ryton Cl. TS17: T Tee 2B **128**

Sabatier Cl. TS17: T Tee. 1C **98**
Sacriston Cl. TS23: Bill 4C **38**
Sadberge Gro. TS19: S Tee . . 5A **72**
Sadberge Rd. TS18: S Tee . . . 3F **97**
Sadberge St. TS3: N Orm. . . . 4C **78**
Saddler Cl. TS17: I Bar 5B **128**
Saddleston Cl.
  TS26: H'pool 2D **13**
Sadler Dr. TS7: Mart 3C **132**
Sadler Forster Way
  TS17: T Tee 4D **129**
Sadler St. TS25: H'pool 5D **15**
Saffron Wlk. TS25: S Car . . . 3E **21**
St Abb's Wlk. TS24: H'pool . . 4C **14**
St Aidan's Cres. TS22: Bill . . 2C **54**
St Aidan's Dr. TS1: Midd 3E **77**
St Aidan's St. TS1: Midd 4E **77**
  TS25: H'pool 1B **20**
St Aidan's Vw. TS12: Boo. . . 3C **112**
St Andrew's Cl. TS16: Eag . . 1C **148**
St Andrew's Gro.
  TS6: Gran 3E **81**
St Andrew's Rd. E.
  TS6: Gran 3E **81**
St Andrew's Rd. W.
  TS6: Gran 3E **81**
St Annes Gdns.
  DL2: M Geo. 3A **144**
St Annes Rd. TS11: N Mar . . . 2A **86**
St Ann's Ct. TS24: H'pool. . . . 4D **15**
ST ANN'S HILL 4C **74**
St Anns Ind. Est.
  TS18: S Tee 4C **74**
St Ann's Ter. TS18: S Tee . . . 4C **74**
St Austell Cl. TS8: Hem . . . 4C **130**
St Barnabas Rd.
  TS5: Midd 1D **101**
St Bees Wlk. TS24: H'pool . . . 4C **14**
  (off Longscar Wlk.)
St Bega's Glade
  TS26: H'pool 3E **13**
St Bernard Rd. TS18: S Tee . . 1A **98**
St Brides Ct. TS17: I Bar. . . . 2F **149**

St Catherines Ct.
  TS3: Midd 1C **102**
  TS24: H'pool. 4C **14**
St Columba's Av. TS22: Bill . . 2C **54**
St Crispins Ct. TS19: S Tee. . . 3E **73**
St Cuthbert Ct. TS17: T Tee . . 3C **98**
St Cuthbert's Av. TS23: Bill. . 2C **54**
St Cuthberts Church
  (Turner Mausoleum) 5A **64**
St Cuthbert's Rd.
  TS18: S Tee 2A **98**
  (not continuous)
St Cuthbert St. TS24: H'pool . . 5E **9**
St Cuthbert's Wlk.
  TS13: Live 1A **116**
St Davids Gro.
  TS17: I Bar 2F **149**
St David's Rd. TS6: Gran . . . 3F **81**
St David's Wlk.
  TS26: H'pool 1D **13**
St Edmund's Grn.
  TS21: Sed 3D **23**
  (not continuous)
St Edmund's Ter.
  TS21: Sed 4D **23**
St Francis Ga.
  TS25: H'pool 2B **20**
St George's Bungs.
  TS6: Gran 3E **81**
St George's Cres.
  TS11: N Mar 2A **86**
St George's Rd. E.
  TS6: Gran 3E **81**
St George's Rd. W.
  TS6: Gran 3E **81**
St Georges Ter. TS13: Live. . 1A **116**
  (off Liverton Ter.)
St Germain's Gro.
  TS11: M Sea 4D **67**
St Germain's La.
  TS11: M Sea 4D **67**
St Helen's Cl. TS6: Est. 1D **105**
St Helen's St. TS24: H'pool . . . 5E **9**
St Helens Wlk.
  TS13: Live 1A **116**
St Hilda Chare
  TS24: H'pool. 1F **15**
ST HILDA'S 1F **77**
St Hilda's Cres.
  TS24: H'pool. 1F **15**
St Hilda's Pl. TS13: Loft. . . . 5C **92**
St Hilda's Ter. TS13: Loft . . . 4A **92**
St Hilda St. TS24: H'pool . . . 1F **15**
St Ives Cl. TS8: Midd 2B **132**
  TS10: Redc 3F **65**
St James Cl. TS21: T The . . . 1D **51**
St James Ct. TS6: Gran 2D **81**
  TS19: S Tee. 2D **73**
St James Gdns. TS2: Midd . . 2F **77**
St James Gro. TS27: Hart . . . 4F **5**
St James Ho. TS18: S Tee . . . 4C **74**
St James' M. TS1: Midd 5D **77**
St Joan's Gro.
  TS25: H'pool 2B **20**
St Johns Cl. TS4: Midd. 3A **78**
  TS18: S Tee 4A **74**
St John's Ga. TS1: Midd. . . . 3A **78**
  (off Woodside St.)
St John's Gro. TS10: Redc. . . 5D **49**
St Johns Pk. TS21: Stil. 2B **50**
St John's Way TS19: S Tee . . 2F **73**
St Josephs Ct. TS10: Redc. . . 5B **48**
  TS26: H'pool 3A **14**
St Leonards Cl.
  TS13: Live 1A **116**
St Leonards Rd.
  TS14: Guis 3C **138**
St Luke's Av. TS17: T Tee. . . . 3D **99**

St Luke's Cotts.
TS4: Midd 2A **102**
St Lukes Ct. TS26: H'pool 2F **13**
St Lukes Cres. TS21: Sed 1C **22**
St Margarets Cl.
DL2: M Geo 3A **144**
St Margaret's Gro.
TS5: Midd 4D **101**
TS6: S Ban 4B **80**
TS10: Redc 1D **65**
TS17: T Tee 1D **129**
TS25: H'pool 2B **20**
St Margaret's Way
TS12: Brot 2B **90**
St Mark's Cl. TS11: M Sea 4C **66**
TS19: S Tee 4B **72**
St Mark's Ct. TS17: T Tee 1B **98**
St Mark's Ho. TS17: T Tee . . . 1B **98**
St Martins Cl. TS13: Live 1A **116**
St Martin's Way
TS15: K'ton 4D **161**
St Mary's Cl. TS18: S Tee 4B **74**
St Mary's Ct. TS5: Midd 3D **101**
TS6: Gran 3E **81**
*TS24: H'pool 1F **15***
(off Union St.)
St Marys Ga. Bus. Pk.
TS20: Nort 4B **74**
St Mary St. TS24: H'pool 1F **15**
St Mary's Wlk. TS5: Midd . . . 4D **101**
St Matthews Ct. TS6: Gran 2D **81**
St Mawes Cl. TS26: H'pool 2D **13**
St Michael's Cl.
TS13: Live 1A **116**
St Michael's Ct. TS20: Nort . . .2B **74**
St Michael's Gro.
TS20: Nort 2B **74**
St Nicholas Ct. TS6: Gran 2D **81**
St Nicholas Gdns.
TS15: Yarm 5E **149**
St Oswald's Cres.
TS23: Bill 2C **54**
St Oswalds St.
TS24: H'pool 2A **14**
St Patrick's Cl. TS6: Gran 3E **81**
St Patrick's Rd. TS6: Gran 3E **81**
St Paul's Ct. TS19: S Tee 4F **73**
St Pauls Rd. TS1: Midd 3D **77**
TS17: T Tee 3C **98**
TS19: S Tee 4F **73**
TS26: H'pool 4A **14**
St Paul's St. TS19: S Tee 5F **73**
St Paul's Ter. TS19: S Tee 4F **73**
St Peter's Gro. TS10: Redc . . .5D **49**
St Peter's Rd. TS18: S Tee 2F **97**
St Peter's Sq.
TS17: T Tee 1D **129**
St Stephens Cl. TS20: Nort . . .3A **54**
St Thomas Gro.
TS10: Redc 5D **49**
St Vincent Ter. TS10: Redc 4B **48**
Salcombe Cl. TS8: Midd 2B **132**
Salcombe Dr. TS25: H'pool . . .5A **20**
Salcombe Way TS10: Redc . . .3E **65**
Salisbury Gro. TS10: Redc 5F **49**
Salisbury Pl. TS26: H'pool 1E **13**
Salisbury St. TS17: T Tee 3D **99**
Salisbury Ter. TS6: S Ban 2F **79**
TS20: Nort 2B **74**
Saltaire Ter. TS25: Grea 4F **31**
Saltburn Bank TS12: Salt 3D **69**
SALTBURN-BY-THE-SEA 4C **68**
Saltburn Gill Nature Reserve
. . . . .1E **89**
Saltburn La. TS12: Salt 4D **69**
TS12: Salt, Skel 3C **88**
Saltburn La. Rdbt.
TS12: Skel 2C **88**
Saltburn Leisure Cen. 5B **68**

Saltburn Rd.
TS12: Brot, Salt 4D **69**
Saltburn Smugglers' Heritage Cen.
. . . . 3E **69**
Saltburn Valley Woodland Cen.
. . . . 5D **69**
Saltcote TS7: Mart 2E **133**
Saltergill La. TS15: K'ton 3A **160**
Salter Ho. Dr. TS22: Wyn 4C **26**
(not continuous)
Salter Ho's. TS22: Wyn 4C **26**
SALTERSGILL 3F **101**
(not continuous)
Saltersgill Av. TS4: Midd 3F **101**
Saltersgill Cl. TS4: Midd 3F **101**
Salter's La.
TS21: Fish, Sed 2D **23**
Saltholme Cl. TS2: P Cla 4E **57**
Saltney Rd. TS20: Nort 5F **53**
Salton Cl. TS5: Midd 2B **100**
Saltram Cl. TS17: I Bar 1B **150**
Saltram Gro. TS7: Mart 2C **132**
Saltscar TS10: Redc 2E **65**
Saltview Ter. TS2: P Cla 5A **58**
Saltwells Cres. TS4: Midd 5B **78**
Saltwells Rd. TS4: Midd 4A **78**
Samaria Gdns. TS5: Midd 2D **131**
Sambrook Gdns.
TS5: Midd 2D **131**
Samphire St. TS2: P Cla 5F **57**
Samuelson Ho. TS3: Midd 2D **103**
Samuel St. TS19: S Tee 4F **73**
Sandalwood Ct.
TS5: Midd 2E **131**
Sandbanks Dr. TS24: H'pool . . .2D **7**
Sanderson's Yd. TS13: Loft . . .5C **92**
Sandford Bus. Pk.
TS6: Gran 2C **80**
Sandford Cl. TS4: Midd 4A **102**
Sandgate Ind. Est.
TS25: H'pool 1D **21**
(not continuous)
Sandhall Cl. TS23: Bill 2E **39**
Sandholme TS12: Ling 4E **113**
Sandling Ct. TS7: Mart 2E **133**
Sandmartin La. TS20: Nort 3B **54**
Sandmoor Cl. TS6: Est 2E **105**
Sandmoor Rd. TS11: N Mar . . .2F **85**
Sandown Pk. TS10: Redc 1D **65**
Sandown Rd. TS23: Bill 4D **39**
Sandown Way TS17: T Tee 2F **99**
Sandpiper Cl. TS10: Redc 3E **65**
Sandpiper Ho.
TS24: H'pool 3D **15**
Sandpiper Wlk. TS2: P Cla 4E **57**
Sandport Wlk. *TS18: S Tee 4C **74***
(off Alnport Rd.)
Sandringham Ho.
TS3: Midd 3D **103**
Sandringham Rd.
TS3: Midd 3D **103**
TS6: Gran 4E **81**
TS10: Redc 4C **48**
TS12: Ling 5F **113**
TS17: T Tee 3D **99**
TS18: S Tee 1F **97**
TS26: H'pool 3A **14**
Sandsend Rd. TS6: Est 5F **81**
TS10: Redc 1A **64**
Sands Hall Rdbt.
TS21: Sed 4B **22**
Sandwell Av. TS3: Midd 3F **103**
Sandwell Chare
TS24: H'pool 1F **15**
Sandwich Gro. TS27: H'pool . . .2D **7**
Sandwood Pk. TS14: Guis 4A **138**
Sandy Bank TS21: Sed 4A **22**
Sandy Flatts La. TS5: Midd . . .2E **131**

Sandy Flatts La. TS5: Midd . . .2E **131**
Sandy La.
TS11: Guis, N Mar 5D **85**
(not continuous)
TS22: Bill 5B **38**
(not continuous)
Sandy La. W. TS22: Bill 3F **37**
Sandy Leas La. TS21: Elt 1A **94**
Sapley Cl. TS17: T Tee 2C **128**
Sarah St. TS25: H'pool 1C **20**
Sark Wlk. *TS14: Guis 3D **139***
(off Hutton La.)
Satley Rd. TS23: Bill 2F **39**
Saunton Av. TS10: Redc 3E **65**
Saunton Rd. TS23: Bill 1F **55**
Sawley Gro. TS18: S Tee 2A **96**
Sawtry Rd. TS3: Midd 3F **103**
Saxby Rd. TS20: Nort 2B **74**
Saxonfield TS8: C New 4B **132**
Scalby Gro. TS10: Redc 2E **65**
TS19: S Tee 5A **72**
Scalby Rd. TS3: Midd 1B **102**
Scalby Sq. TS17: T Tee 4D **99**
Scaling Ct. TS14: Guis 1D **139**
Scampton Cl. TS17: T Tee 2B **128**
Scanbeck Dr. TS11: M Sea 3D **67**
Scarborough St. TS6: S Ban . . .3A **80**
TS13: Loft 5A **92**
TS17: T Tee 3C **98**
TS24: H'pool 3C **14**
Scarteen TS14: Guis 3D **139**
Scarth Cl. TS12: Ling 4E **113**
Scarth Wlk. TS18: S Tee 5F **73**
Scarthwood Cl.
TS17: I Bar 5C **128**
Scawfell Gro. TS25: H'pool . . . 1B **20**
Scholars Ct. TS15: Yarm 3B **148**
Scholars Ga. TS14: Guis 4D **139**
School Av. TS5: Midd 2B **100**
School Cl. TS11: M Sea 4D **67**
TS18: S Tee 2A **98**
TS21: T The 2D **51**
School Cft. TS1: Midd 2F **77**
School La. TS9: G Ayt 2D **167**
TS13: Live 1A **116**
School Wlk. TS18: S Tee 2A **98**
Schooner Ct. TS24: H'pool 3D **15**
Scotforth Cl. TS7: Mart 3F **133**
Scotney Rd. TS23: Bill 5D **39**
Scotswood Ho. TS17: T Tee . . .2B **98**
Scott Dr. TS20: Nort 5F **53**
Scott Gro. TS25: H'pool 2D **19**
Scotton Cl. TS18: S Tee 3A **96**
Scotton Ct. TS3: Midd 2A **104**
Scott Rd. TS6: Norm 2B **104**
Scott's Rd. TS2: Midd 2A **78**
TS3: Midd 2A **78**
Scott St. TS10: Redc 4D **49**
Scrafton Pl. TS11: M Sea 4D **67**
Scruton Cl. TS18: S Tee 2B **96**
Scugdale Cl. TS15: Yarm 1B **160**
Scurfield Rd. TS19: S Tee 1A **72**
Seaford Cl. TS10: Redc 3E **65**
Seaham Cl. TS10: Redc 3F **65**
TS20: Nort 4E **53**
Seaham St. TS20: Nort 4B **74**
Seaham Vw. TS20: Nort 4E **53**
Sealand Cl. TS17: T Tee 3D **129**
Seal Sands Link Rd.
TS23: Bill, C Bew 2D **39**
Seal Sands Nature Reserve
. . . . .2F **43**
Seal Sands Rd. TS2: S San . . . 1B **58**
Seamer Cl. TS5: Midd 4E **101**
Seamer Gro. TS18: S Tee 2D **97**
Seamer Rd.
TS8: Thor, Newb 1B **152**
TS15: Hilt, Seam 1F **163**
Seathwaite TS5: Midd 3B **130**

SEATON CAREW 4E 21
Seaton Carew Rd.
   TS2: P Cla, S San 5A 58
Seaton Cl. TS10: Redc 2F 65
   TS13: Stait 2C 120
   TS19: S Tee. 5A 72
Seaton Cres. TS13: Stait 2C 120
Seaton Gth. TS13: Stait 1C 120
Seaton La. TS10: H'pool 4B 20
Seatonport Ct. TS18: S Tee . . 4C 74
Seaton St. TS1: Midd 4F 77
Seaton Ter. TS12: Ling 5E 113
Seaview Pk. Homes
   TS27: H'pool 1C 6
Sea Vw. Ter. TS6: Gran 1D 81
   TS24: H'pool 5E 9
Second Foulsyke
   TS13: Loft 5F 93
Sedgebrook Gdns.
   TS3: Midd 3A 104
SEDGEFIELD. 4D 23
Sedgefield Ind. Est.
   TS21: Sed 2D 23
Sedgefield Race Course. 5A 22
Sedgefield Rd. TS5: Midd . . 2C 130
Sedgefield Way
   TS18: S Tee 3E 75
Sedgemoor Rd. TS6: Est . . . 3E 105
Sedgemoor Way TS23: Bill. . . 3A 40
Sedgewick Cl. TS24: H'pool . . . 3A 8
Sefton Rd. TS3: Midd 1A 104
Sefton Way TS15: Yarm 5A 148
Selbourne St. TS1: Midd 4D 77
Selby Gro. TS25: H'pool 3A 20
Selby Rd. TS7: Nun 3B 134
Selkirk Cl. TS4: Midd 4F 101
         (not continuous)
Selset Av. TS3: Midd 4E 103
Selset Cl. TS26: H'pool 3C 12
Selwood Cl. TS17: T Tee . . . 2D 129
Selworthy Grn.
   TS17: I Bar 3B 150
Selwyn Dr. TS19: S Tee 2A 72
Semmerwater Gro.
   TS10: Redc 5C 48
Serpentine Gdns.
   TS26: H'pool 2E 13
Serpentine Rd.
   TS26: H'pool 3E 13
         (not continuous)
Severn Dr. TS14: Guis 3C 138
Severn Gro. TS12: Skel 3D 89
   TS22: Bill. 4A 38
Severn Rd. TS10: Redc 4A 48
Severn Way TS10: Redc 4A 48
Severs Dr. TS8: Stain 5C 130
Severs St. TS6: S Ban. 2F 79
Seymour Av. TS16: Eag 2A 148
Seymour Cl. TS11: M Sea . . . 5F 67
Seymour Cres. TS16: Eag . . . 1A 148
Seymour Dr. TS16: Eag 1A 148
Seymour Gro. TS16: Eag . . . 2A 148
Seymour Hill Ter.
   TS13: Loft 5C 92
         (off North Rd.)
Shackleton Cl.
   TS17: T Tee 2D 129
Shadforth Dr. TS23: Bill 3F 39
Shadwell Cl. TS6: Norm. . . . 4C 104
Shaftesbury Rd. TS6: Est . . . 5D 81
Shaftesbury St.
   TS18: S Tee. 2A 98
Shakespeare Av. TS6: Gran . . 3F 81
   TS25: H'pool 1A 20
Shaldon Cl. TS10: Redc 3E 65
Shambles, The
   TS18: S Tee. 1B 98
Shandon Pk. TS8: Mart 5D 133
Shannon Ct. TS25: Grea 3E 31

Shannon Cres. TS19: S Tee . . . 4A 72
Shannon Lea DL2: M Geo . . . 1A 144
Sharp Cres. TS24: H'pool. 4A 8
Sharrock Cl. TS3: N Orm 4B 78
Shaw Cres. TS6: Gran. 4F 81
Shawcross Av. TS6: Gran. . . . 3D 81
Shaw Gro. TS25: H'pool 2D 19
Shearwater La.
   TS20: Nort. 3A 54
Sheepdene TS22: Wyn 4A 26
Sheepfoote Hill
   TS15: Yarm 4B 148
Sheerness Gro.
   TS24: H'pool 4C 14
Sheerness Way
   TS10: Redc 3E 65
Shelley Cl. TS23: Bill. 2D 39
Shelley Cres. TS6: Est 5C 80
Shelley Gro. TS25: H'pool . . . 1F 19
Shelley Rd. TS4: Midd. 3F 101
Shelton Cl. TS3: Midd. 2F 103
Shepherd Cl. TS17: T Tee . . . 5B 98
Shepherd Cl. TS12: Boo . . . 3C 112
Shepherdson Ct.
   TS6: S Ban 2A 80
Shepherdson Way
   TS3: Midd 2B 78
Shepton Cl. TS17: T Tee 5E 99
SHERATON 3A 4
Sheraton Bank TS27: Sher . . . 3A 4
Sheraton Pk. TS19: S Tee. . . . 2E 73
Sheraton St. TS18: S Tee . . . 1F 97
Sherburn Av. TS23: Bill. 3E 39
Sherburn Cl. TS5: Midd 1C 130
Sheridan Gro. TS25: H'pool . . 1F 19
Sheriff St. TS26: H'pool 3A 14
Sheringham Ct.
   TS10: Redc 3F 65
Sherwood Cl. TS7: Orm 1B 134
Sherwood Dr. TS11: M Sea . . 4B 66
Sherwood Rd.
   TS17: T Tee 2C 128
Shetland Av. TS17: T Tee . . . 4D 99
Shetland Cl. TS5: Midd 3D 131
Shevington Gro.
   TS7: Mart 3E 133
Shibden Rd. TS3: Midd 5C 78
Shields Ter. TS24: H'pool. 4C 8
Shildon Cl. TS23: Bill. 4D 39
Shincliffe Rd. TS23: Bill 3F 39
Shinwell Cres. TS6: S Ban . . . 3A 80
Shipham Cl. TS10: Redc 3E 65
Ship Inn Yd. TS18: S Tee . . . 1A 98
Shirley Av. TS5: Midd. 2B 100
Shoreham Cl. TS10: Redc . . . 3E 65
Shoreswood Wlk.
   TS5: Midd 2D 131
Short Cl. TS18: S Tee 4F 97
Shotley Cl. TS23: Bill 4D 39
Shotton Cl. TS23: Bill 5F 39
Showcase Cinemas
   Middlesbrough 1A 100
Shrewsbury Rd.
   TS3: Midd 2F 103
Shrewsbury St.
   TS25: H'pool 1A 20
Shropshire Wlk.
   TS25: H'pool 5B 14
Sidcup Av. TS3: Midd 4E 103
Siddington Wlk. TS3: Midd. . . 1E 103
Sideling Tails TS15: Yarm . . 5B 148
Sidlaw Av. TS12: Skel. 3C 88
Sidlaw Rd. TS23: Bill 5C 38
Sidmouth Cl. TS8: Midd 1B 132
Silton Cl. TS10: Redc 1F 63
Silton Gro. TS18: S Tee 2D 97
Silver Chambers
   TS18: S Tee. 5B 74
         (off Silver St.)

Silver Ct. TS18: S Tee. 5B 74
         (off Silver St.)
Silverdale TS7: Nun 4F 133
Silver St. TS2: Midd 1E 77
   TS9: Stok 1B 168
   TS15: Yarm 3B 148
   TS18: S Tee 5B 74
   TS24: H'pool 4B 14
Silverton Rd. TS14: Guis . . . 4F 139
Silverwood Cl. TS27: H'pool . . 2C 6
Silverwood Ct. TS17: T Tee . . 3C 98
Simcox Cl. TS2: Midd. 2C 76
Simonside Gro.
   TS17: I Bar 2B 150
Simonside Wlk.
   TS7: Orm 4A 104
Simpson Cl. TS6: S Ban 3B 80
Simpson Grn. TS6: S Ban. . . . 3A 80
Simpson St. TS5: Midd. 1E 101
Sinclair Rd. TS25: H'pool . . . 3D 19
Sinderby Cl. TS23: Bill. 4E 39
Singapore Sq. TS16: Eag . . . 4F 125
Sinnington Cl. TS14: Guis . . . 3E 139
Sinnington Rd.
   TS17: T Tee 2C 128
Sir Douglas Pk.
   TS17: T Tee 1C 128
Sir Hugh Bell Ct.
   TS10: Redc 3E 47
Sir William Turner's Hospital
   (Almshouses)
   TS10: K'ham 5A 64
Siskin Cl. TS20: Nort 3A 54
   TS26: H'pool. 1D 13
Sitwell Wlk. TS25: H'pool . . . 2D 19
Skeeby Cl. TS18: S Tee 3B 96
SKELTON 4B 88
Skelton/Brotton By-Pass
   TS12: Brot, Skel 3A 88
Skelton Castle Rdbt.
   TS12: Skel 3A 88
Skelton Cl. TS14: Guis 5E 109
Skelton Dr. TS10: Redc. 1E 65
   TS11: M Sea 4E 67
Skelton Ellers TS12: Skel . . . 2C 110
   TS14: Guis, Skel 4A 110
SKELTON GREEN 5B 88
SKELTON HIGH GREEN 5A 88
Skelton Ind. Est.
   TS12: Skel 3E 89
Skelton Rd. TS12: Brot. 4F 89
   TS17: T Tee 4D 99
Skelton St. TS24: H'pool. 3F 7
Skelwith Rd. TS3: Midd 2C 102
Skerne Rd. TS20: Nort 1A 74
   TS24: H'pool 4A 8
         (not continuous)
Skerries Cres. TS10: Redc. . . 3B 64
Skiddaw Cl. TS16: Eag. 4B 126
Skiddaw Ct. TS7: Nun. 3F 133
Skinner St. TS18: S Tee 1A 98
SKINNINGROVE 2A 92
Skinningrove Bank Rd.
   TS13: Loft 1A 92
Skinningrove Rd.
   TS13: Skin. 3A 92
Skiplam Cl. TS8: Hem 4C 130
Skipper's La.
   TS6: Norm, S Ban 3F 79
Skipper's La. Ind. Est.
   TS6: S Ban 3F 79
         (not continuous)
Skipton Rd. TS23: Bill 5D 39
Skirbeck Av. TS3: Midd 3A 104
Skirlaw Rd. TS15: Yarm 5B 148
Skomer Cl. TS10: Redc 3E 65
Skottowe Cres.
   TS9: G Ayt 1C 166
Skottowe Dr. TS9: G Ayt 1C 166

Stray, The TS21: L New 1A **124**
Streatlam Rd. TS23: Bill 4F **39**
Strensall Cl. TS11: N Mar 2A **86**
Stripe, The TS9: Stok 1B **168**
Strome Cl. TS17: I Bar 1C **150**
Strona Wlk. TS14: Guis 3D **139**
Stuart St. TS24: H'pool 2B **14**
Stubbs Cl. TS23: Bill 3D **39**
Studland Dr. TS24: H'pool 2D **7**
Studland Rd. TS10: Redc 3F **65**
Studley Rd. TS5: Midd 2C **100**
  TS17: T Tee 5D **99**
  TS19: S Tee 4F **73**
  TS25: H'pool 5B **14**
Stump Cross TS14: Guis 2D **139**
Sturt Dr. TS20: Nort 5F **53**
Sudbury TS8: Mart 4E **133**
Sudbury Rd. TS20: Nort 5C **54**
Suffield St. TS2: Midd 1E **77**
  TS25: H'pool 1B **20**
Suffolk Cl. TS12: Skel 5B **88**
  TS25: H'pool 1B **20**
Suffolk Rd. TS5: Midd 2F **101**
Suffolk St. TS18: S Tee 1F **97**
Sugar Loaf Cl.
  TS17: I Bar 1F **149**
Suggitt St. TS26: H'pool 3F **13**
Sulby Av. TS3: Midd 2D **103**
Summerhill Country Pk. 1D **19**
Summerhill Country Pk. Vis. Cen.
  . . . . 5D **13**
Summerhill La.
  TS25: H'pool 5E **13**
Summerhouse Sq.
  TS20: Nort 5A **54**
Sundell Ct. TS18: S Tee 1F **97**
Sunderland Rd.
  TS22: Wolv 2C **38**
Sundial M. TS22: Wolv 2C **38**
Sun Gdns. TS17: T Tee 3B **98**
Sunley Av. TS4: Midd 2A **102**
Sunningdale Ct. TS6: Est 1E **105**
Sunningdale Dr.
  TS16: Eag 5C **126**
Sunningdale Gro.
  TS27: H'pool 3D **7**
Sunningdale Ho.
  TS4: Midd 4F **101**
  TS6: Est 2E **105**
Sunningdale Rd.
  TS4: Midd 4F **101**
  TS11: N Mar 2A **86**
Sunningdale Wlk.
  TS16: Eag 5C **126**
  (not continuous)
Sunniside TS24: H'pool 1F **15**
Sunnybank Rd.
  TS7: Orm 5B **104**
Sunnybrow Av. TS23: Bill 3D **55**
Sunnyfield TS7: Orm 4A **104**
  TS9: G Ayt 2C **166**
Sunnyfields Gdns.
  TS13: Eas 2A **118**
Sunnygate TS6: Est 1A **106**
Sunny Row TS13: P Mul 4E **121**
Sunnyside TS8: C New 4F **131**
  (not continuous)
Sunnyside Av. TS4: Midd 3F **101**
Sunnyside Gro. TS18: S Tee . . 3C **96**
Sunstar Gro. TS7: Mart 2C **132**
Sun St. TS17: T Tee 3B **98**
  TS18: S Tee 2F **97**
Surbiton Rd. TS18: S Tee 4F **71**
  TS19: S Tee 4F **71**
Surgery La. TS24: H'pool 4A **8**
Surrey Rd. TS20: Nort 1C **74**
Surrey St. TS1: Midd 5D **77**
Surrey Ter. TS23: Bill 2E **55**
Surtees St. TS18: S Tee 1A **98**
  TS24: H'pool 4C **14**

Sussex St. TS2: Midd 2E **77**
  (not continuous)
  TS25: H'pool 1B **20**
Sussex Wlk. TS20: Nort 2C **74**
Sutherland Gro. TS20: Nort . . . 3A **54**
Sutton Pl. TS23: Bill 5F **39**
Sutton Way TS4: Midd 4F **101**
Swainby Cl. TS5: Midd 5E **101**
Swainby Rd. TS20: Nort 3B **74**
  TS25: S Car 5E **21**
Swainson Pl. TS24: H'pool . . . 3B **14**
Swainson St. TS24: H'pool . . . 3B **14**
Swainston Cl. TS5: Midd 1B **130**
  TS22: Wyn 3A **26**
Swale Av. TS17: T Tee 5D **99**
Swalebrooke Av.
  TS25: H'pool 1E **19**
Swale Cl. TS16: Eag 2B **148**
Swaledale Cl. TS17: I Bar 2B **150**
Swaledale Cres. TS23: Bill . . . 2D **55**
Swaledale Ho. TS4: Midd . . . 3F **101**
Swale Rd. TS20: Nort 5A **54**
Swallow Ct. TS14: Guis 2A **138**
  TS26: H'pool 5D **7**
Swallowfields
  TS8: C New 1A **154**
Swallow La. TS20: Nort 4A **54**
Swanage Cl. TS8: Midd 2B **132**
Swanage Dr. TS10: Redc 3F **65**
Swanage Gro. TS24: H'pool . . . 2D **7**
Swancer Ct. TS22: Wyn 4B **26**
Swan Ho. TS17: T Tee 1C **98**
Swart Hole Rdbt.
  TS22: Wyn 5E **27**
Swift Gro. TS25: H'pool 2E **19**
Swilly La. TS12: Skel 4B **88**
Swinburne Ho.
  TS25: H'pool 2E **19**
Swinburne Rd. TS16: Eag . . . 3C **126**
  TS25: H'pool 2E **19**
Swinburn Rd. TS20: Nort 3A **74**
Swinburn's Yd.
  TS15: Yarm 3B **147**
Swindale La.
  TS12: Ling, Moor 3A **142**
Swinton Rd. TS18: S Tee 3B **96**
Swyfte Cl. TS21: Sed 4D **23**
Sycamore Av. TS12: Salt 5A **68**
  TS17: T Tee 5C **98**
Sycamore Cres.
  TS6: Norm 5C **80**
Sycamore Dr. TS12: Brot 2A **90**
Sycamore Lodge
  DL2: M Geo 1D **145**
Sycamore Rd. TS5: Midd 2E **101**
  TS7: Orm 5B **104**
  TS16: P Tee 2D **127**
  TS19: S Tee 2E **73**
Sycamore Rd., The
  TS10: Redc 4E **49**
Sycamores, The
  TS25: H'pool 2F **19**
Sycamore Ter. TS2: P Cla 4E **57**
Sycamore Wlk.
  TS13: Loft 4C **92**
Sycamore Way
  TS19: S Tee 1C **72**
Sydenham Rd.
  TS18: S Tee 2E **97**
  TS25: H'pool 1B **20**
  (not continuous)
Sydney Cl. TS5: Midd 2B **100**
Sydney Rd. TS7: Mart 3D **133**
Sydney St. TS18: S Tee 5A **74**
  (not continuous)
Sylvan Wlk. TS3: Midd 4E **103**
Symons Cl. TS18: S Tee 1A **96**
Synthonia Sports Ground 3F **55**
Syon Gdns. TS20: Nort 4E **53**

T

Tailrigg Cl. TS19: S Tee 4F **73**
Talbenny Gro. TS17: I Bar. . . . 2F **149**
Talbot Ho. TS24: H'pool 1F **15**
Talbot M. TS6: Est 4D **81**
Talbot St. TS1: Midd. 4A **78**
  TS20: Nort 3B **74**
Talgarth Rd. TS20: Nort 4B **54**
Talisker Gdns. TS10: Redc . . . 3D **65**
Talisman Cl. TS16: Eag 4A **126**
Talland Cl. TS27: H'pool. 3C **6**
Talybont Gro. TS17: I Bar . . . 1F **149**
Tamarisk Cl. TS17: I Bar 4B **128**
Tame Rd. TS3: N Orm 3C **78**
Tameside TS9: Stok 5B **164**
Tame St. TS23: Bill 3D **57**
Tamworth Rd. TS23: Bill 4E **39**
Tanfield Rd. TS25: H'pool 2A **20**
Tanhill Wlk. TS3: Midd. 2D **103**
Tankersley Rd.
  TS11: N Mar 2A **86**
Tankerville Ct.
  TS26: H'pool 3A **14**
Tanner Cl. TS17: I Bar 5B **128**
Tansley Av. TS3: Midd 1E **103**
TANTON 2B **164**
Tanton Gro. TS22: Bill. 5A **38**
Tanton Rd. TS9: Seam 3A **164**
  TS9: Stok 4C **164**
Tanwell Cl. TS19: S Tee 4B **72**
Tanya Gdns. TS5: Midd. 2E **131**
  TS19: S Tee 5C **72**
Taransay Vw. TS17: T Tee . . . 4D **99**
Tarell Ct. TS17: I Bar 2F **149**
Tarnston Rd. TS26: H'pool . . . 2D **13**
Tarran St. TS5: Midd 5C **76**
Tarring St. TS18: S Tee 1F **97**
Tarr Steps TS17: I Bar 3B **150**
Task Ind. Est. TS18: S Tee . . . 4B **74**
Task Rd. TS18: S Tee 4C **74**
Tasman Dr. TS18: S Tee 2B **96**
Tasmania Sq. TS7: Mart 3E **133**
Tatham Ct. TS7: Nun 4A **134**
Taunton Cl. TS8: Midd 2B **132**
Taunton Gro. TS26: H'pool. . . 1D **13**
Taunton Va. TS14: Guis 4E **139**
Tavistock Cl. TS27: H'pool 3C **6**
Tavistock Rd. TS5: Midd 1D **101**
Tavistock St. TS5: Midd 1D **101**
Tawney Cl. TS6: Est 4D **81**
Tawney Rd. TS6: Est 4D **81**
Taybrooke Av.
  TS25: H'pool 1F **19**
Teak St. TS1: Midd 4F **77**
Tealby Wlk. TS3: Midd 2A **104**
Teal Ct. TS10: Redc 3E **47**
Teare Cl. TS1: Midd 4D **77**
Teasel Ct. TS19: S Tee 3C **72**
Tebay Cl. TS7: Orm 4A **104**
Tedder Av. TS17: T Tee. 2D **129**
Tedworth Cl. TS14: Guis. 4E **139**
Tees & Hartlepool Yacht Club
  . . . . 3D **15**
Tees Bank Av.
  TS16: P Tee. 3D **127**
Tees Barrage Way
  TS17: T Tee 5E **75**
Tees Bay Bus. Pk.
  TS25: H'pool 3D **33**
Tees Bay Retail Pk.
  TS25: H'pool 3C **20**
Teesbrooke Av.
  TS25: H'pool 2F **19**
Tees Cl. TS6: S Ban 4F **79**
TEESDALE 1C **98**
Teesdale Av. TS23: Bill. 2D **55**
  TS26: H'pool 4F **13**

Teesdale Lodge—Tofts Farm E. Ind. Est.

Teesdale Lodge
TS17: T Tee 1C 98
Teesdale Ter. TS17: T Tee . . . 3D 99
Tees Dock Rd. TS6: Midd 2C 60
Teesgate TS17: T Tee 5E 99
Teeside Ho. TS17: T Tee 1C 98
Teesmouth Field Cen. 4E 33
Tees (Newport) Bri. App. Rd.
TS18: S Tee 2A 76
TEESPORT 2C 60
Teesport Commercial Pk.
TS6: Midd 5F 59
Teesport Rd. TS6: Midd 3F 61
Tees Reach TS17: T Tee 1C 98
Tees Rd. TS10: Redc 5B 48
TS14: Guis 3C 138
TS25: H'pool 2C 42
Teesside Crematorium
TS5: Midd 1E 131
Teesside Ho. TS1: Midd 3F 77
Teesside Ind. Est.
TS17: T Tee 4E 129
Teesside Leisure Pk.
TS17: T Tee 2A 100
Teesside Pk. Dr.
TS17: T Tee 2F 99
Teesside Pk. Interchange
TS17: T Tee 2E 99
Teesside Retail Pk.
TS17: T Tee 2F 99
Teesside Trade Pk.
TS18: S Tee 3E 75
Tees St. TS6: S Ban 1A 80
TS13: Loft 5D 93
TS23: Bill 3D 57
TS24: H'pool 3B 14
Tees Viaduct TS18: S Tee 3A 76
TEESVILLE 5B 80
Teesway TS18: S Tee 3F 75
Tees Yd. TS17: T Tee 1E 99
Teignmouth Cl.
TS27: H'pool 3C 6
Telford Cl. TS24: H'pool 5C 8
Telford Rd. TS3: N Orm 3E 79
Temperance Ter.
TS24: H'pool 5F 9
Tempest Ct. TS22: Wyn 1E 37
Tempest Rd. TS24: H'pool . . . 3E 7
Templar St. TS18: S Tee 2F 97
Templeton Cl. TS20: Nort 4B 74
Tenby Cl. TS6: Est. 5E 81
Tenby Rd. TS10: Redc 2A 64
Tenby Wlk. TS26: H'pool 1E 13
Tenby Way TS16: Eag 1C 148
Tennant St. TS18: S Tee 5A 74
Tennyson Av. TS6: Gran 3E 81
TS25: H'pool 1F 19
Tennyson Cl. TS6: Gran 4E 81
Tennyson Rd. TS23: Bill 2D 39
Tennyson St. TS1: Midd 5E 77
Ternbeck Way TS17: T Tee . . 3E 129
Terrace, The TS27: D Pie 1F 17
TS27: Elw 4C 10
Terry Dicken Ind. Est.
TS9: Stok 3D 169
Tetcott Cl. TS14: Guis 4E 139
Tewkesbury Av. TS7: Mart . . . 4D 133
Thackeray Gro. TS5: Midd . . . 3E 101
Thackeray Rd.
TS25: H'pool 1D 19
Thames Av. TS14: Guis 3C 138
TS17: T Tee 5D 99
TS24: H'pool 5A 8
Thames Rd. TS10: Redc 5A 48
TS12: Skel. 3C 88
TS22: Bill. 4A 38
Thatch La. TS17: I Bar 4C 128

The . . . .
Names prefixed with 'The' for
example 'The Acres' are indexed
under the main name such as
'Acres, The'
Theakston Gro.
TS18: S Tee 2A 96
Theatre Yd. *TS18: S Tee* *5B 74*
(off Calvert's La.)
Thetford Av. TS3: Midd 3F 103
Thetford Rd. TS25: H'pool . . . 1E 31
Thinford Gdns. TS5: Midd . . . 2D 131
Thirlby Cl. TS3: Midd 2C 102
Thirlby Way TS14: Guis 5E 109
Thirlmere Av. TS5: Midd 4C 100
Thirlmere Ct. TS23: Bill 5E 55
Thirlmere Cres.
TS6: Norm 2D 105
Thirlmere Dr. TS12: Skel 4B 88
Thirlmere Rd. TS10: Redc . . . 5B 48
Thirlmere St. TS26: H'pool . . . 5A 14
Thirsk Gro. TS25: H'pool 3B 20
Thirsk Rd. TS9: Stok 3A 168
TS15: K'ton, Yarm. 5C 148
Thirwall Dr. TS17: I Bar 2A 150
Thistle Grn. TS18: S Tee. . . . 5B 74
Thistle Ri. TS8: C New 3F 131
Thistle Rd. TS19: S Tee 1E 73
Thistle St. TS1: Midd 4F 77
Thomas St. TS3: N Orm 4C 78
TS12: Skel. 4D 89
TS18: S Tee 4A 74
Thomlinson Rd.
TS25: H'pool 1C 20
Thompson Gro.
TS24: H'pool 5A 8
Thompsons Cl. TS22: Wolv . . 2C 38
Thompson's Rd.
TS12: Skel. 5B 88
Thompson St. TS18: S Tee . . . 4A 74
TS24: H'pool 5B 14
Thomson Av. TS5: Midd 1B 100
Thomson St. TS14: Guis 2D 139
Thorgill Cl. TS4: Midd 3F 101
Thorington Gdns.
TS17: I Bar 1C 150
THORNABY-ON-TEES 5D 99
Thornaby Pl. TS17: T Tee . . . 2B 98
Thornaby Rd. TS17: T Tee . . . 2C 98
Thornaby Swimming Baths
. . . . 4B 98
Thornberry Ct. TS5: Midd . . . 2C 100
Thornbrough Cl.
TS18: S Tee 3B 96
Thornbury Cl. TS10: Redc. . . . 4F 65
TS27: H'pool 2C 6
Thorn Cl. TS17: I Bar 4B 128
Thorndike Rd. TS6: Est. 5E 81
Thorndyke Av. TS4: Midd . . . 3A 102
Thornfield Cl. TS16: Eag 5A 126
Thornfield Gro. TS5: Midd . . . 3C 100
Thornfield Rd. TS5: Midd. . . . 3C 100
Thornhill Gdns.
TS26: H'pool 2E 13
Thornhill Pl. TS26: H'pool . . . 2E 13
Thornley Av. TS23: Bill 2E 39
Thorn Rd. TS19: S Tee 1E 73
Thorn Side TS17: I Bar. 4B 128
Thornthwaite TS5: Midd. . . . 3B 130
Thornthwaite Cl.
TS12: Skel. 3B 88
THORNTON. 1B 152
Thornton Cl. TS8: Thor. 1B 152
Thornton Cotts. TS8: Thor . . . 1B 152
Thornton Cres. TS22: Bill . . . 5B 38
Thornton Gth. TS15: Yarm . . 5C 148
Thornton Gro. TS20: Nort. . . . 2A 74
Thornton Rd.
TS8: Thor, Stain 1B 152

Thornton St. TS3: N Orm 4C 78
TS26: H'pool 4A 14
Thornton Va. TS8: Thor 1B 152
THORNTREE 1F 103
Thorntree Av. TS3: Midd. 4E 79
(not continuous)
Thorntree Ct. TS17: T Tee 5D 99
Thorntree Ho. TS3: Midd . . . 1E 103
Thorn Tree La. TS25: Grea . . . 4F 31
Thorntree Rd.
TS17: T Tee 4C 98
Thornville Rd.
TS26: H'pool 3A 14
Thornwood Av.
TS17: I Bar 4B 128
THORPE LARCHES. 1B 34
Thorpe M. TS20: Nort. 5B 54
Thorpe Rd. TS21: Car. 4D 51
TS24: H'pool 5D 9
THORPE THEWLES 2E 51
Thorpe Thewles Station Vis. Cen.
. . . . 5E 35
Thorphill Way TS23: Bill 3E 39
Three Tuns Wynd
TS9: Stok 1B 168
Throckley Av. TS5: Midd. . . . 1C 130
Thropton Cl. TS23: Bill 3C 38
THROSTON. 5E 9
Throston Cl. TS26: H'pool. . . . 5F 7
THROSTON GRANGE 5E 7
Throston Grange Ct.
TS26: H'pool 1E 13
Throston Grange La.
TS26: H'pool 1D 13
Throston St. TS24: H'pool . . . 1F 15
Thrush Rd. TS10: Redc 4C 48
Thrushwood Cres.
TS11: M Sea 5E 67
Thruxton Way TS20: Nort . . . 5F 53
Thurlestone TS8: Mart 4F 133
Thurlow Grange TS21: Sed . . 4D 23
Thurlow Rd. TS21: Sed 4D 23
Thurnam Gro. TS7: Mart. . . . 3E 133
Thursby Dr. TS7: Orm. 4A 104
Thursby Gro. TS25: H'pool. . . 1D 31
Thurso Cl. TS19: S Tee 5F 71
Thwaites La. TS10: Redc. . . . 5D 49
Thweng Way TS14: Guis. . . . 3C 138
Tibbersley Av. TS23: Bill. . . . 4E 55
Tibthorpe TS7: Nun. 3F 133
Tick Hills La. TS13: Live 5A 116
Tidkin La. TS14: Guis. 3C 138
Tilbury Rd. TS6: S Ban 2F 79
Tilery Cl. TS20: Nort 3B 74
Tilery Ct. TS20: Nort 3B 74
Tilery Rd. TS20: Nort 3B 74
Tilery Way TS20: Nort 3B 74
Tilery Wood TS22: Wyn 4B 26
Timbercombe Cl.
TS17: I Bar 3A 150
Tindale TS14: Guis 3A 138
Tindale Cl. TS15: Yarm 1B 160
Tindale Wlk. TS5: Midd 2C 130
Tintagel Cl. TS27: H'pool 3C 6
Tintern Av. TS23: Bill 5D 39
Tintern Rd. TS12: Skel. 4D 89
Tipton Cl. TS17: T Tee 5E 99
Tirril Way TS7: Mart 4F 133
Tithebarn Ho. TS19: S Tee . . . 1B 72
Tithe Barn Rd. TS19: S Tee . . 1A 72
Tiverton Gro. TS26: H'pool . . . 1E 13
Tocketts Mill Cvn. Pk.
TS14: Guis 2B 110
Tocketts Watermill. 2B 110
Toddington Dr. TS20: Nort. . . 5E 53
TOD POINT. 3C 46
Tod Point Rd. TS10: Redc. . . . 3E 47
Tofts Cl. TS11: M Sea 4E 67
Tofts Farm E. Ind. Est.
TS25: H'pool 1D 33

Weston Av. TS3: Midd 4E **79**
  (not continuous)
Weston Cres. TS20: Nort 2B **74**
WEST PARK 3C **12**
West Pk. TS26: H'pool 4D **13**
West Pk. Av. TS13: Loft 5B **92**
West Pk. La. TS21: Sed 4C **22**
Westpoint Rd.
  TS17: T Tee 1C **98**
Westport Cl. TS18: S Tee . . . 4C **74**
West Pct. TS23: Bill 1D **55**
Westray TS8: Mart 5E **133**
Westray St. TS13: C How . . . 3F **91**
West Rd. TS23: Bill 4D **55**
West Row TS5: Midd 2B **100**
  TS6: Est 1F **105**
  TS18: S Tee 1A **98**
  TS25: Grea 4E **31**
West Scar TS10: Redc 2D **65**
West Side TS7: Mart 2D **133**
  TS7: Nun 2C **156**
West St. TS1: Midd 1E **77**
  TS2: P Cla 5F **57**
  TS6: Est 1F **105**
  TS6: Norm 2D **105**
  TS11: M Sea 3D **67**
  TS15: Yarm 2B **148**
  TS21: Stil 1A **50**
West Ter. TS3: N Orm 4B **78**
  TS9: G Ayt 2C **166**
  TS10: Redc 3C **48**
  TS11: N Mar 2A **86**
  TS12: Skel 4A **88**
WEST VIEW 3E **7**
West Vw. TS10: Redc 4D **49**
West Vw. Cl. TS16: Eag 5B **126**
West Vw. Rd. TS24: H'pool . . . 3E **7**
  TS27: H'pool 3B **6**
West Vw. Ter. TS16: Eag . . . 1B **148**
  TS25: S Car 4E **21**
Westward Cl. TS1: Midd 3E **77**
Westwick Ter. TS4: Midd . . . 1B **132**
Westwood Av. TS5: Midd . . . 3D **101**
  TS7: Nun 3B **134**
Westwood La. TS17: I Bar . . . 1C **150**
Westwood Way
  TS27: H'pool 2C **6**
Westworth Cl.
  TS15: Yarm 5E **149**
Wetherall Av. TS15: Yarm . . 1B **160**
Wetherby Cl. TS18: S Tee . . . 3E **75**
Wetherby Grn. TS7: Orm . . . 3A **104**
Wetherell Av. TS11: M Sea . . 5E **67**
Wetherfell Cl. TS17: I Bar . . 3A **150**
Weymouth Dr. TS24: H'pool . . . 2D **7**
Weymouth Rd. TS8: Midd . . 1B **132**
  TS18: S Tee 1C **96**
Whaddon Chase
  TS14: Guis 3F **139**
Wharfdale TS12: Skel 2C **88**
Wharfdale La. TS23: Bill 3D **55**
Wharfedale Cl.
  TS17: I Bar 3B **150**
Wharf St. TS18: S Tee 1B **98**
Wharton Cl. TS15: Yarm 5E **149**
Wharton Cotts. TS12: Boo . . 5B **112**
Wharton Pl. TS12: Boo 2C **112**
Wharton St. TS12: Skel 5F **89**
  TS24: H'pool 3B **14**
Wharton Ter. TS24: H'pool . . 1A **14**
  (not continuous)
Wheatacre Cl.
  TS11: M Sea 5E **67**
Wheatear Dr. TS10: Redc . . . 3D **65**
Wheatear La. TS17: I Bar . . 5A **128**
Wheatfields Ho. TS6: Est . . . 3E **105**
Wheatlands Cl.
  TS14: Guis 3F **139**

Wheatlands Dr.
  TS11: M Sea 4C **66**
  TS13: Eas 3A **118**
Wheatlands Pk.
  TS10: Redc 3D **65**
Wheatley Cl. TS5: Midd 2D **131**
Wheatley Rd. TS19: S Tee . . 1B **72**
Wheatley Wlk.
  TS19: S Tee 1B **72**
Wheeldale Av. TS10: Redc . . 1A **64**
Wheeldale Cres.
  TS17: T Tee 5D **99**
Wheldrake Cl. TS14: Guis . . . 5E **109**
Whernside TS7: Mart 4F **133**
  TS12: Skel 3B **88**
Whernside Cres.
  TS17: I Bar 3B **150**
Whessoe Rd. TS19: S Tee . . . 1C **72**
Whessoe Wlk. TS19: S Tee . . . 1C **72**
Whickam Rd. TS19: S Tee . . . 1B **72**
Whickham Cl. TS3: N Orm . . . 3C **78**
Whinchat Cl. TS17: I Bar . . . 5B **128**
  TS26: H'pool 5F **7**
Whinchat Tail TS14: Guis . . . 2B **138**
Whinfell Av. TS16: Eag 4B **126**
Whinfell Cl. TS7: Mart 4F **133**
Whinfield Cl. TS19: S Tee . . . 3A **72**
Whinflower Dr. TS20: Nort . . . 4F **53**
Whingroves TS17: T Tee 4F **99**
Whinlatter Cl. TS19: S Tee . . 5F **73**
Whin Mdws. TS24: H'pool . . . 3E **7**
WHINNEY BANKS 3B **100**
Whinney Banks Rd.
  TS5: Midd 2A **100**
Whinny Bank TS9: G Ayt . . . 1E **159**
WHINNY HILL 5A **70**
Whinston Cl. TS26: H'pool . . . 2C **12**
Whinstone Dr. TS8: Stain . . . 5C **130**
Whinstone Vw.
  TS9: G Ayt 1D **167**
Whinstone Vw. Camping & Cvn. Site
  TS9: G Ayt 4F **157**
Whin St. TS1: Midd 3E **77**
Whisperdale Ct.
  TS3: Midd 1E **103**
Whitburn Rd. TS19: S Tee . . 1B **72**
Whitburn St. TS24: H'pool . . 5B **14**
Whitby Av. TS6: Est 5E **81**
  TS14: Guis 2F **139**
Whitby Cl. TS12: Skel 4D **89**
Whitby Cres. TS10: Redc . . . 1F **65**
Whitby Gro. TS24: H'pool 4C **14**
Whitby Rd. TS7: Nun 3B **134**
  TS13: Loft 5D **93**
  TS14: Guis 2F **139**
Whitby St. TS24: H'pool 3C **14**
Whitby St. Sth.
  TS24: H'pool 4C **14**
Whitby Wlk. TS24: H'pool . . . 4C **14**
Whitchurch Cl.
  TS17: I Bar 3A **150**
Whitebeam Ct. TS4: Midd . . 3F **101**
Whitecliffe Ter. TS13: Loft . . . 5B **92**
Whitecliff Wood Nature Reserve
  . . . . 5A **92**
Whitegate Cl. TS13: Stait . . . 2C **120**
Whitehall Rd. TS16: Eag . . . 3A **126**
Whitehaven Cl.
  TS10: Redc 2B **64**
White Ho. Cft.
  TS21: L New 5A **94**
White Ho. Dr. TS21: Sed . . . 4D **23**
Whitehouse Dr.
  TS19: S Tee 4D **73**
White Ho. Rd.
  TS17: T Tee 1B **128**
Whitehouse Rd. TS22: Bill . . 4A **38**
Whitehouse St. TS5: Midd . . 4C **76**
Whiteoaks Cl. TS10: Redc . . . 4F **65**

Whitestone Bus. Pk.
  TS4: Midd 4A **78**
White Stone Cl.
  TS10: Redc 2E **65**
White St. TS3: Midd 5C **78**
White Water Way
  TS17: T Tee 5E **75**
Whitfield Av. TS4: Midd 4A **78**
  (off Angle St.)
Whitfield Bldgs. TS4: Midd . . 4A **78**
  (off Park Va. Rd.)
Whitfield Cl. TS16: Eag 5B **126**
Whitfield Dr.
  TS25: H'pool 2B **20**
Whitfield Rd. TS20: Nort 4F **53**
Whithorn Gro. TS8: Hem . . . 3E **131**
Whitley Rd. TS17: T Tee . . . 2D **129**
Whitrout Rd. TS24: H'pool . . . 3E **7**
Whitstable Gdns.
  TS10: Redc 3A **64**
WHITTON 3A **50**
Whitton Cl. TS5: Midd 5B **100**
Whitton Gro. TS21: Stil 2A **50**
Whitton La.
  TS21: Stil, Whit 3A **50**
Whitton Rd. TS19: S Tee . . . 5C **72**
  TS21: Redm 4A **50**
Whitwell Cl. TS18: S Tee . . . 2A **98**
Whitwell Pl. TS12: Ling 4F **113**
Whitwell Ter. TS14: Guis . . . 1E **139**
Whitworth Gdns.
  TS25: H'pool 3F **19**
Whitworth Rd. TS6: Gran . . . 2D **81**
  (not continuous)
Whorlton Cl. TS14: Guis . . . 4D **139**
Whorlton Rd. TS2: Midd . . . 5D **57**
  TS22: Bill 5B **38**
Wibsey Av. TS3: Midd 4E **103**
Wickets, The TS7: Mart . . . 2C **132**
  TS25: S Car 5E **21**
Wicklow St. TS1: Midd 5C **76**
Widdrington Ct.
  TS19: S Tee 2A **72**
Wigton Sands TS5: Midd . . . 3B **130**
Wilder Gro. TS25: H'pool . . . 1D **19**
Wilfred St. TS18: S Tee 1F **97**
Wilken Cres. TS14: Guis . . . 5F **109**
Wilkinson St. TS12: Ling . . . 4D **113**
  TS20: Nort 3B **74**
Willerby Grn. TS5: Midd . . . 3C **100**
WILLEY FLATT 1B **160**
Willey Flatt La.
  TS15: Yarm 5B **148**
William Crosthwaite Av.
  TS17: T Tee 1D **151**
Williams Av. TS5: Midd 2B **100**
Williams St. TS12: Skel 4F **89**
William St. TS2: Midd 2E **77**
  TS6: Est 1F **105**
  TS10: Redc 4D **49**
  TS12: Skel 4D **89**
  TS18: S Tee 1A **98**
  (not continuous)
  TS24: H'pool 4C **14**
William Ter. TS20: Nort 2B **74**
Willington Rd. TS19: S Tee . . 1B **72**
Willow Bank TS8: C New . . . 5B **132**
Willow Chase, The
  TS21: L New 1F **123**
Willow Cl. TS12: Salt 5A **68**
  TS17: T Tee 5C **98**
Willowdene Av.
  TS18: S Tee 3E **97**
Willow Dr. TS6: Norm 3C **104**
  TS26: Brot 2A **90**
Willow Flats TS26: H'pool . . . 4D **7**
Willow Gro. TS24: H'pool . . . 1A **14**
Willow Lodge
  DL2: M Geo 1D **145**

Willow Rd.—Works Rd.

Willow Rd. TS14: Guis 1E **139**	**Windsor St.** TS1: Midd 4E **77**	**Woodburn Cl.** TS8: Hem 3E **131**
TS19: S Tee 3F **73**	TS23: Bill 3D **57**	**Woodchester Gro.**
Willows, The TS7: Mart 3D **133**	TS26: H'pool 4B **14**	TS17: I Bar 4E **127**
TS10: Redc 5E **49**	**Windsor Ter.** TS13: Loft 5D **93**	**Woodcock Cl.** TS6: Est 3E **105**
TS19: S Tee 3D **73**	(off Whitby Rd.)	**Wood Ct.** TS13: Loft 5C **92**
TS21: Sed 5C **22**	**Windward Way** TS3: Midd . . . 2F **77**	**Woodford Cl.** TS11: M Sea . . . 4B **66**
Willows Av. TS8: Malt. 1F **151**	**Windy Hill La.**	**Woodford Grn.** TS16: Eag. . . 1C **148**
Willows Ct. TS17: T Tee 5E **129**	TS11: M Sea 4D **67**	**Woodford Wlk.**
Willows Rd. TS6: Midd 2E **101**	**Wingate Av.** TS23: Bill 3F **39**	TS17: T Tee 3C **128**
Willow Ter. TS2: P Cla 4E **57**	**Wingate Rd.** TS19: S Tee . . . 1B **72**	**Woodgate Cl.** TS25: Grea 2E **31**
Willow Wlk. TS13: Loft 4B **92**	**Wingate Wlk.** TS3: Midd 5E **103**	**Woodhall Gro.** TS18: S Tee . . 3B **96**
TS24: H'pool 1A **14**	**Wingrove** TS15: Yarm. 3B **148**	**Woodham Grn.**
Wilmire Rd. TS22: Bill 5C **38**	**Winlaton Cl.** TS19: S Tee . . . 1B **72**	TS19: S Tee 1B **72**
Wilson St. TS1: Midd 3E **77**	**Winpenny Cl.** TS15: Yarm . . . 5E **149**	**Woodham Rd.** TS23: Bill. 3E **39**
TS12: Brot. 2B **90**	**Winsdale Av.** TS3: Midd 4F **79**	**Woodhay Av.** TS5: Midd . . . 3A **100**
TS12: Ling 4E **113**	**Winsford Cl.** TS17: I Bar 3B **150**	**Woodhouse Rd.**
TS14: Guis 2D **139**	**Winston Av.** TS23: Bill 3E **39**	TS14: Guis 1C **138**
TS17: T Tee 2D **99**	**Winston Churchill Cl.**	**Woodhouse Rdbt.**
TS26: H'pool 3F **13**	TS17: T Tee 2D **129**	TS14: Guis 2B **138**
Wilson Ter. TS13: Skin 2A **92**	**Winston Ct.** TS24: H'pool 4D **9**	**Woodland M.** TS21: Sed . . . 2D **23**
Wilstrop Grn. TS3: Midd . . . 4D **103**	**Winston Dr.** TS6: Est 1E **105**	**Woodlands, The**
WILTON 4F **83**	**Winston St.** TS18: S Tee 2F **97**	TS7: Nun. 5B **134**
Wilton Av. TS10: Redc 1D **63**	**Winterbottom Av.**	TS17: T Tee 5C **98**
TS26: H'pool 4F **13**	TS24: H'pool 4A **8**	**Woodlands Dr.** TS6: Norm . . 3E **105**
Wilton Bank TS12: Salt. 5A **68**	**Winter Cl.** TS15: Yarm 1A **160**	TS15: Yarm 4D **149**
Wilton Grn. TS6: Laze 4B **82**	TS25: H'pool 2B **20**	**Woodlands Grn.**
Wilton La.	**Wintersweet Gdns.**	DL2: M Geo. 1A **144**
TS11: Wilt, Guis 3E **83**	TS20: Nort 1F **73**	**Woodlands Gro.**
TS14: Guis. 3E **83**	**Winterton Cotts.** TS21: Sed . . 1D **23**	TS26: H'pool 3D **13**
Wilton Rd. TS26: H'pool. 4A **14**	**Winthorpe Gro.**	**Woodlands Hall** TS1: Midd. . . . 4F **77**
Wilton St. TS1: Midd 5E **77**	TS25: H'pool. 1D **31**	**Woodlands Rd.** TS1: Midd . . . 5F **77**
TS10: Redc 3C **48**	**Wisbech Cl.** TS25: H'pool . . . 2D **31**	TS6: Norm 4D **105**
Wilton Way TS6: Est 5F **81**	**Wiske Cl.** TS19: S Tee 3B **72**	**Woodland St.** TS18: S Tee . . . 2F **97**
TS12: Brot. 2C **90**	**Witcombe Cl.** TS17: I Bar . . . 4E **127**	**Woodlands Wlk.**
Winchester Rd. TS5: Midd . . 1F **101**	**Witham Av.** TS16: P Tee 3C **126**	TS9: Stok 5C **164**
TS10: Redc 1F **65**	**Witham Gro.** TS25: H'pool . . . 1E **31**	**Woodland Way**
TS12: Brot. 2C **90**	**Witham Ho.** TS16: P Tee 3C **126**	TS21: L New 1F **123**
Winchester Wlk.	**Witham Lodge**	**Woodlea** TS8: C New 5B **132**
TS26: H'pool 1E **13**	TS16: P Tee. 3C **126**	**Woodley Gro.** TS7: Orm . . . 1B **134**
Windermere Av.	**Witton Ct.** TS23: Bill 5F **39**	**Woodmere Rd.**
TS10: Redc 5C **48**	**Woburn Gro.** TS3: Midd 3F **103**	TS19: S Tee 4D **73**
TS21: Redm 1B **70**	TS25: H'pool 5A **20**	**Woodrow Av.** TS7: Mart 3D **133**
TS23: Bill 4E **55**	**Woking Cl.** TS6: Norm 4D **105**	TS12: Salt 4B **68**
Windermere Dr. TS12: Skel . . 3B **88**	**Wolfe Rd.** TS20: Nort 1A **74**	**Woodrush** TS8: C New 2C **154**
Windermere Rd.	**Wollaton Rd.** TS23: Bill. 5F **39**	**Woodside** TS7: Orm 4F **103**
TS5: Midd 2D **101**	**Wolsey Dr.** TS20: Nort 4E **53**	TS10: Redc 3C **64**
TS18: S Tee. 5D **73**	**Wolsey Ho.** TS24: H'pool . . . 1F **15**	TS12: Brot. 2A **90**
TS25: H'pool 2B **20**	**Wolsingham Dr.**	TS17: I Bar 4B **128**
(not continuous)	TS5: Midd 2D **131**	TS22: Wyn 4B **26**
Windleston Cl. TS19: S Tee . . 1B **72**	TS17: T Tee 5E **99**	**Woodside Gro.**
Windleston Dr. TS3: Midd . . . 4D **103**	**Wolston Back La.**	TS18: S Tee 3C **96**
Windlestone Ho. TS23: Bill. . . . 5F **39**	TS23: Bill, C Bew. 2A **40**	**Woodside St.** TS1: Midd. . . . 3A **78**
(off Windlestone Rd.)	WOLVISTON 2C **38**	**Woodstock Way**
Windlestone Rd. TS23: Bill. . . . 5F **39**	**Wolviston Bk. La.**	TS27: H'pool 2C **6**
Windmill Ter. TS20: Nort 2B **74**	TS23: Bill 2D **39**	**Wood St.** TS1: Midd 2F **77**
Windmill Way	(not continuous)	TS6: Gran 2D **81**
TS17: H Lev 3C **150**	**Wolviston Ct.** TS22: Bill 5B **38**	TS13: C How 3F **91**
Windsor Ct. TS5: Midd 2E **101**	**Wolviston Interchange**	TS24: H'pool 1F **15**
TS6: Gran 4E **81**	TS22: Wyn 1A **38**	TS26: H'pool 5D **15**
TS12: Salt 4D **69**	**Wolviston Mill La.**	**Woods Yd.** TS12: Skel 4B **88**
Windsor Cres. TS7: Nun. 3A **134**	TS22: Bill, Wolv. 4A **38**	**Woodvale** TS8: C New 4D **133**
Windsor Dr. TS12: Ling. 4F **113**	(not continuous)	(not continuous)
Windsor Gdns. TS2: Midd. 2F **77**	**Wolviston Rd.**	**Wood Vw.** TS13: Loft 5C **92**
Windsor Oval TS17: T Tee . . . 5C **98**	TS22: Bill, Wolv. 4C **38**	**Woodville Av.** TS4: Midd . . . 3F **101**
Windsor Rd. TS5: Midd 1D **101**	TS23: Bill. 1C **54**	**Woolcotts Cl.** TS17: I Bar . . . 3B **150**
TS6: Est 2D **105**	TS25: H'pool 1A **20**	**Wooler Cres.** TS23: Bill 4E **55**
TS10: Redc 1E **65**	**Wolviston Rdbt.**	**Wooler Rd.** TS26: H'pool 3E **13**
TS12: Salt 4C **68**	TS22: Wolv 2D **39**	**Woolsington Dr.**
TS17: T Tee 5C **98**	**WOLVISTON SERVICES** 1B **38**	DL2: M Geo. 1A **144**
TS18: S Tee. 2E **97**	**Wolviston Wlk.**	**Worcester Gdns.**
Windsor St. TS1: Midd	TS19: S Tee 1B **72**	TS25: H'pool 1B **20**
	Woodale Cl. TS14: Guis 5E **109**	**Worcester St.** TS1: Midd 5D **77**
	Woodbank Rd. TS7: Orm . . . 5B **104**	**Wordsworth Av.**
	Woodbine Cl. TS9: G Ayt . . . 1D **167**	TS25: H'pool 1F **19**
	Woodbine Ter. TS25: Grea . . . 3E **31**	**Wordsworth Cl.** TS23: Bill 2D **39**
	Woodborough La.	**Wordsworth Rd.** TS6: Est . . . 5D **81**
	TS19: S Tee 3D **73**	**Wordsworth Va.**
	Woodbrook Cl.	TS5: Midd 5B **100**
	TS11: N Mar 2F **85**	**Works Rd.** TS3: Middlesbro . . 3D **79**

HOSPITALS and HOSPICES
covered by this atlas
with their map square reference

N.B. Where Hospitals and Hospices are not named on the map, the reference given is for the road in which they are situated.

BUTTERWICK HOSPICE & BUTTERWICK HOUSE
    CHILDREN'S HOSPICE 2C **72**
Middlefield Road
STOCKTON-ON-TEES
TS19 8XN
Tel: 01642 607742

CARTER BEQUEST HOSPITAL 3D **101**
Cambridge Road
MIDDLESBROUGH
TS5 5NH
Tel: 01642 850911

EAST CLEVELAND HOSPITAL 3B **90**
Alford Road
Brotton
SALTBURN-BY-THE-SEA
TS12 2FF
Tel: 01287 676205

GUISBOROUGH GENERAL AND
    MATERNITY HOSPITAL 1E **139**
Northgate
GUISBOROUGH
TS14 6HZ
Tel: 01287 284000

HARTLEPOOL AND DISTRICT HOSPICE 4A **8**
Alice House
Wells Avenue
HARTLEPOOL
TS24 9DA
Tel: 01429 855555

JAMES COOK UNIVERSITY HOSPITAL, THE
.... 3B **102**
Marton Road
MIDDLESBROUGH
TS4 3BW
Tel: 01642 850850

ST LUKE'S HOSPITAL 3B **102**
Marton Road
MIDDLESBROUGH
TS4 3AF
Tel: 01642 850850

SEDGEFIELD COMMUNITY HOSPITAL 2C **22**
Salter's Lane
Sedgefield
STOCKTON-ON-TEES
TS21 3EE
Tel: 01740 626600

STEAD PRIMARY CARE HOSPITAL 4B **48**
33-37 Kirkleatham Street
REDCAR
TS10 1QR
Tel: 01642 282282

TEES NUFFIELD HOSPITAL 4E **53**
Junction Road
STOCKTON-ON-TEES
TS20 1PX
Tel: 01642 360100

TEESSIDE HOSPICE CARE FOUNDATION
.... 3D **101**
1 Northgate Road
MIDDLESBROUGH
TS5 5NW
Tel: 01642 816777

UNIVERSITY HOSPITAL OF HARTLEPOOL 5F **7**
Holdforth Road
HARTLEPOOL
TS24 9AH
Tel: 01429 266654

UNIVERSITY HOSPITAL OF NORTH TEES 2C **72**
Hardwick Road
STOCKTON-ON-TEES
TS19 8PE
Tel: 01642 617617

WEST LANE HOSPITAL 1C **100**
Acklam Road
MIDDLESBROUGH
TS5 4EE
Tel: 01642 352000

RAIL

with their map square reference